Trial by Ordeal

Trial by Ordeal takes a sharp look at central aspects of the critical reception of Thomas Hardy. It demonstrates how critical appropriations of Hardy's work often provide a simplifying, conventional, or conservative image of the writer, which a sophisticated view of his creative intentions by no means confirms. Edward Neill discusses the dangers inherent in interpreting Hardy's writings in terms of his life; the limitations of criticism that views his work as nostalgic reaction; approaches to the poetry; and the critical response to *Jude the Obscure*.

Edward Neill teaches literature at Middlesex University, London.

Literary Criticism in Perspective

James Hardin (*South Carolina*), General Editor

Stephen D. Dowden (*Brandeis*), German Literature

About *Literary Criticism in Perspective*

Books in the series *Literary Criticism in Perspective* trace literary scholarship and criticism on major and neglected writers alike, or on a single major work, a group of writers, a literary school or movement. In so doing the authors — authorities on the topic in question who are also well-versed in the principles and history of literary criticism — address a readership consisting of scholars, students of literature at the graduate and undergraduate level, and the general reader. One of the primary purposes of the series is to illuminate the nature of literary criticism itself, to gauge the influence of social and historic currents on aesthetic judgments once thought objective and normative.

Edward Neill

Trial by Ordeal

Thomas Hardy
and the Critics

CAMDEN HOUSE

First published 1999
Camden House
Drawer 2025
Columbia, SC 29202–2025 USA

Camden House is an imprint of Boydell & Brewer Inc.
PO Box 41026, Rochester, NY 14604–4126 USA
and of Boydell & Brewer Limited
PO Box 9, Woodbridge, Suffolk IP12 3DF, UK

ISBN: 1–57113–140–x

Library of Congress Cataloging-in-Publication Data

Neill, Edward, 1941–
    Trial by ordeal : Thomas Hardy and the critics / Edward Neill.
        p.   cm. – (Studies in English and American literature,
linguistics, and culture (Unnumbered). Literary criticism in
perspective)
    Includes bibliographical references (p.   ) and index.
    ISBN 1–57113–140–X (alk. paper)
    1. Hardy, Thomas, 1840–1928 – Criticism and interpretation -
-History. 2. Criticism – Great Britain – History – 20th century.
3. Criticism – Great Britain – History – 19th century. I. Title.
II. Series.
PR4754.N39   1998
843.8—dc21   98-37818
                                                                        CIP

This publication is printed on acid-free paper.
Printed in the United States of America

Contents

Preface   vii

Acknowledgements   xiii

1: Sitting In Judgement: 1
   The Biographical Assize

2: Convergence of the Twain? Hardy and   21
   the Forms of Critical Appropriation

3: Smock-Frock'd Boor, *Bricoleur*, or   53
   Engineer? Hardy's Poetry Assayed

4: *Jude the Obscure*: The "Untimely Text"   89

Works Cited   115

Index   139

Preface

HOWEVER SERIOUS AND SIGNIFICANT THE reflections on a critical process as a necessary mediating activity may be, our sense of its importance will necessarily derive from the relative significance accorded to the
subject of its procedures. But such processes are already, at least in part,
"about" just such an ascription of value. It is, indeed, hardly possible to escape from such assaying even when the critic's procedure turns out to be
either hermeneutic, concerned with interpretation and the rules which
should govern it, or occupied with the means and techniques by which
meaning is constructed or projected.

In the case of Thomas Hardy, I shall argue that, although the persistent
denigration that accompanies his work can act as an obfuscation of his
achievement, the forms of praise his work seems to attract, not to speak of
its sources, are in themselves often an obstacle in the way of understanding,
appreciation and even enjoyment. This is partly a product of the fact that
earlier forms of argument which expressed outrage were at least responding
to Hardy's capacity to make mischief, if only in the interests of more liberal
forms of understanding. Later, a somnolent "yea-saying" in the critical tradition is rather inclined to turn all to favour and to prettiness in Hardy, to
stress the more reassuring qualities ascribed to him — tenderness, nostalgia,
picture-card rusticity — and to exhibit, if unwittingly, its own intellectual
limitations in its ascription of them to him.

Schoenberg, in the strange English that adds to a sense of the pathos of
his deracinated exile, seems to have claimed that his best friends were his
enemies. One can see what he means, and presumably they provided an artistic stimulus, a "stimulus" being originally military parlance for something
unpleasant and painful ("stimuli" were small spikes fixed in the earth to
deter cavalry deployments). It might be possible, here, to reverse the figure
and claim that Hardy's worst enemies are his friends, who tour the Hardy
country, more a textual event than a place to hold picnics (or conferences),
in chartered buses. They know "Hardy," but not Hardy in relation to
modern thought and theory which validates the critical process, and the
Hardy they know is largely a phantom of their own figuring, a product of
an inadequate process of critical production.

However, even if the large, wallowing (possibly, "waddling") movement "against theory" mainly brings to bear an anti-intellectualism hardly
worthy of respect or even attention, despite its prominence in what Paul

Bové has called the cultural tabloids, there is still a claim, I think a legiti-
mate one, that critical insight may be communicated in a way that looks
relatively informal. It is not always required of critique that it should
threaten the world with high astounding terms, certainly. However, this is a
dangerous maxim, and can do nothing to justify what Nicholas Tredell has
described as the "proudly paraded ignorance" and useless ironies of academic reaction among those perennial fogeys who await the whirligig of
taste's justification for their collective sloth.

Unfortunately, such people are still well to the fore in conveying (or
convoying) our sense of "Hardy," partly through their association with the
official cultists who, strategically placed *in situ* (the Heart of Wessex, "qui
pourtant n'existe pas"), and their conservative sense of Hardy undercuts his
own radical intellectuality, while their conservative procedures also contrive
to fashion an image of a traditional author whose techniques are conventional and whose philosophical upshot is an innocuous sense of mis-hap
without significant ideological coefficients or historical antennae. (I should
prefer to characterize this as a sense of what is allowed to enter or to con-
stitute history as writing. Hardy has, in fact, a dialectic sense of what is presented as "famous" or "obscure" as regards their claims on our attention
and right to be represented that would have appealed to Walter Benjamin.)

Perhaps more than any other author, Hardy has been attacked for what
may prove to be his virtues. His transitional position as an inheritor of a
High Romanticism which promised liberation through cultural advance
and found itself traduced by the aftermath of the Napoleonic Wars, and as a
post-Victorian novelist whose desertion of realism pointed to the experimental writing to follow, led to his being querulously handled (instead of
being praised for the variousness of his artistic experiments and his own independence of authorial example). He was also commended for a kind of
anti-intellectual parochiality when his texts in fact offer a prismatic refraction
of all manner of phrases and philosophies. He was a liminal figure whose
liminality adds to and does not, as has so often been hastily assumed, de-
tract from, his achievement.

"What do they know of Hardy who only Hardy know?" might consti-
tute a good summary here, except that the question infolds the Hardy already constituted as an object of knowledge by a determined clique-ishness
in the critical response itself. It might have been healthier in this respect if
the exponents of Hardy, already intrigued by biographical possibilities (by
comparison, perhaps with the Renaissance period in which giants like
Shakespeare came and went in maddening obscurity) had followed the example of Ernest Brennecke, a researcher inquisitive enough to call on
Hardy in person and record his impressions of Dorchester, but with genuine and wide-ranging intellectual interests, rather than Carl Weber, an en-

dearing personage but a perpetrator of much in the way of bluff belle-lettrist inconsequence.

Hardy hails the writing of Darwin as primarily an ethical advance. This is because he seems to provide a sense that the idea that "all life is one" (sustained in various ways by the major Romantic poets) has been given a certificate of scientific authentication, and such attitudes always challenge the advocate who prefers an ideological no less than an artistic orthodoxy. Indeed, he himself noted how an apparent artistic scrutiny was always already contaminated by an unavowed interest in ethical conventionalities and constricting orthodoxy. It is difficult to reckon up the ingredients of a response, particularly if they consist mainly of those howls of outrage which may merely announce that form of homage which mediocrity and conventionality pay to those who challenge received ideas of what is good in the way of belief or social dispensation, or is directed mainly at that which "makes it new," as modernism's most jaded tag has it, by way of Poundian or Nietzschean paradigms of aesthetic release or enhancement.

What follows here is hardly a grand narrative of critical emancipation; indeed it may positively encourage postmodernist doubt about progress and all such linear transitivities of critical and cultural initiative in a relay of enlightenment which moves to one great goal (in that Tennysonian idiom parodied by Joyce), of complete eradication of hermeneutic or evaluative error. That is not possible.

It is possible to feel that a certain kind of reader might be disappointed at the relative faintness of epistemic imprint left by such powerful intellectual currents as those of negative dialectics, structuralism, post-structuralism, postmodernism, feminism, or psychoanalytic critique, initiated or exemplified by intellectual eminences from Adorno and Benjamin through Barthes and Derrida, Lacan, Foucault and co. here, although the more literary mediators of such movements do indeed survive to make their collective voice and presence felt in a critical reception still perhaps dominated by simple questions and requirements. Still, only a fairly faint figure, it seems, stands beside us to attest to such magisterial currents of thought.

The fault lies partly in the state of criticism of the novel. As the Henry James epigone Percy Lubbock reminded us, novels are unusual as works of art in that not many can be comprehensively mastered and held in the head, which encourages an ancillary industry which acts as a collective *aide-memoire*, an essentially parasitic activity which Frank Kermode, doubling for Derrida here, calls "doubling." Implicitly, such non-criticism asks, with Robert Lowell in a late poem, "Why not say what happened?" Well, quite, for certain purposes, but this is a somewhat desolating and demoralizing role for critique. Hence, in Hardy's case, those Hardy-intensive critical industrialists, "all habit and memory," as Yeats put it of his senators, who carry their points by parochial appropriations which bracket larger issues of intellectual stewardship and responsiveness. They may be felt to involve Hardy in a conservatism which is that of their own ideological affinities but also associated with the simplistic conservatism of their own procedures and pronouncements.

The work which follows is, frankly, not a comprehensive investigation of all the material which might be considered relevant to such a study. Although proprietors of Hardy may be feline enough for this, nine lives would hardly be sufficient to master the material and lick its unbridled proliferations into shape. In general, I have sought to favour discussion of recent forms of response which show a sense of sophistication in their own and Hardy's ways of working, intellectual complexity at the service of Hardy's own interrogative and subversive procedures. However, the reader will derive some sense of the outraged (and occasionally outrageous) responses of what for Hardy himself was contemporaneity: for example, in the case of *Jude the Obscure*, attacks included that by Mrs Oliphant, "The Anti-Marriage League," *Blackwood's Magazine* (Jan., 1896, clix), 135–49; and those by Jeanette Gilder in the New York *World* (8 December 1895), an anonymous critic in the New York *Critic* (28 December 1895), and A. J. Butler on "Mr Hardy as a Decadent," *National Review* (May, 1896), xxvii: 384–90. There is a very neatly constructed paragraph on the pejorative remarks Hardy had to endure here in Paul Turner's *The Life of Thomas Hardy. A Critical Biography* (144). Citing Jowett's advice, which the less confident Hardy tried to heed — "Never retract. Never explain. Get it done and let them howl," — he crisply adds that "the howling started promptly. Even the friendly Edmund Gosse's first review called it "a grimy story." The *Pall Mall Gazette* retitled it "Jude the Obscene." The Anglican *Guardian* called it "a shameful nightmare," *Blackwood's* Mrs Oliphant described it as "a nauseous tragedy" — "intended as an assault on the stronghold of marriage," and almost ran out of words like "foul," "shameful," "disgusting," "sickening," "unsavoury," "filth," "garbage," and "depravity." (144)

Secondly, especially in my first chapter, I try to give some sense of the depredations of biography, an approach still inclined to try to list everything Hardy experienced, though hardly either as he may be assumed to have experienced it, or as that experience may be felt to have entered his texts. However, as I attempt to argue, the assumptions which underlie all such procedures are fatally flawed in any case, and often flagrantly (if occasionally fragrantly), pursue an agenda transparently enfeebled and hopelessly tangential. In my second chapter I give some sense of the ideologies of cultural production which act to appropriate Hardy in a kind of inverse "skimmity ride" (the famous satirical procession of *The Mayor of Casterbridge*), intended to exhibit him fairly and favourably but in fact creating difficulties of apprehension and engagement.

Chapter Three follows the theme in relation to the reception of the poetry, which precipitates strange forms of cultural intervention which vie with one another in patronizing pseudo-compliments. The worst of them, indeed, appear to salute the mysterious achievements of his ineptitude and feeble-mindedness, either through possessing no sense of the difference of a good poem from a bad one, or through the deployment of mysteriously motivated criteria persistent only in their attempts to "sanitize" Hardy and minimize his capacity for *miching mallecho* or ultimately well-meaning mischief against a constricting social and cultural dispensation.

In this connection the final chapter takes *Jude* as a cultural "event," using the Nietzschean and Deleuzian overtones sounded by John Hughes, giving equitable treatment and regard to those who salute him for his ability to represent a problem and those who point out that he problematizes representation. Once again it is necessary to point out, among brilliant writing ousted in the struggle for existence by simpler and more tendentious performances, the strange inadequacy of the cultural convoy for this inherently provocative brew. *Jude* certainly offers much in the way of exposure of ideologies — whether "dominant," "emergent," or "residual," to cite the terms of Raymond Williams's still interesting characterisation.

But much in the critical practice in relation to Hardy is busily engaged in covering it all up again. Its political provocativeness is perhaps not separable from its unusual techniques, called "expressionist" by some critics. Yet, so far from containing some Munch-like "primal scream," the characters discuss the fiction in which they are immured at such length that a conventional critic does not know quite where to begin with such a text, discursive, but "flying crooked," in Robert Graves idiom, a "wild, Polonial" novel which touches down at various genres and highly volatile in tone and register. As the critic John Goode puts it, it is "simply not fit for consumption." One feels that many Hardy critics may have felt such things, and worked hard to turn him into something more acceptable and convenient — what might be called "fast food" produced by critical processings. Caveat emptor.

Acknowledgements

I MUST THANK PROFESSOR BENJAMIN FRANKLIN V for scrutinizing my work so carefully and helpfully, and also the other professional and conscientious members of the team at Camden House including Jim Hardin and James Walker. Many engaging and talented colleagues at Middlesex helped keep me sane while I finished this, and I am grateful to Professor Christopher Ricks and Stephen Wall of *Essays in Criticism* for being generally supportive. My family has also been a mainstay, and I could accomplish but little without Heather, Edmund and Gregory.

E. N.
October 1998

1: Sitting In Judgement: The Biographical Assize

Introduction

T HE BIOGRAPHICAL TRADITION IN THE reception of Hardy, as with most modern (postromantic) authors, but even more so in his case, is immensely powerful in controlling and convoying his cultural processing. It constitutes a parochial cloud of knowing, a reductive and distorting refraction of the import of his work. For most readers, at least in England, the critical reception of Hardy *is* this biographical tradition, and it may be indicative of its dominance that a large bookshop in London, a specialist in "fiction" had on its shelves of "Author Criticism" the two major biographies of Hardy by Millgate and Gittings *and nothing else*. It is hardly possible, then, to explore criticism of Hardy and the painful contours of his critical reception without noting not only the fact of this "great tradition" but its overall impact on Hardy's critical processing.

Hardy's very reticence and defensiveness seemed to combine with a late Romantic sensibility, an inquisition into the nature of desire and the pursuit of happiness, which in turn, united with a quasi-confessional streak, made him appear the ideal subject for such a venture. He seemed to be the ideal prey to stalk, given that the very lightness of the spoor made him something of a challenge to pertinacity no less than perspicacity.

In the field of modern cultural production Hardy bulks almost farcically large as the chronicler of the cultural change from "agrarian" to "industrial," from immemorial rustic ways to urbanised modernity, from what Weber would have called *Gemeinschaft* to *Gesellschaft*. Fredric Jameson inadvertently describes well the kind of change that Hardy (ambiguously) celebrates and sorrows over. He equally inadvertently makes the point that the official critical convoy for canonic figures is very far from supplying the unique repository of critical acumen about them. Indeed, the fact that he doesn't have Hardy in mind makes this, as a point about him, potentially the more telling. He observes that "the older village structure and precapitalist forms of agriculture are now systematically destroyed, to be replaced by an industrial agriculture whose effects are fully as disastrous as, and analogous to, the moment of enclosure in the emergence of capital . . . [and] the 'organic' social relations of village societies are now shattered, an enormous landless preproletariat produced,' which migrates to the urban areas."[1]

Interestingly, Jameson then salutes Marx for his "dialectical ambivalence" in describing such "developments," an ambivalence fully registered in Hardy's own texts. However, not only is Hardy not generally thought of as a "radical" writer, his dominant critical idiom has worked to re-process him as an avatar of single- or even simple-minded conservatism. What we call his "world," which may bring the illusion of strolling in the fields, is in fact constructed of textual traces, a prismatic refraction of everything from Shelley's failed utopian hopes to Comte's doggedly positivistic (but still equivocal) narrative of cultural "progress." At once a graveyard of dead romanticisms and a theatre of bleak and vaguely congruent world-views of his own time from Darwin to Schopenhauer, Hardy's writing, with its peerless autodidactic intensity, is at once host and parasite to the numberless phrasings and philosophisings he hoarded. That's to say, he was an intensely intellectual author, if one committed to popular forms.

In a book worthy to be hailed as a significant advance in understanding the complex linguistic processing which his procedures entailed, *The Descent of the Imagination* (1990), Kevin Z. Moore has well characterised this "second degree writing," calling on figures like Barthes to indicate the palimpsest-like "always already textualised" nature of his literary processings,[2] yet such pertinent and sophisticated work never figures in the clique-like musings of Hardy's official curators.

As Craig Raine has pointed out in a (1994) article on *The Mayor of Casterbridge* (1886), that novel is least as "allusive" as T. S. Eliot's *The Waste Land*.[3] As a version of his own "Jude," the strenuous seeker after "culture," coming from behind, who effortfully overtakes his pampered peers, Hardy is, above all, a study in intertextuality. Even his celebrated Wessex is a kind of text, closer to the brochure than the reality, a house of hospitalities to books rather than people, a weave of signifiers rather than a thatch over your head, traversed by the traces of other men's texts rather than the spoors of smock-frocked agriculturalists.

Unfortunately, the Biographical Industry which has attached its suckers to the Hardy who was as pathologically discreet in his mores as he was provocative in his texts is scarcely up to all this. One suspects that, having, like Angel's brothers in *Tess of the D'Urbervilles*, certain investments in the status quo, Hardy's biographers' and curators' attitude to his provocative undercurrents remains profoundly ambiguous.

It is often implied, for example, that Leslie Stephen, who published *Far from the Madding Crowd* (1874) in a carefully expurgated version in the *Cornhill Magazine* — though, due to editorial timidity he accepted nothing from him subsequently — was the supremely necessary intellectual "presence" for Hardy.

But Rosemarie Morgan, for example, in her *Cancelled Words* (1992),[4] shows that Leslie Stephen, the Eminent Victorian par excellence, was at best an ambiguous gift to Hardy, not the paternalist godsend he has been taken to be by Robert Gittings in particular (see below). Gittings, not exactly a biographer-critic in the hagiographical tradition, patronises Hardy and takes both Emma and Florence (wives who vie with the other in being fairly unclever), under his wing. A brilliant scholarly researcher who virtually decreed subsequent attitudes to Hardy among the conventional and the unwary, Gittings creates Hardy as a culture villain rather than a culture hero. Like Patricia Beer,[5] he makes fairly critical remarks about Hardy's snobbery while stigmatizing him as a "peasant," creating a kind of "aporia of Englishness" which it is more instructive than pleasant to behold. This may sound provocative, but whence does provocation proceed if one is merely reporting what happens to be the unfortunate case?

So instead of a warm welcome for Kevin Moore's soundings and trawlings of Hardy's complex traffic in ideas as mediated by the popular narratives of this "Rousseau of Egdon Heath" (a description of the underdeveloped character of Damon Wildeve in *The Return of the Native* [1878]), a front-page TLS welcome for Michael Millgate's edition of yet more correspondence of Hardy's witless wives (1996)[6] was perhaps inevitable (see the issue of 1st November 1996, in which the work is reviewed by Samuel Hynes). And here again is poor, slightly mad Emma, who usually sounds a little like a bowdlerized Molly Bloom (a bowdlerized Molly Bloom is not much fun). A spirited, if scatterbrained figure, Emma is followed by dull, depressive Florence, acting out a role of high-minded loyalty, but secretly committed to compulsive disloyalty — addicted, indeed, to the furtive expression of all manner of petty, fretful resentments, and pining for her dead lover, the aspiring Enfield journalist Alfred Hyatt. Many little notes of complaint concerning the Max Gate regime were fired off to the ironclad rationalist, banker, and felicitously-named Edward Clodd and many another. As Martin Seymour-Smith has pointed out, she was actually unable either to like the man she had elected to live with (out of a "nice," but fundamentally self-serving strategy), or to appreciate his achievement.[7]

Hardy's recent biographers and the Thomas Hardy Society people who cite each other much and others but little, move quickly and effectively to exclude anything that might seem to threaten the artificially promoted pre-eminence of their own patronising and paradoxically repressive cult. (Lest this tendency be thought residual, in Raymond Williams' sense, it should be observed that James Gibson's highly readable *Thomas Hardy* (1996) in Macmillan's "literary lives" series is almost excessively true to type. Indeed, not only does it pointedly exclude anything that would rank as progressive intellectual inquiry, it also omits for the most part from its bibliography even Hardy's more enthusiastic American promoters in favour of pure Englishmen faithfully presented.)[8]

Much of the damage was indeed done by Robert Gittings, who reported in *Young Thomas Hardy* (1975)[9] and *The Older Hardy* (1978),[10] but also in another "bite" at the author who was feeding him (*The Second Mrs Hardy* [1979])[11] on Hardy as a "peasant" who also had the misfortune to be an enormous snob, a cringing, insignificant fellow towered over by Oxbridge men, metropolitan editors, and worldly, sophisticated Lords and Ladies.[12] "For such a provincial adolescent as Hardy, this was a plunge into the very deep end of sophistication," etc. To take the measure of Gittings's unsuitability for the role he adopts, one must experience the full wince-inducing social perspective of a sentence like "little Miss Campbell, the daughter of a naval officer, duly danced with the strange peasant boy" — that's to say, Hardy (1975: 12). Curiously, it is against such perspectives that much of Hardy's work is aimed, but this is not altogether welcome news to bow-tied experts.

Gittings's treatment of the remoteness and savagery of young Hardy's world was as breathtaking as an act of scholarly entrepreneur-ship as his discussion of Hardy's texts was heavy-handed and critically unsophisticated. He found good words for Emma and Florence and harsh words for Hardy's treatment of them. In doing so, he reproduced not only their malicious critiques of him but also Hardy's slightly hangdog attitude to himself. As Jacqueline Rose complained in her *Haunting of Sylvia Plath* (1991)[13] that the accomplished biography of Sylvia Plath by Anne Stevenson (1989)[14] was written from a position of chilling normalcy, almost as if Sylvia were a kind of anti-self to be purged away, Gittings's work is written from an unreal patronage of the supposedly ultra-susceptible male — that's to say, from the Olympian viewpoint of one who cannot admit any inquisition into the nature of desire, language and society. He thus becomes what Shelley would call a "thought-executing minister." He speaks with journalistic aplomb of "[Hardy's] intense and original treatment of words" (1975: 124), only to spend much of his time complaining about the way he used them. With a complacency reminiscent of the Oxonian patronage Hardy memorably noted in *Jude*, he complains that the use of "for" in the line "And dicing time for gladness casts a moan" is not only clumsy but obscure — "one has to substitute 'in place of' for the word 'for' to make any sense of it." In general, it might be said that, if Christopher Ricks is, as Auden claimed, the critic whom every poet dreams of finding, Gittings is par excellence the type of the biographer about whom one might legitimately have nightmares.

Michael Millgate, who wrote about Hardy's career as a novelist in a factually awesome, if, in literary terms, conventional, perspective (1971),[15] produced a similarly "magisterial" biography (1982),[16] as well as editing (7 vols., 1978–88) the dismally diminished correspondence, *"veteris vestigae flammae"* (the celebrated bonfires of Max Gate) as they mostly turned out to be.[17] There are also interesting "offcuts" or "offshoots" in Millgate's *Testamentary Acts* (1994).[18] The biography itself was undoubtedly intended as something of a corrective to Gittings, and Millgate pointed out, for example, that Emma was not very bright, that she could be a bit of a bully, and that her unbridled expressions of snobbery and resentment might just suggest that Hardy was, on the whole, a man more sinned against than sinning. In this way, and in its superior literary urbanity and suavity, the biography was a decided advance on its predecessors.

Unfortunately, however, Millgate also reproduces Gittings's patronage at strategic points, describing, for example, Hardy's "sullen peasant anger" (1982: 371) in the face of often outrageous as well as outraged critical responses, particularly to *Tess* (1891) and *Jude* (1896). As Martin Seymour-Smith ingeniously conjectures, perhaps Millgate was anxious not to offend Richard Purdy, doyen of Hardy scholars, who made him a gift of his informative notes, and whose "bibliographical study" (1954) is still useful (Seymour-Smith, 1994: 520).[19] Purdy was much indebted in his researches to the ailing Florence ("far too reliant on . . . her suburban view of her husband" as Seymour-Smith roundly expresses it [520]), and also, with his old-fashioned academic primness, not entirely the right man to construe Hardy's positively Lacanian dealings with the dance of desire (520). (See Terence Wright's *Hardy and the Erotic* [1988][20] for attempts to come to terms with this, although on the whole it is a less than satisfactory book, if a highly readable one, marrying a strain of critical naivety to the wilder stock of its quasi-Lacanian "treatment.")

Seymour-Smith's 900-page riposte (*Hardy* [1994]) is a recent addition to the heavy industry of biographical effort. He is, effectively, without his realising it, writing a tirade against the possibility of biography at least as much as he is writing a biography. If one can reverse the emphases and the conclusions of fifteen hundred pages by one's immediate biographical predecessors without apparent absurdity, how much can be assumed to have been established about the true verity of the life of Thomas Hardy from all those "trivial fond records" in the first place? Has the hermeneutic scepticism induced by deconstruction not a claim on the attention of even the most mercenary writer of lives? (It is the latest clerical treason to pretend that nothing has happened in this respect, and even that there is something instrinsically unsound about theory, in order to keep the world safe for what Paul Bové has called "the cultural tabloids," apparently.)

After all, as Roland Barthes has remarked, what is a biography but a
novel that dare not speak its name? The idea is suggestive, and could be
devastating. Yet it is slightly unfortunate in its lack of discrimination: some
biographies really are a bit more like novels than even he may have envis-
aged, and it seems churlish not to concede that at least some are like good,
where many are like bad, novels. In Hardy's case the most extreme example
is the case of *Providence and Mr Hardy* (1966),[21] in which, as if in response
to the urgings of good Quaker Lois Deacon, Hardy's cousin Tryphena, the
"lost prize" of the "Thoughts of Phena" poem, becomes (a) his half sister
(b) mother of a illegitimate child, the all-too-appositely named "Randy" (c)
the "totalized" explanation for his whole *oeuvre*. In view of Hardy's virtuoso treatments of the vagaries of desire over the whole range of his fiction
which precipitates out in *The Well-Beloved* (1897), it is hard to think of
anyone who is equally resistant to this abject "*cherchez la femme*" literalism,
and the whole *procédé* is almost comically inapposite. Yet much of this tendentious material has leaked into critical discussion, dogging J. O. Bailey's
doggedly quasi-biographizing accounts of the poems (1970),[22] spilling into
F. B. Pinion's similarly "factitious" guide *A Commentary on the Poems of
Thomas Hardy* [1976][23] — a chilling anticipation of what Joyce might have
called his "chaffering, allinclliding" and deeply inconsequential *Thomas
Hardy: His Life and Friends* (1992). For example:

> After recovering from a severe chill and violent cough in May, Hardy had
> several visitors, including Cockerell, and Lady Ilchester and her mother,
> from whom he learned that Mrs. Fortescue and her husband, the military
> historian whom she first met by the Druid stone at one of Emma's tea-
> parties, had been staying with them at Melbury House.[24]

Hardy once complained that he found it difficult talking to Browning as the
latter kept glancing round the *salon* in search of bigger social game. A sentence like Pinion's seems almost to be about the same task. It also evokes
the postmodernist feeling that "it parodies itself" (although Hugh Kenner
[1985] traces this topos [or cliché?] back to the era of Eisenhower's presi-
dential pronouncements).[25] Pinion seems to have hundreds of such sen-
tences here.

It is possible to become bogged down in these biographical positions,
and Pinion gives the impression of someone who has long since abandoned
the possibility of critical inquiry, never mind outright scepticism, as to what
it might be one thinks one is achieving in this mode. The tendency continues in his "Questions Arising from Hardy's Visits to Cornwall" (in Pettit,
1994, 191–208), with its claim to the effect that "some uncertainty must
remain on the number of times Hardy visited Cornwall" (191),[26] to which
one might reply, in Yeatsian idiom, that one is satisfied with that.

Such work might in turn call to mind the almost equally factitious bio-graphical forays into Hardy country by Harold Orel.[27] The Deacon and Coleman virus emerges, even, in Donald Davie's cranky, intelligent *Thomas Hardy and British Poetry* (1973), and perhaps Davie allowed himself to be influenced by the impassioned irrationality of F. R. Southerington's defence of this work in the Hardy-dedicated number of *Agenda* which he guest-edited in 1972.

The "Phena" legacy thus combines with tendentious explanation and explication, which is always referring complex textual operations which make of Hardy a "culture hero," an intellectual and aesthetically ethical force to be reckoned with, to some rather simple point of origin — usually in his "peasant" background. Gittings makes very free use of the word, though we have it on the authority of Raymond Williams that there were no peasants as such in Thomas Hardy's England. (Amusingly, perhaps, the Marxist critic Arnold Kettle, who described the subject of *Tess* as "the de-struction of the peasantry,"[28] seems also to have accepted the point that there were, in fact no peasants in England at the time)[29] Alternatively, Hardy's relationships with his wives, or mentors who are invariably more sophisticated, or educated, or (the implication is plain) more intelligent than Hardy was himself may serve to explain his artistic output, which is made to subtend in a simplistic way the gross and obvious signposts to sig-nificance provided by the "life". Gittings may have taken his cue from the Oxonian tones of J. I. M. Stewart in *Thomas Hardy: A Critical Biography* (1971). Stewart, a nice man in propria persona but every inch The Don, weighs in again with a word Hardy must have found offensive, ascribing his sense of ancestral pathos as the mistaken regard for "some shambling peas-ant."[30]

As frequently noted, there seems to be some carry-over from a social to a critical note of patronage here. As Charles Lock points out (1992), when Stewart embarks, as he frequently does, on a comparison of Hardy with other writers, Hardy invariably comes off worse.[31] However, unfortunately, Charles Lock himself is also an eminent example of a Hardy Expert, a Dor-set-born Oxonian who joined Millgate's English Department in Toronto. Lock's contribution to the Criticism in Focus series, while well informed and obviously intelligent, is not consistently focussed, and also reproduces the equivocal endorsements and blusteringly ambiguous rhetorical patron-age we expect from the cultists who cluster protectively but smotheringly round their disappointing deity.

His rhetoric of literary inflation is very much in tension with his rhetoric of social patronage. We hear, for example, of Hardy's home "on an eleva-tion overlooking the valley of his modest origins" (125–6). The most re-warding result of his critical enquiry is a persuasive sketch of the purveying of "Wessex" as a cultural commodity, and indeed we may almost call it Hardy's cultural capital, particularly as this enters into the categorising of Hardy's novels as major or minor according to the degree of their partici- pation in this myth of "Wessex," a rather late-flowering concept in the context of his novel-writing career, as Lock makes clear. Having decon- structed this notion of Hardy's major novels as growing out of Wessex as naturally as leaves come to a tree, however, he is inclined to re-invoke its canons implicitly when new and challenging critical interpreters arrive on the scene. Peter Widdowson, for example, is firmly put in his place for finding the lack of interest shown in *The Hand of Ethelberta* ideologically suspicious (115).

However, much of his discussion is of earlier critical responses, and a good deal of the information concerns critics of the period between Lionel Johnson's study of 1894 and Joseph Warren Beach's majestic summaries and critical probings of 1922. His reference to more recent work, which requires nuanced and complex responses, tends to be loosely adjectival. One wouldn't wish to be too hard on the book, especially as it looks as though a requirement of the series is to emphasise earlier critical responses. He unpicks some of Lawrence's contentious "re-readings" (or one may say virtual re-writings) of Hardy, relating them usefully to the Abercrombie text on Hardy Lawrence used. But in general he gives short shrift to re-readings of Hardy which suggest that Hardy produces interrogative texts, so that critics like Williams, Wotton, Widdowson and Goode are subject to sum- mary, tell-tale dismissal; conventional perspectives are re-animated to quash those very perspectives which promise to "make it new" in precisely the ways he seems to think desirable elsewhere. In general, Lock's book, though well-intentioned and scholarly, has some of those disconcerting features which serve to confirm the feeling that custodians of Hardy and his environment are in some respects strangely unsuited to the task, almost as if the officious collegian "T. Tetupheny," who stands like a small dragon to forbid all entrance to the aspiringly scholarly Jude, had subsequently been commissioned to write his biography.

In this tradition too, in a different way, is the earlier biography by Evelyn Hardy, who writes under the aegis of Lord David Cecil and takes her social cues from him, spending much time and detail on the aristocratic people surrounding Hardy in his early world — we hear of Lord Grey, Pitt, Mrs Martin and Susan Fox-Strangeways, and little about Hardy's immedi- ate kith, kin and environment.[32] However pronounced Hardy's *prédilection d'artiste* (in his own phrase) for the aristocrat — *An Indiscretion in the Life of an Heiress* (1876), from which the phrase is taken, will itself vouch for the fact — there was another "lower" tradition associated with his own family which Hardy wished to be respected which his Cecilian namesake is reluctant to dabble in. It took a Raymond Williams to reverse the emphasis and express the wish (in *The Country and the City*) that Hardy should never have gone near the aristocratic world, and Williams also looks on the great country houses as great bad, not good places for which it is appropriate to express what Milton calls "distance and distaste" (1973: 199). The effect is refreshing, and enacts a healthy alienation both from the Hardy created by his critical response and his official cult and a re-alignment of the intention of Hardy's work as a whole.

Also at Toronto, and, as it would appear, more intellectually open, Marjorie Garson was able to write a quasi-Lacanian account of Hardy's work, probing Hardy's presentations of male somatic anxieties and fears of dispersal in a highly intelligent fashion. For example, as a study in various kinds of returning repressions, *The Return of the Native* offers an almost paradoxical triumph of the feminine, as the Silent Woman (the comically misogynist name of Damon Wildeve's pub) is, as Garson puts it, "still talking."[33] It's possible that a tendentious "bio-graphical" sub-text writes a Hardy assailed by and doomed to project the same somatic phantoms of his own figuring as representations of femininity, something of an immanent will stirring and urging everything here, work against their own subaltern stereotypicalities to thwart or overwhelm maleness. Even on the impossible semiotic terrain of *Tess*, committed apparently to dramatizing male predation, what particularly arrests Garson's attention is the structural homology between Tess, Angel and an unproblematically "historical" Hardy himself, in pessimism, religious scepticism, intellectual superiority to his family matrix, and dispossession from certain key rights, including those of educational advancement (135–6).

Despite her promising approach and material (this is, without doubt, one of the most brilliant books written about Hardy), Garson's equivocally feminist theme elaborates, then dissipates itself, partly by repetition: a character in *Under the Greenwood Tree* speaks of the formidableness of "united 'ooman" (woman) and *Jude the Obscure* is still broaching something like the same idea, apparently. It isn't "myth criticism," exactly, but displays something of the same kind of limitation of that particular approach. Garson is extremely well up in and an astute reader of critics of Hardy. If all Hardy critique were this intelligent, things would be a good deal healthier down on the organic farm of Hardy studies.

Yet even here the pupil of Lacan soon shows her paces as the pupil of Millgate and (her Ph.D supervisor) John Bayley, the former Thomas Warton Professor at Oxford whose opposition to "theory," despite his glancingly illuminating discussion and formidably wide range of literary reference, soon grows obscurantist. The trouble is that he comes to offer in its place (see *An Essay on Hardy* [1978]) a home-grown patrician mysticism

which is at least as difficult to follow as "theory."[34] This is accompanied in
Garson's text by fleeting visits, which grow more frequent and less fleeting,
from the work of Northrop Frye, a presence from the outset, really, given
her conviction of a "mythic subtext" (2). Subtexts are fine but "mythic"
suggests the return of the correctly repressed — de-'class'ifying, de-
historicising genealogies. This conservative aspect of her textual formation
soon surfaces strongly, particularly as one soon comes to realise that the
demand that Hardy cannot be made "politically correct," an ambition she
presumably ascribes to Peter Widdowson, John Goode and George Wotton, which quickly declares itself more plainly as a categorical repression of
"the political" as such.

The critics' characteristic failure here may entail the denial that there is a
significant political vector to Hardy, and involve a muted but unmistakable
hostility consequent on the realisation that Hardy may not mean intensely
and mean good for those of conservative critical idiom or temperament.
The feeling that Hardy is hardly politically acceptable, let alone correct,
feeds into the recuperative ferocity of Philip Collins in his article, following
hard upon an article of a quite opposing tendency by Raymond and Merryn
Williams[35] in a heterogeneous collection of critical pieces by Norman Page
(1980). Page might have remarked on such ideological variables in his introduction to this much-used collection. Yet, though immensely scholarly
(in his magnificent Norton edition of *Jude the Obscure*, for example), he
seems to be another of those strange "everything is grist" Hardy people
who works in the "unweeting way" of one of Hardy's own hypothetically
somnambulistic deities. Collins's article has a number of what might be
known (admittedly in a rather popular idiom) as cheap cracks and little digs
whose "purport wry," in Hardy's idiom, might be summed up in his claim
that

> Hardy's childish antagonism to the Established Church can provoke the
> mildest agnostic to rejoice in G. K. Chesterton's description of Hardy as "a
> sort of village atheist brooding and blaspheming over the village idiot."[36]

Behind Hardy here is the ghost of Shelley, and his attacks on religion as
part of an unctuous but grasping Establishment (in, for example, "The
Mask of Anarchy," "England in 1819" and many other poems). Indeed
Hardy's announced "program" in poetry is that of a "bold inquirer into
morals and religion" after the manner of Shelley's Milton — the great liberator of the "Preface" to *Prometheus Unbound* [1820]). Hardy might have
been glad to have been made one with the execrated Shelley.

Indeed, in Hardy's own *Life* he points out that cultural productions are
often scrutinized with unavowed reference to their political and theological
proprieties.[37] In fact if Hardy had as a prospective architect's apprentice (as

Seymour-Smith avers [1994: 30]), to listen to a sermon preached by his vicar Shirley which followed the readily intelligible theme of the censorious Mrs Norris in *Mansfield Park* (" . . . people are never respected when they step out of their proper sphere"), he surely had more than enough to put up with. If this sermon really was preached, it seems to entail an attempt at Althusserian "interpellation" in an almost farcically pure form.

That Collins is not exactly the critic Hardy might have dreamed of finding is shown by persistent little animadversions like his reference to "Hardy's sad proclivity for firing off his popguns of knowledge indiscriminately in his novels" (51). Comparable patronage is found in J. A. Sutherland's widely-used reference work, *Victorian Novelists and Publishers* (1976), where he takes what might be felt to be a slightly complacent view of the young incipient novelist Hardy's dealings with Macmillan. As he himself points out, "Hardy submitted all three of his first novels to Macmillan's . . . [but] they accepted none of them."[38] Nevertheless, he hastens not only to exonerate but to lavish praise upon them for their timidity, reserving his acidulousness for the presumptuous young cottager ("The first thing that Hardy had to learn was that he had something to learn," etc.).

But finally he is forced to concede that the young Hardy was bombarded with a ridiculous excess of that kind of good advice with which it is as difficult to comply as it is easy to dispense. In particular, he was being offered so many models to follow that, as Sutherland himself concedes, "a literary Proteus would have had difficulty in adapting to all these roles" (216). He then arrives at the slightly perverse conclusion that "it is hard not to feel rather sorry for Macmillan's and Tinsley," the former because they had invested their valuable "'time' in the developing author" (224). In fact one should feel irritated with Macmillan and extremely sorry for Tinsley. He published three of Hardy's novels — *Desperate Remedies, Under the Greenwood Tree,* and *A Pair of Blue Eyes* and yet not even the extremely favourable notices accorded to the second could prevent his later (1878) bankruptcy. Macmillan were then able to move in and clean up.

Indeed, faced with all this ideologically cued pseudo-bantering, one might well be tempted to declare that *Enfin* Seymour-Smith *vint*, to write with polemical ferocity on behalf of the entrepreneurial man of letters (that's to say, himself and Hardy, or himself as Hardy) against the securely pensioned academic (he does not hesitate, one might say scruple, to make such points, and indeed he permits himself a tone of abusiveness which is injudicious but understandable given the notes of patronage and evasiveness of orthodox Hardy specialists). For example, a suggestion of a certain epicene quality in Hardy initiated by Gittings but somewhat incautiously developed by Millgate leads to an unacceptable jibe at what he describes as "well-hung professors" (1994: 460) who, it's implied, suffer no insecurity about their virilities as they go about the business of finding a good deal of it for Hardy himself. Unfortunately, these lunging polemics occlude what he wants to say, which is that biographies written from a rigid position of unimaginative normality occlude a proper examination of the inquisition into instabilities in language, desire, and society which Hardy's writing conducts. This rather bluff tone also combines with the idea that one mustn't be "left wing" or "radical," so instead of appearing as the Promethean liberator of Hardy's reputation, his fogeyish perspective corresponds to the unhappily "Victorian" moments of Hardy's own more unguarded political pronouncements. As Lucille Herbert has remarked in an interesting article (ELH, 1970), Hardy's "philosophy" is more radical than his "sociology."[39]

Seymour-Smith is lively reading, but he does have problems of tone and register. He keeps referring to Hardy as "Tom," to insinuate a biographerly solidarity missing in previous efforts, one assumes, but this grates, especially when combined with the strange publisher's decision to call the book *Hardy*. His intimations that Hardy was "normal" and, as in the personal testimony of Robert Graves, actually lovable (803), is an understandable counter to Gittings's insinuations of dark, alienating morbidity. He might have been better advised to emphasise Hardy's achievements and their ideological coefficients rather than embark on the abusive course of (or in) an original mode of bad-tempered hagiography which comes of being, as Samuel Hynes put it in his review of the book in the TLS, paranoid on someone else's behalf.

Hynes is an equable, even-handed sort of critic, but he himself can hardly be exonerated for his part in the creation of a Hardy who eschews experiment and who, particularly in poetry, is king of the *arriere-garde*.)[40] Peter Widdowson notes how influential his somewhat apodictically limiting view of Hardy's poetical achievement has become due to his magisterial, repetitive introductions to various editions.

Reacting against second wife Florence's posthumous control of Hardy's reputation, Seymour-Smith makes Florence and Emma a binary, with Emma as a pure plus, so that we are made to understand that "Emma, unlike Florence, had a sense of humour" ( ). It was, to put it mildly, not always in evidence, and Florence's own reference to Emma as Hardy's "late espoused saint" attracts a high score for comedy at the price of casting severe doubt on the *tendresse* she "professed." What he unwittingly establishes is the limitations of biography itself, both ontologically and contingently, as it is particularly in Hardy's case that it becomes little more than an egregious peep-show with little to show for it. Beyond a certain limited intellectual horizon biography, it's clear, though loved by publishers, inhibits thinking, including thinking about just what it is one thinks one is achieving when one writes a biography.

Hardy was a writer, which means, inter alia, that "he" was written by writing in the first place. Attempts to grapple with the ectoplasm of "Hardy" apart from his texts are doomed to the disappointments of the ineluctably aporetic. Hardy seems to have attracted much biographical writing dedicated to proving that he had "the hard coldness of the genuine artist," to cite Hawthorne as cited by T. S. Eliot, and then to reprove him for it. Much of the appearance of cloistered imperturbability might as well derive from anxiety as aloofness, and speculation along these lines seems as fruitless as it is, at least potentially, uncharitable. Yet huge investments of cash and time seem to say otherwise. Attempts to calibrate this may find themselves engaged in an increasingly desperate attempt to conceal a growing awareness of the essential irrelevance of their procedures no less than the unreliability of their instruments.

Indeed, what Seymour Smith himself seems to illustrate is the impossibility of biography, by writing the opposite of well researched versions of Hardy by Hardy scholars and finding that this "other one" is equally true, provides equally a plausible narrative which, claiming to be superior as fact becomes superior as fiction. Hardy in propria persona always seemed rather reluctant to get a life. Fortunately his followers have offered to fetch a choice of several for him.

What Seymour-Smith is writing is less a biography based on the results of independent scholarly research than a "black hole" version of Millgate in which his positivities are cashed out as negatives, and vice versa, and especially where the latter is following Gittings (and indeed the former substitutes for the latter just as Hardy substitutes for Seymour-Smith.) J. M. Barrie, for example, becomes a grotesque gnome in Seymour-Smith (794), not for having perpetrated anything untoward, but for having been praised at Hardy's expense by Gittings. Perhaps Hardy becomes a whipping-boy for the putative ethical derelictions involved in becoming a writer (even if only a writer of biographies). Just as biographers are a prey to the factual basis of their narratives, they secrete ressentiment that Hardy can write about such things as trysts and assignations without actually having them. In a sense, even in confronting these empiricisms, there is no escape from the politics of writing, a native who returns no matter how high one raises the stakes in his repression.

It may be conceded, certainly, that Hardy's political vectors are hard to establish, partly because the whole matter of whether, or to what extent, the work of art might be said to have ideological coefficients, is a contentious (if highly interesting) one. Also Hardy, unlike the imposing W. B. Yeats, was not imperious in his fashion of re-creating himself textually. Raymond Williams is, significantly, a critic rarely cited by the ingrown "keepers of Hardy" people, although he made significant critical interventions in both *The English Novel from Dickens to Lawrence* (1970) and *The Country and the City* (1973) and elsewhere. He points out that characteristic words of critical response to Hardy ("gauche," "clumsy," etc.), reproduce the social patronage which he often had to undergo, a "rhetoric of origins": even a friendly contemporary critic, Charles Kegan Paul, was at pains to point out that the author of *Under the Greenwood Tree* (1872) was "sprung from a race of laboring men,"[41] which bespeaks a whiskered, cultivated disdain which seems to be, in all its toxicity, alive and well and living in current biographical responses.

Perhaps if the response to Hardy had taken the route indicated by Ernest Brennecke (1924, 1925)[42] things might have been healthier. Brennecke stressed Hardy's intellectual growth and affinities, even if his championship of Schopenhauer as influence drew forth a would-be rebuttal from Hardy that native thinkers like Hume, Mill and Darwin were more germane than Schopenhauer in attempts to plot his intellectual development.[43] His stress on Hardy's intellectual debts and complex sense of intertextuality would at least have avoided the absurdities of making his main intellectual and creative rivals Emma and Florence. Brennecke incurred the wrath of Florence in making Hardy a smoker, and in confusing the indifferent meal which he had in his Dorset hotel with the five-star one he must have had at Max Gate. In fact there seems to be some kind of correlation between Brennecke's relative lack of interest in circumstantial detail (although he has a good eye and ear for the tawdry thespian ineptitudes of the "Hardy players," a more relevant consideration [1925: 19]), and his subtle appreciation of Hardy's achievement. Even an observation like "a single human intelligence, detached, aloof, penetrating, pitying, has sent forth in certain printed pages an ectoplasm that has penetrated the Kingdom you see" (1925: 26) could lead into a sophisticated apprehension of the meaning of "Wessex," not exactly a place on the map.

Unfortunately, Carl Weber, who achieved greater *éclat* and authority as a biographical reader of Hardy in the earlier days of his cultural transmission was, although well-meaning enough, a bluffer character much given to sentiments like "he continues today to inspire readers to strive towards noble conduct in an imperfect world,"[44] which is nice, but a little hearty — and not very helpful. Like many of Weber's well-meaning remarks, it doesn't take you far into what Hopkins would have called Hardy's *haecceitas* or uniqueness.

Paul Turner comes most lately to hand with what purports to be a biography which, in its strengths relates to Hardy's reading, a story of a life in or as writing which deconstructs the received idea of biography. Turner has an ear for literary reminiscence over a wide scholarly range. By taking texts which Hardy devoured, re-used, cunningly deployed sometimes throughout his writing career, he shows that in terms of his own width of (inter)textual focus, Hardy is at least as bookish as Eliot, with a particular autodidactic intensity which makes his "could not go to Oxford" situation seem something of a godsend. Although scholarly in a traditional, if after his fashion perspicacious way, Turner's simple re-allocation of emphasis on the writings Hardy perused and purloined, re-used and revised looks revolutionary in its stultified context.

In general, the volume follows the contours of his texts rather than the ley-lines of his imputed passions and proclivities, showing how, from *Desperate Remedies* to *The Well-Beloved*, he wasted nothing, a quality also ascribed to his great (but now much diminished) adversary, T. S. Eliot, by Peter Ackroyd. Some of these intertextualities are interesting for the sheer persistence of the trace elements they leave — Longus' *Daphnis and Chloe*, St. Pierre's *Paul et Virginie*, the Greek Dramatists, Virgil especially in Dryden's rendering, but also, incontrovertibly, Horace, along with modernities from *Lady Audley's Secret* through Tennyson, Arnold, Browning and Swinburne and many another — "there" in minute verbal reminiscences but so significant they make one wonder how very original in its exoskeleton of intertextuality even a supposedly radical modernist work like *The Waste Land* is by comparison. Unusual for a novelist, perhaps, is the direct use of poetry in his work: Jude's obscurity comes courtesy of Thomas Gray, and the Shelley of *The Revolt of Islam* and "Epipsychidion" and the Browning of "The Statue and the Bust" are everywhere.[45] Turner is steeped in the literature of Victorian England and this in turn is backed by an awareness of the classical world which challenges a modern sociological approach.

Such an approach can dismiss even those classical tragedies Hardy (cued by Horace Moule, perhaps), found so suggestively inspiring, as merely an "alien" mode. This is going much too far in directions suggested by Marx's *Dix-Huite Brumaire*, assuming that all literary sociologists will have read this. But despite all that may be said for this, the scholarly "formatting" of the series to which Turner is a contributor is not, on the whole, encouraging. These Blackwell products are general-edited by Claude Rawson, and pursue an implicitly "against theory" line, which suits biography-making rather well, as theory resists the assumptions which underpin the lucrative pursuit of bio-graphy, or "my life as written" — and by others at that. The authors in the series are asked to pursue their aims without "programmatic assertions or strenuous point-making." And this is altogether more dubious. "Programmatic assertions" becomes less attractive when you realise this might just be construed to mean "anything radical, subversive, political, intellectual or original," and "strenuous point-making" may be read off as "the intellectual passion or conviction which validates scholarly procedure and gives it an underlying raison-d'être." If an unhappy program, we must concede that the results are felicitous in the case of Hardy's biographer, who provides a kind of corrective to the more novelistic biographies which preceded his.

Apart, then, from a generally admirable bookishness (although this often begs the question of what a specific reminiscence may be said to signify), the work repeats at least some features of the anti-intellectual and ideologically recuperative mode of this dominant strain in Hardy studies. Although it retreats from philistine patronage which disfigures Hardy, it emphatically declines to achieve any rapport with a growing body of critical writing which conscripts Hardy, more legitimately, for its a more intellectually open (and also radical) tradition. This tradition is more alert to the special constraints and constrictions under which Hardy laboured to become an author, to change, in Mallarméan idiom, *en lui-même enfin*, as a "written" self. But Turner, without being at all polemic in the matter, so emphasizes the strenuous nature of Hardy's intellectual formation that the patronage which still visits the presumptuous cottager ("peasant") is at least implicitly rebuked.

But biography perhaps denigrates intrinsically as well as accidentally, whether or not it has a "peasant" in its clutches. It seems to step forward in an awkward sort of phenomenologico-empirical doublet, deducing feelings from "facts" which are always under erasure from a correctly Nietzschean scepticism in such matters, and a quasi-Husserlian inwardness with an "Other" who is present only in reflection and representation, "shade more than man, more image than a shade." If phenomenology was doomed to dissolve in the acid of deconstruction, biography melts like an emperor of ice cream in the glare of rigorous poststructuralist inquisition.

In particular, biography predicates a sequence event — feelings/ emotions — writing which ignores the idea that the sequence is equally likely to be reversed. Perhaps an image for the writerly world that biography can only regard as topsy-turvy can be found in the figure of Boldwood, staring at the text of Bathsheba's ill-starred valentine until overwhelming emotions create strange and terrible events, or perhaps the short story "An Imaginative Woman," in which emotions grow into huge and shadowy shapes as a result of purely textual "intercourse."

In fact, as J. Hillis Miller, in *Thomas Hardy: Distance and Desire* has pointed out, Hardy's supreme antecedent was Shelley ("our most marvellous lyrist," Hardy called him).[46] Shelley was not only some kind of Marxist *avant la lettre*: he wrote, in "Epipsychidion" in favour of a kind of imaginative promiscuity much flirted with by Hardy himself, and specifically warned that, in settling down, one might find one would "with one chained friend, perhaps a jealous foe,/The dreariest and the longest journey go." That journey is, of course, marriage. As an image of Hardy's marital states, Shelley seems to have outsoared the shadow of subsequent biographical attempts to "capture" Hardy in an — at least for us — brilliantly anticipatory account of what was to happen to him. If, as Margaret Whitford says, writing of Irigaray (1991), "one way of neutralizing a woman thinker whose work is radically challenging is to 'reduce' her to her biography,"[47] it is difficult to see that the claim is "gender-specific." Surely, now, what we need in relation to Hardy, and others, is more intertextuality and less biography.

Notes

[1] Fredric Jameson, "Periodising the Sixties," in *The Ideologies of Theory: Essays 1971–86*, reproduced in *Postmodernism: A Reader*, ed. Patricia Waugh (London: Edward Arnold, 1992), 131.

[2] Kevin Z. Moore, *The Descent of the Imagination: Postromantic Culture in the Later Novels of Thomas Hardy* (London: New York UP, 1990).

[3] Craig Raine, "Conscious Artistry in *The Mayor of Casterbridge*," in Charles P. C. Pettit (ed.), *New Perspectives on Thomas Hardy* (London: Macmillan, 1994), 156–171.

[4] Rosemarie Morgan, *Cancelled Words: Re-Discovering Thomas Hardy* (London: Routledge, 1992).

[5] Patricia Beer. *Wessex: A National Trust Book* (London: Hamish Hamilton, 1985), 79–84.

[6] Michael Millgate, *Letters of Emma and Florence Hardy* (Oxford: Clarendon Press, 1996).

[7] Martin Seymour-Smith, *Hardy* (London: Sinclair-Stevenson, 1994), e.g. 745.

[8] James Gibson, *Thomas Hardy: A Literary Life* (Basingstoke: Macmillan, 1996).

[9] Robert Gittings, *Young Thomas Hardy* (London: Heinemann, 1975). Rev. Ed. Harmondsworth: Penguin, 1978. Some of the points of protest made here are also mooted in Peter J. Casagrande's "'Old Tom and New Tom': Hardy and His Biographers," *Thomas Hardy Annual* 1 (1982), 1–32.

[10] Robert Gittings, *The Older Hardy* (London: Heinemann, 1978).

[11] Robert Gittings and Jo Manton, *The Second Mrs Hardy* (London: Heinemann, 1979).

[12] Note, for example, how much better Horace Moule seems to be able to approach the business of writing than Hardy — as reported by Gittings (1975: 69).

[13] Jacqueline Rose, *The Haunting of Sylvia Plath* (London: Virago, 1991).

[14] Anne Stevenson, *Bitter Fame: A Life of Sylvia Plath* (London: Viking, 1989).

[15] Michael Millgate, *Thomas Hardy: His Career as a Novelist* (London: Bodley Head, 1971).

[16] Michael Millgate, *Thomas Hardy: A Biography* (Oxford: Oxford UP, 1982).

[17] Thomas Hardy, *The Collected Letters of Thomas Hardy*, edited by R. L. Purdy and Michael Millgate (Oxford: Oxford UP, 1978–88).
[18] Michael Millgate, *Testamentary Acts: Browning, Tennyson, James, Hardy* (Oxford: Clarendon Press, 1992).
[19] R. L. Purdy, *Thomas Hardy: A Bibliographical Study* (Oxford: Oxford UP, 1954).
[20] Terence Wright, *Hardy and the Erotic* (Basingstoke: Macmillan, 1989).
[21] Lois Deacon and Terry Coleman, *Providence and Mr Hardy* (London: Hutchinson, 1966). F. R. Southerington saddles himself with these findings in his *Hardy's Vision of Man* (London: Chatto and Windus, 1971), 253–72.
[22] J. O. Bailey, *The Poetry of Thomas Hardy. A Handbook and Commentary* (Chapel Hill: North Carolina, 1970).
[23] F. B. Pinion, *A Commentary on the Collected Poems of Thomas Hardy* (London: Macmillan, 1976).
[24] F. B. Pinion, *Thomas Hardy: His Life and Friends* (London: Macmillan, 1992), 340. In the same tradition, but more parochially anchored in fascinating tittle-tattle and anecdotage, often with the accent on the dotage, is *Concerning Thomas Hardy*, ed. D. F. Barber (London: Charles Skilton, 1968).
[25] Hugh Kenner, *The Mechanic Muse* (New York: Oxford UP, 1987).
[26] F. B. Pinion, "Questions Arising from Hardy's Visits to Cornwall," in *New Perspectives on Thomas Hardy*, ed. Charles P. C. Pettit (London: Macmillan, 1994), 191–208.
[27] Harold Orel, *The Final Years of Thomas Hardy* (London: Macmillan, 1976) and *The Unknown Thomas Hardy: Little-Known Aspects of His Life and Work* (London: Macmillan, 1988).
[28] See "Hardy the Novelist: A Reconsideration" (W. D. Thomas Memorial Lecture, University College, Swansea [1966]). Reprinted in *The Nineteenth Century Novel: Critical Essays and Documents*, Edited by Arnold Kettle (London: Heinemann Educ. Books, 1972), 262–273; see also Arnold Kettle, *An Introduction to the English Novel*. 2nd. ed. London: Hutchinson, 1967.
[29] Raymond Williams, *The Country and the City* (London: Chatto and Windus, 1973), 199.
[30] J. I. M. Stewart, *Thomas Hardy: A Critical Biography* (London: Oxford UP, 1971), 45. Lance St. John Butler correctly defines and attacks the patronage in all such "peasant 'wisdom' merely confirmed by reading" perspectives in "'Bosh' or: Believing Neither More Nor Less," in *New Perspectives on Thomas Hardy*, 101–116: 101–102. Curiously, Stewart comes closer to accuracy and generosity when he defines Hardy as offering "ambivalent contructs . . . satisfying to the imagination rather than to the logical faculty" in "The Major Novels," a short piece in *The Genius of Thomas Hardy*, ed. Margaret Drabble (London: Weidenfeld and Nicholson, 1976), 58. But the persiflage is sustained, for example in *Eight Modern Writers* (Oxford: Clarendon Press, 1963), 19–70. As Hardy's forte is felt to be irony, he obviously feels the need to repay in the same coin. However, we may at least enjoy the idea that "just as each of

Dickens' novels is a sort of Christmas hamper so is each of Hardy's a Pandora's box" (51).

[31] Charles Lock, *Thomas Hardy* (Bristol: Bristol Classical Press, 1992), 108.

[32] Evelyn Hardy, *Thomas Hardy: A Critical Biography* (London: Hogarth Press, 1954). For Lord David Cecil, who has eloquent passages correlating the awkwardness of Hardy's prose style with the lowliness of his rustic background, see his *Hardy the Novelist* (New York: Bobbs-Merrill, 1946).

[33] Marjorie Garson, *Hardy's Fables of Integrity: Woman, Body, Text* (Oxford: Clarendon Press, 1991), 79.

[34] John Bayley, *An Essay on Hardy* (Cambridge: Cambridge UP, 1978).

[35] Merryn and Raymond Williams, "Hardy and Social Class," in Norman Page (ed.), *Thomas Hardy and His Background* (London: Bell and Hyman, 1980), 29–40: 31.

[36] Philip Collins, "'Hardy and Education," in *Thomas Hardy and His Background*, 412–75: 60. For the too-often-cited G. K. Chesterton jibe, see his *The Victorian Age in Literature* (London: Williams and Norgate, 1913), 43.

[37] *The Life of Thomas Hardy*. by F. E. Hardy. 2vols. As reprinted (London: Studio Editions, 1994): vol. 2, 183.

[38] John Sutherland, *Victorian Novelists and Publishers* (London: Athlone Press, 1976), 212.

[39] Lucille Herbert, "Hardy's Views in *Tess of the D'Urbervillles*," in *ELH: A Journal of English Literary History* 37 (1970): 77–94; also cited in Penny Boumelha, *Thomas Hardy and Women: Sexual Ideology and Narrative Form* (Brighton: Harvester, 1982).

[40] Samuel Hynes, ed. *Thomas Hardy* (Oxford Authors Series). Oxford: Oxford UP, 1984; Samuel Hynes, "The Hardy Tradition in Modern English Poetry," in *Thomas Hardy and His Background*, 173–91.

[41] See, e.g. Seymour-Smith, *Hardy*, 246.

[42] But see, e.g. Helen Garwood's *Thomas Hardy: An Illustration of the Philosophy of Schopenhauer* (Philadelphia: John C. Winston, 1911) for confirmation that Schopenhauer enters deeply into Hardy's intellectual matrix.

[43] See Ernest Brennecke, *Thomas Hardy's Universe: A Study of a Poet's Mind* (London: T. Fisher Unwin, 1924); and Ernest Brennecke, *Thomas Hardy: A Biography* (New York: Greenberg, 1925).

[44] Carl Weber, *Hardy of Wessex: His Life and Literary Career* (New York: Columbia, 1940), 295. As Richard H. Taylor puts it, this is "the work of a disciple" with consequent "difficulty in objective interpretation." As a kindly critic who finds it difficult to find hard words for anyone, the statement, coming from him, that Weber's "erratic critical judgement and lapses into journalese irritate" may be taken to be an extraordinary piece of scholarly severity here. See his "Thomas Hardy: A Reader's Guide," in *Thomas Hardy: The Writer and His Background*, edited by Norman Page (London: Bell and Hyman, 1980), 219–258.

[45] Paul Turner, *The Life of Thomas Hardy* (Oxford: Blackwell, 1998).

[46] J. Hillis Miller, *Thomas Hardy: Distance and Desire* (Cambridge, MA: Harvard UP, 1970).

[47] Margaret Whitford, *Luce Irigaray: Philosophy in the Feminine* (London: Routledge, 1991), 31.

2: Convergence of the Twain?
Hardy and the Forms of
Critical Appropriation

THAT THERE IS SUCH A THING AS A "Hardy Industry" (even if only a cottage one) few would doubt. Donald Davie (1989) ironically claimed he had seen the phrase used un-ironically[1] (but how would one establish that?) Curiously, though, it might seem that it is the official Hardy cult associated with such organisations as the Thomas Hardy Society (with its journal, newsletter, guaranteed biennial publication by a major London publisher of conference proceedings, and the small body of influential editors and biographers who cluster round the shrine) which in certain ways may impede rather than facilitate the recognition of the nature of Hardy's achievement.

Although scholarly and industrious after their fashion — there are prominent, indeed distinguished names in this world of Hardy studies — such eminent writers positively strive to achieve unity in yea-saying, as gatekeepers of the informatic flow about Hardy. Despite much meritorious scholarship, there is an all too obvious desire to "stop things happening" in the intellectual "eweleaze" of precisely that section of Thomas Hardy studies which most strenuously lays claim to official custodianship. In general, there are institutions and individuals, culturally conservative in a way that Hardy himself was not, which undertake to represent and to make representations of him, which mingle incidental scholarly help with the more dubious forms of cultural intervention which lead to the results just touched on.

It might be said, then, that a slightly ironic discovery awaits anyone interested in Hardy's critical reception who brings to it what Barthes describes as a "modern gaze."[2] It would indeed be a highly hypothetical (or, to speak plainly) impossible she who would attempt to map the various intellectual fields of force here. As no one will have read all which has been written about Hardy it seems important that the potential peruser of some of those writings should at least set off in what would seem to be the more congenial intellectual directions. Still dominant strains in this wide-ranging discourse about Hardy sometimes offer positively anti-intellectual ones as, precisely (and rather damagingly) the most authentic.

This is a world of disputes and diversions, of occasional theoretical interventions and those forms of apparent resistance to the theoretical which
may, as Paul de Man implies,[3] secrete their own theory. In general, it is
those forms of critical practice which are least progressive, least in touch
with intellectual developments, which often offer themselves as and actually
win out in being accepted as the most authentic in presenting a "good little
Thomas Hardy" who is more reassuring than exciting, closer to received
ideas than to troubling or original ones. As this chapter will show, the idea
that things are improving is sustainable but it is obvious that it is still largely
untheorised and critically "inert" approaches which bulk large in treatments
of a novelist and poet who was, in his day, at once an experimental and a
polemical writer, a "*succès de scandale*" whose experimental program was
inseparable from an inquiry, if usually a fairly polite one, into social arrangements and ideological assumptions. In this connection, see e.g. Widdowson (1988),[4] Goode (1976, 1979, 1988, 1990),[5] Williams (1970,
1973, 1980)[6] Ingham (1976, 1989),[7] Ebbatson (1993),[8] Wotton (1985),[9]
Feltes (1986)[10] and Fisher (1992)[11] offer rewardingly sophisticated approaches and suggestions which will attract some attention in appropriate
contexts here, partly because in their various ways they impel the recognition that Hardy's texts "mean mischief," as his publisher Macmillan put it.

Even if all of these works are, in various ways, flawed, all contrive to
suggest the inherently provocative and subversive qualities of Hardy's work
which are muted or even occluded by those who, if tacitly, offer themselves
as mainstream Hardy critique, replaying him on apparently authentic instruments ("serpents," perhaps). The irony of the critical reception of
Hardy is that the homespun modalities of Hardy criticism, the cottage industry with its basically "recuperative" agenda still pursued and embodied
in recent work by Lock (1992),[12] Pettit (1994),[13] Pettit (1996)[14] Millgate
(1996)[15] and Gibson (1996)[16] — still offers itself as the authentic route, or
rather lane, to Hardy. The list includes a recent biography, yet more biographical contextualizing, and "appreciative" conference essays by Thomas
Hardy Society members (Pettit, 1996), and all this activity rewrites Hardy
so as to make him fairly reassuring. Despite the alarms and incursions of recent forays into Wessex, then, there is still a dominant, "hegemonic" feeling
about so much of this pseudo-homage in which, in Eliot's idiom, "the giving famishes the craving."

Consider, for example, the contribution by Edward Blishen (Pettit,
1996), "Hardy, *The Hand of Ethelberta*, and Some Persisting English Discomforts" (177–195), which might have been penned in the remote English village of Much Wittering. Indeed, much of what Blishen says is, as
usual, about himself considered as a personage in whom we will all have a
profound interest. It should be noted that Edward, who died fairly recently,

was an absolutely charming man who wrote a string of entertaining autobiographical books which involve you in his unresolved oedipality and intellectual formation at High School level. And he has certainly not gone
amiss in the text he has chosen. Margaret Higonnet has claimed that *The
Hand of Ethelberta* (1876) is "one of Hardy's most underrated novels,"[17]
and Blishen is surely right to defend it, just as Charles Lock (1992) is
wrong to cavil at Peter Widdowson's prolonged defence of it (1989: 115),
accepting in his attack on Widdowson the conventional valuations he elsewhere seems to be challenging.

The "challenge," it must be conceded, *is* quite implicit. We have already
seen how great authorities on poetry and on Hardy like Harold Bloom and
J. Hillis Miller have pointed out how "Shelleyan" he is in terms of his
whole literary inception. But Kevin Moore, whose work was also described
in chapter 1, was right to qualify this with an account, more thoroughgoing
and more nuanced, of Hardy's response to Shelley and to Romanticism. In
this, he announces a Shelleyan program based on a passion for reforming
the world, literally avant la lettre,[18] before, that is, becoming a man of letters
or (literally) a man made out of words, and deconstructs it. He then leaves
the reader to mourn his compulsion to repeat gestures which, returning as
farce or textuality (the corpus becomes a corpse, the native eternally returns
to find himself gone), are always already cancelled, disallowed or disavowed.

Biographically speaking, this might be said to cash out as a frantic social
sycophancy which already secretes the *ressentiment* he craves. If he offers
subversiveness, it needs must appear as a Shelleyan ("insider's") commodity. Shelley, quite conscious of belonging to a "good family," as he puts it,
however ironically, in the "Preface" to "Julian and Maddalo," belongs in a
distinctly English and rather strange tradition of aristocratic radicalism.
Moore analyses in some detail how High Victorian culture has traduced
these original models of enlightenment and emancipation. What Kevin
Moore ignores, having already more than enough to do in his magnificently
ambitious book, is how Hardy hesitates between such postures as these and
others, including the quite differently inflected plebeian radicalisms which
the actuality of Puddletown seemed to offer him in the versions of him presented by Gittings [1975] and Seymour-Smith [1994]).[19] Yet he wished to
observe defiantly, defiantly even of the Shelleyan revolutionary, if it came to
that, that in his own way he himself came of a good family with traditions
which might be respected. Indeed, part of what he has to atone for, despite
his claim that his treatment of village life would be "without caricature," is
precisely that he traduces that culture as one largely of yokels, however
sympathetically perceived, for the delectation of Leslie Stephen and people
of his social standing and privileged intellectual formation. Marjorie Garson

in work already alluded to in chapter 1 has helped define this combination of defensiveness and independence.

Here one might also consult Rosemarie Morgan (1992)[20] and Martin Seymour-Smith (1994: 182) for disquieting accounts of the baleful influence and requirements of Stephen, which may be felt to feed into the point made by Jan Jedrzejewski (which constitutes in fair measure the thesis of his book here) that such patronage "resulted in the emergence of an image of Hardy as an epigone of mainstream Victorian agnosticism rather than as an original thinker in his own right."[21]

But no simple account of Hardy's "intentions" will pass muster, as Peter Widdowson notes as the basis of his latest writing about Hardy, offering an overall argument which correctly concludes that he is in this respect the "slipperiest" of customers,[22] and one can certainly concede something to James Gibson's point that Hardy as hired to be "a good hand at a serial" was not in a position to stir up trouble in a way that he claims "comfortable Marxist professors" would like him to be (1996: 143), and hence that his subversiveness is submerged and canny. Indeed, James Gibson, a searching critic on the right occasion, offered an introductory essay (cited in chapter 1 [1980]) in the definition of such "canny" moments.

Here, indeed, not entirely un-Hardy-ishly, if by accident, Blishen considers only the problem of one's own social mobility, not the radicalism, the fierce contempt for mere rank which glows with animation and unusual lack of ambiguity in *The Hand of Ethelberta*, combined with a sense of the needful solidarity and mutually supportive roles of humble families under pressure from generally untoward social arrangements. Instead of seeing the highly charged irony in the working man's contempt for the aristocratic brother of the future husband of Ethelberta as equal to and more authentic than his for him, Blishen makes the book simply embody the pathos that attends the rite of passage from one class to another — that "going up into the next class" of which Frances Widdowson made such a good title in her study of the teaching profession.[23] Blishen then trails off into typical critical inconsequence: "Hardy is marvellous always about the sea" (186). What leaps into life here is, typically, Blishen's schoolboy account of his Headmaster's assaults on Hardy's pessimism in the interests of *esprit de corps*. This turns out to be Blishen's characteristic approach to things made into an unusual way of proselytizing for Hardy (182). In this limited sense we may even conclude that his treatment of *Ethelberta* is actually successful.

We might also note, for example, how a discussion of Hardy's poetry by James Gibson (Pettit, 1996), ("Thomas Hardy's Poetry: Poetic Apprehension and Poetic Method" [1–21]) ignores previous discussions, often at a high pitch of critical sophistication. Gibson is of course an editor of enormous distinction and should be honoured for his real achievements — the

"Variorum" edition of a *Complete Poems* of Hardy in particular. But as a critic, to judge by these recent performances, he very much "abides our question," in Arnold's idiom. This particular essay is very much of a piece with his procedures in his contribution to the earlier collection by Pettit (1994), "'The Characteristic of All great Poetry — The General Perfectly Reduced in the Particular': Thomas Hardy" (1–15).

Without his overtly claiming this, an ex cathedra quality is imparted to his pronouncements simply because no sense is conveyed of his being a latecomer to critical disputes, even if those are confined somewhat parochially to Hardy's poetry alone: "he finishes his painting of the scene with the introduction of the animal world" ("Domicilium"), while in "An August Midnight," "what is so impressive about this poem, as it is about so much of Hardy's writing, is its authenticity. This, we feel, really did happen and his descriptive ability is largely responsible here" (4–5). He argues that Hardy wishes to transcend the particular when it seems clear that he does better when not doing that, while "transcend" suggests the idealist tradition which has dogged Hardy studies — he transcends society and sociology, class and ideology, history and actuality to be "pinnacled dim in the intense inane." Although he rightly notes Hardy's "compassion" as an attractive feature in the context of a modern literature in general not strong on tenderness, Hardy's pity is often released as a response to his own sense of the macabre or secreted as a specific response to his own sardonic plottings.

James Gibson is a distinguished editor and almost everything he says about Hardy is of interest. But he refuses to entertain the idea that critical discourse (no less than poetic) is inherently problematic, or consider Hardy's (ineluctable) intertextuality. He does not have a "differing" idea of critique, the sense that how to practice criticism is always on the point of definition, always a place of tension and a contested area. He assumes that Hardy is simply describing something which we all recognise, or, perhaps better, "precognise."

While critique does not elect either to follow or to compose elegant variations on a given theme, and although critics may, as George Watson points out,[24] interrupt rather than simply continue discussion by previous critics, they generally show some awareness of what they are "sidelining." Critical discussion might consider challenging accounts considered elsewhere here, those of Donald Davie (1972, 1973, 1997, 1989)[25] or Harold Bloom (1975)[26] and J. Hillis Miller's (e.g. 1970, 1972, 1984, 1985)[27] 'situating' of Hardy's poetry, or Eric Griffiths's careful, Ricksian consideration of Hardy as a printed voice of Victorian poetry (1989),[28] or Peter Sacks's (1985) discussion of him in the context of the English elegy.[29]

By comparison, Laurence Lerner's pretty untheoretical discussion of the 1912–13 "Emma" sequence) "Moments of Vision — and After," in the same collection (22–38) performs an elementary service in carefully un-shackling them once more from biography, or the kind of interest biogra-phers take in his poems — or, one might say, are doomed to take in poems.

It is a serviceable essay, very clear but also very simple, and it deals, once more, with this domestic Victorian sequence of Hardy's which has perhaps been "too much discussed, too much explained." Naturally it's a crowd-puller, not to say a tear-jerker, and Lerner can hardly be blamed for picking it out again in the special context of an annual conference. Yet an exclusive focus on this sequence, apparently innocuous, may have the effect of oc-cluding considerations of Hardy's range as a poet of wider social horizons, where his rural preoccupations are less involute and not necessarily less in-timate.

Ronald Blythe broaches the idea in another glancingly comparative es-say on Hardy's congruence, or, finally, lack of congruence, with John Clare. "Thomas Hardy and John Clare: A Soil Observed, a Soil Ploughed" (Pettit, 1996: 54–67) gives the honours to Clare as the more authentically "rural" poet. It isn't entirely clear that he doesn't perpetuate the prejudice he is combatting though, with rhetoric like "Clare's poetry is the English field given voice" (59), which maintains an inappropriate "beyond ideology" clause for "rural" poetry he himself seems set on challenging in its reference to enclosures (the endless encroachments by the gentry on "common" land).

For example, he notes Clare's sarcasm in the face of bourgeois wonder over where this particular peasant had picked up poetry — "I kicked it out of the clods." Defending Hardy, by comparison with Clare, he is neverthe-less defensive: "Much of Hardy's work defends the dispossessed. But it has to do so from a height" (62). He claims that "being what he was, he could not be what he had come from." But the answer to Hardy's defensiveness lies in his own essay when he observes that "the indigenous writer or artist of any kind blows his own and his neighbours' cover" (55), which com-bines with the upward mobility he was bred to to create an inevitable defen-siveness. Nor does he sufficiently consider the conditions under which Hardy was allowed to become a writer, nor that the conditions Clare en-dured led him to the lunatic asylum — suggesting the forms of desperation which might easily underlie Hardy's own quest for literary success. If he is saying that Hardy should have achieved authenticity by courting the fate of John Clare, we may be grateful that Hardy himself didn't see the necessity to conduct himself in that particular way.

If we return, then, to James Gibson as the presiding scholarly eminence of this collection, we must note that, despite his charm and scholarship, such appreciation as he seems to be encouraging takes pride in having no new critical or theoretical bearings and in taking no note of what has been going on in various theoretical and critical areas. Such an approach, usually, though not always, without overt polemicizing, excludes provocative, useful, and sophisticated studies which in fact "threaten" nothing but the conferencers' own claims to act as authoritative mediators of Hardy. (Indeed, even the American critics who have been accepted as one of themselves like Dale Kramer [1975, 1979, 1990][30] and Peter Casagrande [1982, 1987])[31] seem curiously untouched by those critical approaches which have left traces and "tell-tale articles" all across "America," at least in their own writings, despite the fact that as editors they may usefully play host to them, as Kramer certainly has — in *Critical Essays on Thomas Hardy* in particular, where contributions by John Goode, Mary Jacobus, Kathleen Blake and Philip M. Weinstein are all admirably "advanced."

Kramer's obvious desire to include advanced work in the field, and which compels respect, is itself highly respectable.[32] His recent addendum to the literature on *Tess* (1991)[33] is hugely well informed in terms of the cultural matrix for the creation of *Tess*, particularly perhaps on the relation of Hardy to Richard Jefferies, if still fairly unadventurous in theoretical, hermeneutic, and critical terms.

There is, though, a startling moment in an essay by Peter Casagrande in Pettit's 1994 collection, which, unlike its successor, intermittently promised "new threshholds, new anatomies." Here Casagrande suddenly observes that

> Because Hardy instinctively wrote against the grain, his writing challenged precedent, tradition, convention, and custom — the already-existing in all its forms — in ways that the writing of contemporaries such as Dickens, Meredith, the Brontes, and even Eliot and Butler did not (18).

It's a muted note, certainly, in the context of the collection itself, nor, characteristically, is it followed through or convincingly illustrated in the essay on "'Something more to be Said': Hardy's Creative Process and the Case of *Tess and Jude*" (16–40), which, disappointingly in view of that sudden flash of scholarly provocation, consists of expressions of scholarly respect based on structural parallels of *Tess* and *Jude*, eking out an original insight of D. H. Lawrence but partly based on the procedures of his earlier book (1982), and finally portraying *Jude* as a "parody" (37) of *Tess*. He also explores the decay in romantic claims for the artist as creator — from Sidney and Tasso to Shelley — to the acceptance of the idea of the artist as mere creature a hollow or empty way of conceiving subjectivity, traversed, moment by moment, by various (semic?) codes (18–21).

Yet when James Gibson observes of "During Wind and Rain" in "Thomas Hardy's Poetry — Intention and Method" that "the feeling is so intense, the choice of detail so right, that it becomes universal," (11) everything depends on Hardy as a man noticing such things, hardly at all on the textual operation by which they are preserved or rather created, not to mention the de-historicising and de-"class"-ifying nature of the "move" here which a Roland Barthes would be quick to note. Gibson unguardedly quotes William Archer's observation (1898),[34] originally picked up by Edmund Blunden (1942)[35] that he regards "all the words in the dictionary on one plane, so to speak" and regards "them all as equally available and appropriate for any and every literary response." He reads this off as purely complimentary, when in fact it is well on the way to supplying the critical patronage which has often visited, perhaps at times vitiated, the critical response to him. See, for example, Leavis (1932, 1940),[36] Blackmur (1940),[37] and, carefully explicating and explaining all this, Williams (1973, 1970, 1980).[38]

Gibson himself, though interesting on his own "Robinson Crusoe" terms, cites only parochial authorities who ignore sophisticated considerations of poetic language and textuality, so that his would-be inflations turn easily to deflations. Although he may well be an extremely winning presence as a lecturer, there is a curious arrogance in the apparent assumption of critical modesty itself, the certainty that recent writing in particular can safely be, or is perhaps best ignored.

As Peter Rothermel shows, in an essay in Pettit (1996) certainly not without charm — "The Far and the Near: On Reading Thomas Hardy Today" — another, and cognate, weakness is the construction of a unilaterally bourgeois-sentimental perspective for the reader of Hardy, as if Hardy himself had simply arranged this:

> Hardy knew and loved the value and significance of things as they had been: the old churches, cottages and roads, the trees and springs and wells, the old ways of toil and soil, of pasture and pleasure, of shepherd and sheep (163).

In Hardy, the somnolence of these complacent perspectives is always in tension with destabilizing, disconcerting, unreassuring and un-"bourgeois" points of view. Raymond Williams's quietly devastating first sentence in his chapter on "Wessex and the Border" in *The Country and the City* might be cited here:

> Thomas Hardy was born a few miles from Tolpuddle, a few years after the deportation of the farm labourers who had come together to form a trade union. This fact alone should remind us that Hardy was born into a

changing and struggling rural society, rather than the timeless backwater to which he is so often deported (197).

That Hardy was born into a struggling rural society does not, of course automatically mean that he must obviously reflect or refract it, still less that he was necessarily committed to reflecting or refracting it in such a way as to stir up trouble. K. D. M. Snell might feel that Hardy's romantic subjectivity precludes much of a look at the worst as that might be chronicled in statistics of suffering (1985),[39] although his and Ebbatson's (1993) view of this is surely overdemanding to the point of harshness ("The Dorset labourer is effectively silenced in the seamless flow of Hardy's meditative prose . . . when the labourers found a voice . . . their conversation was marked by bitterness and class animosity" &c.).[40]

Nevertheless, in Hardy's work there is always a pressure from the "other side" (or underside) of that rural idyll the genteel critic has been too concerned to emphasize. And in consigning the rural poor to an "objective" existence Snell ignores the fact that they too, exist as "subjectivities," and it is in allowing "them" some access to the bourgeois condition of subjectivity that Hardy's claims to radicalism finally rest. And even if, as Michael Valdes Moses argues, "Hardy's regionalism carries a conservative or antimodern charge" and "functions as an imaginative bulwark against the globalizing and homogenizing tendencies of modernity,"[41] the "effort to exhume a pre-modern world often leads to bizarre reconstructions"(32) which, as he fails to note, may have the effect of deconstructions. The complications of Hardy's text may finally feed into the subtle perspective of a Walter Benjamin conjuring a "revolutionary nostalgia."

Kevin Z. Moore's (1990) work has already been referred to as wide-ranging, well-informed criticism which, alert to Hardy's textuality, to wider intellectual horizons, reads him as, supremely, a graveyard of dead romanticisms, screeds no less than creeds.[42] There is an unavoidable political undertow here concerning the extinguishing of Utopian hopes. He is perhaps too indebted to the kind of formalism associated with Harold Bloom (1961, 1971).[43] It's obvious that, for his own purposes, or his own responsiveness to traits of his mentors, who would certainly include Eliot and Nietzsche, he forgets the radicalities that come with his own holistically anamnesic ingestion of the poetry of romanticism. Behind Bloom, after all, also stands Northrop Frye (1957)[44] and what Eagleton has excessively but not irrelevantly styled "The Idealism of American Criticism" [1986]).[45] (And yet, as one article has astutely noted, Frye is, in a curiously "boneless" way, a "Utopian Marxist").[46]

Or one might consider, for yet another example, Marjorie Garson's (1991) study,[47] to which a Michael Millgate (1971, 1982)[48] and John Bayley (1978)[49] stood godfather. It is still Lacanian enough to show the more

startling side of Hardy's treatment of a hay-wain named desire, and thus
with considerable capacity for stirring things up, if not in the world, at least
in the world of Hardy critique. As a result, despite her tilting at those who
wish to make Hardy politically correct (but the phrase is inadmissable), she
does not overinvolve Hardy with any kind of conservative consensus.

Another book on Hardy which had its origins as a dissertation under
John Bayley's supervision, by Jan Jedrzejewski, produces interesting arguments about Hardy's "phased withdrawals" from churchiness and subsequent approaches to it (rather like T. S. Eliot's search for the teasing
rhythms which never quite arrive at metrical orthodoxy). And the book is
informative but traditional in its critical assumptions and the constricted
ambit of its scholarly procedures.)[50] It helps define the inherent instability
volatility, as well as he relative independence of Hardy as creative thinker.
The conservative critical matrix for such work as that of Garson and Jed-
zejewski does not ensure that the healthy offspring are so ideologically constrained.

Curiously, Pettit's previous collection (1994)[51] moved a little in the direction of critical innovation and genuine intellectual debate, though small
signs like the extended title of Peter Widdowson's essay in that particular
Festschrift ("'Moments of Vision': Postmodernising *Tess of the D'Urbervilles*,
or, *Tess of the D'Urbervilles* Faithfully Presented by Peter Widdowson" [80–
100]) may well reflect some tussling between the essayist and his conservative editor. But in general the conference papers of the THS can confidently
be expected to emit little but the usual "pizzicati of hosanna" (Wallace
Stevens), or incense to fume at the altar of their mutilated god. Biography,
context appreciation, belle-lettristic suavity and the mode of "celebration"
by "mindless rote," rather as if the rural English novelist required a "rustic"
response is made to appear the dominant and the correct one in this scholarly but strange, wide-ranging yet recuperative world well lost of official
Hardy studies.

The malaise is partly a matter of what Frank Kermode (1990),[52] explaining Derrida with characteristic clarity, calls "doubling," itself echoing
(doubling) Derrida's complaint about conventional literary criticism, and in
particular also allowing the novelist to be taken on what appears to be his
own terms. In fact Hardy as critic hardly steps forward with magisterial
claims to critical attention. In work already mentioned in chapter 1, Charles
Lock (1992) is inclined to see it otherwise, but he is committed to giving
what might be felt to be an undue prominence to early criticism that this
only underlines the slightly perverse nature of his program, in which recent
sophisticated items are, effectively, although formally listed, quashed.

Lock also wishes to give some prominence to Hardy's own "theoretical" and discursive writing as something of a clue to his creative intentions,

which is salutary to a degree. But as it is, Hardy's critical observations, even on fairly formal occasions, are plainly inadequate as a guide to responding to his own work, hardly claim to be, and could hardly be thought of as that novelist's present-day perspective. Indeed, as Walter Benjamin has remarked, the words of the novelist are "precisely suited to diverting rather than permitting privileged entrée" to the meaning of his work.[53]

Peter Widdowson (1989) is still suggestive on the way these critical appropriations or reappropriations are "always already" misappropriations, calling, in vain, it would seem, for a "critiography" (1989: 12) to replace biography, chartings of the way "Hardy" is a series of seemings, uncoordinated impressions which are the product of critical processings which may well turn out to be a misrepresentation of his representations. Widdowson's thesis consists largely of a series of scholarly snipings at all those who attach a conservative tag to a novelist who attracted savagely dismissive attacks and the indrawn breath of orthodox outrage as a [would be] "bold enquirer into morals and religion" (Shelley "Preface" to *Prometheus Unbound* [1820]). (See, for example, Moore [1990] and Miller [1970] on Hardy as Shelleyan), whose work, as Hardy himself wryly noted, was often scrutinised for its ethical and ideological coefficients (*Life*, Vol. 2: 183), even, that is, he implies, when the explicit criteria were esthetic.

This is, to be sure, in tension with a rural nostalgia which would appear to have conservative implications, although it should be remembered that the hegemonic practices of the ruling order are by no means always "conservative," and may be destructive of things held to be valuable by those powerless to intervene. Curiously, if, as Barthes says, literature is written by relatively powerless social group,[54] they may recognise that part of their task is to record a vanishing way of life. Radicalism is masked as conservatism here, and the tone of Hardy's poetic thought is also caught by Baudrillard's indignation on behalf of "the vanquished dead crying out for justice . . . ."[55]

This is an inadvertently accurate rendering of this curious, almost paradoxical "counter-radical" radicality of Hardy's which much critique has failed to catch in its sightings or citings, and this emphasizes in a slightly different way that the best critique of Hardy will not necessarily, or even easily, be felt to proceed from his official custodians. We might pursue the sense, advanced in the reference to Jameson, that critique which is inadvertently cognate with what Hardy seems to be saying is sometimes more illuminating than that which the official critical convoy provides. For example, one of Baudrillard's most often-quoted maxims, "that when the real is no longer what it was, nostalgia assumes its full value" is so obviously applicable to Hardy's *oeuvre* as a whole, which the effect of his fictions is so complex that we feel in reading him, as Terry Eagleton puts it, again without

specific reference to Hardy, that "a whole traditional ideology of representation is in crisis."[56]

But if we seem to speak of Hardy as a rural recorder of a "world 'out
there'" we need to negotiate the work of the social historian with a distinct
interest in those lower orders who, though undeniably a part of history,
hardly enter the pages of the historian. As we saw, K. D. M. Snell claimed
(1985) that Hardy is not interested in portraying specific conditions of deprivation and distress so much as the realm of subjectivity, although he does
at least endow with subjectivity those who had often been seen as mere objects. However, not to speak of the surprising ideological bearings and political importings of the novels themselves, "The Dorsetshire Labourer"
(1883) is a rousing, if necessarily ambiguous document for one forced, determined in both senses, to be a purveyor of nostalgia to the gentry, or at
least the incipiently genteel. Yet again, as John Piper interestingly remarks
"Hardy taught us to be nostalgic without being sentimental" (cited by Gibson in Pettit [1996], 9).

As already remarked, and in this context it will bear repeating, his world,
an ineluctably textual realm, is equally a graveyard of dead screeds, a realm
of dereliction, effaced inscription, a wan aftermath even the vital glories of
which are, so to speak, posthumous. Kevin Moore is perhaps most attuned
to this fact, although J. Hillis Miller has noticed such things over a temporal
and thematic range of work in which the sense of "il(l)](-)literacy" conveys
and mediates a palpable world in decline and development — whether
leaving the old, both worlds at once he views, in Waller's idiom, or is
"wandering between two worlds, one dead, the other powerless to be
born," in the toweringly desolated phrases of Arnold one suspects Hardy
took so very much to heart. Hardy falls between the sociological insistences
of the excellent historian Snell and the highly distinguished, displayfully deconstructive idealisations of J. Hillis Miller.

Nevertheless, I am still inclined to give the palm here to Kevin Z.
Moore (1990), who has conducted a magisterial investigation of Hardy's
"investment" in Wessex as a superannuated, sunken realm of never quite
extinguished romantic hopes unleashed by the intellectual harvest of the
Enlightenment and the revolutionary decade of the 1790's. That Hardy's
imagination is drawn to this romantic dawn Moore does indeed show in an
exciting but also useful display of scholarly panache.

But he also demonstrates how Hardy's appropriative re-readings are often but wan, retrospective visitations parodying the romantic cult of *anamnesis* or recollection. Hardy is summoned here as a deployer of burnt-out
hopes and tropes which, unlike Shelley, can summon no energizing sense of
incipience after the triumph of the forces of "liberticide" (to cite Shelley's
memorable coinage). Kevin Moore insists we compare his melancholy ret-

rospections with Wordsworth's art of memory, much possessed by "spots of time" (*Prelude* [1850],12.208) which fructify in the speaker's present, with proto-Nietzschean strength through joy.

In Hardy's world Shelleyan hope always already, as it were, "lies slain" ("Hap," *Wessex Poems*, 1897), or is at the very least, *sous rature*, as Peter Casagrande also points out in his summary of the relationship between the two poets.[57] As John Goode has remarked in another sketch of Hardy's annulling repetitions of Romantic teleologies and aspirations, "*The Dynasts* [1903–8] is the morning after to *Prometheus Unbound's* night before,"[58] and wallows in crushed utopian hopes finally hopelessly invested in the original "Eurotrash" of Napoleonic swaggering. Goode, interestingly, reads "Dynasts" as, roughly, "oppressors" (36–7), while Isobel Armstrong also indicates that *The Dynasts*, if ambivalent in this respect, offers the notionally radical reader a position not often remarked.[59] Neither piece, of course, pursues the other issues the Dynasts might seem to provoke — the idea of wholesale plagiarism, not merely healthy "intertextuality" (see, Moore [1990: 12]), and that of botched execution (fustian, etc.) — the issues are raised by Norman Page and briefly by Edward Neill).[60]

Critics who succeed best, then, may be those who recogise that the unscrambling of the ideological and the artistic in representation is fraught with difficulty. If, as Jim Reilly avers in a complicated argument (1991) over Hardy's most effortfully historicized novel,[61] *The Trumpet-Major* (1880) somehow fails of its promised charm, this failure is very much involved with his interest in the history of representation as the representation of history, and specifically in that it commits Hardy to flag-waving, ideological simplicity (and complicity). "Thank God I have seen my King," rhapsodizes nice Mrs Garland over the man who lost us America.

Reilly, pursuing his interesting agenda, is a little hard on the book. Hardy's sense of life's little ironies is clumsily energized by the entanglements of passion in relation to a wider sense of value (or values) in a lurching period-piece: but the whole issue of wholesale militarization and its effects is prettified if not petrified, and Reilly does seem generally justified here in getting his teeth into its representations.

He seems to be arguing that the ideological basis of the fiction seems inseparable from its artistic failure. Here, it may be felt, the besetting intellectual parochialism of Hardy studies has hardly equipped them to cope with these fundamental issues in "historical" writing. How many Hardy critics, for example, are aware of the specific emphasis put by Lukacs on the Napoleonic period? As Jim Reilly usefully puts it later, "the Hardy of *Tess of the D'Urbervilles* makes rather than finds form and truth, whereas the Hardy of *The Trumpet-Major* has seemed to expect to discover and reproduce it" (60). Worried about the history of representations no less than representations of history, and confronting variously Eliot's *Romola,* Conrad's gloriously uncompleted *Suspense* as well as *The Dynasts* and *The Trumpet-Major,* he concludes, a little hectoringly, that "few would want to contradict the view that these works are variously strained, turgid, slight or overblown and rarely redolent of their authors' characteristic brilliancies" (2–3).

In general the theme of national survival decrees unprobing loyalism and much clumsy jesting apparently (as Valentine Cunningham notes in his odd singling-out of this vulnerably programmatic novel as characteristic of Hardy at work [1993]).[62] National survival decrees the imprisoning of ironic nuance and scruple, and we are here shown a Hardy untrammelled by those supple and subtle ideological imbroglios and confusions characteristic of his greater works, at least at the level of world history if not of that of intimate relationships.

Roger Ebbatson, citing Lukacs, describes such moments in Hardy as resulting from "a deadening preponderance of antiquarianism" (1993: 47). It is, rather, a deadening preponderance of *ancien régime*-ism, and the nationalism it evokes. As Glen Wickens has remarked in the central point in his discussion of *The Dynasts,* "such blind patriotism is only another symptom of Europe's great problem."[63]

All in all, it's just as well that *The Trumpet-Major* has not been trumpeted as major by too many modern critics, despite worthy attempts by to make the best of this relatively bad job by jobbing builder of novels and *Bildung*-builder Hardy, himself the son of a jobbing builder whose defensiveness could lead him to speak of "a master-mason employed by his father."

But all of these people are, at the least, offering genuine critical enquiry. As we have seen, the overwhelming impression the reader in England still receives is critical appropriation by a gentle, exclusive, anti-intellectual sect which, whatever its final insidiousness does indeed carry out its agenda of "boosting Hardy" — a phrase adapted from the fierce Q. D. Leavis. The point here is that it does so, it may be felt, at the expense of misrepresenting Hardy's creative implication. The paradox of the central response to "Hardy" as that is measured in public attention and critical consensus about status, is the initial and long-range effect of the work of F. R. Leavis, who rejected Hardy as a novelist (1948)[64] and patronised him as a poet (1932, 1940).[65] The irony is that, while Leavis is usually discussed as an avatar of blinkered reaction (for example by Hawkes,[66] Easthope,[67] Widdowson,[68] Belsey,[69] Baldick,[70] Mulhern),[71] the peerless militancy with which he armed himself may still be felt to contain a "moment" in the sense of a force of untimely meditation tilting against intellectually recessive forces.

Instead of moving forward to new perspectives offered by poststructuralist, feminist or postmodernist developments, particularly after the débâcle at Cambridge (where Leavis had held court) following the advent there in the English Faculty of a radical or "Continental-ised" professorate, there was something of a return to habits of belle-lettrist "appreciation" — anti-Leavisian only in the sense of being pre-Leavisian, opposing even that in Leavis which could be construed as intellectually progressive.

Curiously, Leavis had put Hardy in a *salon des refusés* precisely because, as Lawrence's primal artistic ancestor (see Lawrence [1914/1985]),[72] he came to function as a kind of anti-Lawrentian to be purged away. Nicely defined by John Maynard as Lawrence's "potently impotent" predecessor (for his discussion of *Jude* and its effect on Lawrence see chapter 4), the predecessor or precursor (Hardy) certainly suffered in the comparison. But the critical balance might still be redressed by pointing out that Lawrence owed him so much he is unthinkable without Hardy as his example. Indeed, it might also be pointed out that while Leavis championed Lawrence, his Jamesian affiliations showed the incoherence of his project. Leavis "refused" Hardy, then accepted Lawrence.

He ignored the debt to Hardy which would have led him to pay at least that degree of homage. Similarly, he also "refused" modernism and thus made little of the fact that Lawrence was undeniably part of the constellation of "modernists": however unsatisfactory as a label (see Emig, 1996),[73] the term has stuck (all that one asks of labels, after all), so that Leavis's eventual refusal of modernism except in highly "strained" (Anglo-centric) forms also sits oddly with his rain-dance for Lawrence and rejection of Hardy. Hardy and modernist experiment combine to form a Lawrence. Yet in Leavis's account, in themselves neither Hardy nor modernism are commendable.

It would also appear that as a result of this wilful self-blinkering Leavis also fails to recognise the experimental side of Hardy himself in categorising him so firmly as a Victorian when, as David Lodge points out, he is, technically speaking, a kind of "liminal" modernist, or at the least a "post-Victorian" in the sense briefly suggested much earlier by Morton Dauwen Zabel.[74] Lodge presents well the precise stationing of a Hardy, one in which the author as narrator, not quite dead, fades into impalpability like Joyce's slightly misleading figure preoccupied with his manicure set in *Portrait of the Artist*, or the Cheshire Cat of *Alice in Wonderland* fame, or flails about with self-cancelling inconsistency. Writing on Hardy's productively troubled diegesis, Lodge describes how "Hardy hedges his bets, equivocates, qualifies or contradicts his own authorial dicta, uses tortuous formulae to avoid taking responsibility for authorial description and generalization."[75]

A typical Leavis's-Cambridge-influenced judgement, then, like that of W. W. Robson that "Hardy's technique was old-fashioned even in its

time," is perhaps itself rather old-fashioned in its idea of what technique[76] is
in ours.

Critics may in fact lose themselves in critical air-pockets, not quite modern and not quite ancient. A recent book by Robert Langbaum, is susceptible to influence from recent critique, and thus probing and less than
critically inert after the manner of that too-hardy plant, the traditional
Hardy scholar, but still interested in fulfilling the Leavisian project (Hardy
as the missing link between George Eliot and D. H. Lawrence Leavis neglected to honour, etc.) But Langbaum also "slaloms" with virtuoso shifti-
ness between quasi-concepts like major and minor to conclude that Hardy
is mainly minor but a bit major occasionally in his poems, but more major
and possibly even more than major at times in his novels.[77] Although in
general his writing communicates well, it might also be argued that the
choice of poems which lead to his placing of Hardy here does not inspire
confidence, and the time seems long past when this Eliot-inspired high literary version of a Victorian parlour game could be offered as a serious contribution to scholarly and critical debate. The ghosts of Leavis and Eliot
haunt the book, but show that the evasion of subsequent critical and theoretical complexities does not necessarily issue in critical problem-solving or
critical cogency.

The book discusses various issues associated with Hardy including his
relationship with Lawrence. It attempts to show "how his innovations in
fiction reach through Lawrence into the twentieth century, how his critique
of marriage and his portrayals of women have entered into current contro-
versies over feminism, how his social criticism, humanitarianism and interest
in science meet our concerns as does his treatment of nature and of the unconscious and sexuality," guaranteeing that "Hardy remains a commanding
presence in our time" (155). The book is unsatisfactory but lively, differen-
tiates itself quite clearly from the spectre-gray critique of the official custodians of Hardy,[78] but in its critical scaffolding is, one would hope, outmoded,
unless you wish to insist that Hardy himself belongs in a timeless backwater
which critique, by imitative fallacy, should somehow resemble.

And indeed even this Eliot-inspired if hardly more than journalistic formalism is less in evidence than such approaches as sustain an idea, itself naive, of "Hardy the naive Countryman" to the irritation of Davie [1977]).
The irritation is misplaced if applied to Hardy himself, who can hardly be
denied his place as a countryman of sorts, even if, crucially, this doesn't preclude his having wider intellectual horizons than the term is usually allowed
to connote. The idea is insidious only when as an avatar of rural Englishness
Hardy is immediately saddled with an essentially conservative, perhaps
"neo-Georgian" mind-set.

Indeed, one can even glimpse him as something of a "failed" Georgian (*avant la lettre*, one might say, of their failure), in David Gervais's recent book, in which, comparing him with Edward Thomas, he claims that Hardy "was too much the ironist to capture such sadness" (as Thomas does).[79] And for a Hardy produced as the effigy of a parochial anti-modernism, see Frank Kermode.[80] Hardy is often troubled by ritual invocations of "'folk-ways" (in both senses)[81] put in partnership rather than tension with a "bourgeois" perspective Hardy was born to "trouble." See, for example, the work of Douglas Brown, once head-master of the Perse School, Cambridge [1954]),[82] fostering a sense of "national unity" which provides an imaginary resolution of social contradictions (in Althusser's idiom). An early sniper against Brown was J. C. Maxwell, in "The Sociological Approach to *The Mayor of Casterbridge*,"[83] and sociology is relevant to advances in Hardy criticism, as we have already been able to show.

But if Davie himself bridled at the idea of Hardy the countrymen, this was merely because he wished to replace the concept with an image which applied to Hardy's procedures rather than his context, as a poetic engineer, an Isambard Kingdom Brunel of poetry — poetry of a hard-driving, experimental, progressive edge made by an imperious shape-cutter. Perhaps if Davie had not chosen the title *Ezra Pound: Poet as Sculptor* (1965), he might have pursued the image of Hardy as "sculptor" (the apocalyptic member of the triad "jobbing builder/stoneworker (*autrement* "master-mason") — architect's apprentice — sculptor," which becomes the image for the sketch of the artistic temperament Jocelyn in *The Well-Beloved* (1897). By contrast, John Powell Ward, in a book which leaps into life when he considers other critics (87–98), comes forward with the quite suggestive and seductive notion of Hardy as poetic "bricoleur,"[84] tinkering with and *collage*-ing all manner of linguistic "prefabrications." This is a deliberate attempt to sideline Davie's imperious engineering metaphor, but Ward lacks the critical stamina to make the idea stick and thus register in the cumulative critical consciousness.

The idea might be used to suggest what motivates attacks on Hardy as a Robinson Crusoe of philosophic ready-mades by the more institutionally articulated G. K. Chesterton and T. S. Eliot, a precious pair. The comparison of the two in their intellectual weavings is pursued by Craig Raine in an article on "Conscious Artistry in *The Mayor of Casterbridge*," although it finally perpetuates critical patronage about Hardy's compulsively erudite procedures which could just as well be pinned on the "provincial" T. S. Eliot himself[85] (Pettit [1994: 156–7]). Raine's highly prejudicial claim is that in the novel there is an "anxious show of learning which, by its very anxiety, lends support to Chesterton's and Eliot's insinuation of intellectual narrowness" (157). Taking the anxiety as what Hardy would describe as a "phantom of his own figuring," we may feel that the whole idea of a case against Hardy here is a baseless expression of intellectual prejudice which continues a tradition of academic bullying against which Hardy himself aimed some admirable blows, and which derives from an idea no more creditable than that, in order to have the authority necessary to invoke intellectual authorities, one must have attended an ancient university, especially as Raine writes from New College Oxford after his distinguished stint as poetry editor at Faber and Faber.

But Davie's implied concept of Hardy as an experimental "Victorian modernist" is still quite instructive, if not wholly convincing. For Hardy as a resounding proto-modernist *avant la lettre*, see Davie [1972/ 77]).[86] Curiously, Davie himself has been pigeon-holed as a reactionary (see for example Alan Durant [1988]),[87] and Widdowson [1989, 70–2],[88] but although he fled radical Essex university and Harold Wilson's England, Davie's sardonic attitude to the official custodians of Hardy is surely on the right side here.

One senses that the construction of modern "Englishness"[89] entailed the appropriation of Hardy for the creation of an image consonant with its conservative bias. Anthony Easthope [1988] has powerfully projected the sense of an England specifically sought by educated but relatively right-wing (Jewish) refugees from Europe who related to the idea of England as a bulwark against "the radical" in an almost Conradian way; these were the "White" (as Perry Anderson called them) counter-revolutionaries of extraordinary intellectual distinction and influence — he names Wittgenstein, Malinowski, Namier, Popper, Berlin, Gombrich, Eysenck and Klein[!])[90] Through critical processing Hardy is made to participate in this image of an England strong against progressive currents of thought or action.

Here, however, nostalgia for a nostalgic Hardy very much distorts the flexibility, and, to say the very least, ambiguity of Hardy's forms of response to his own culture. As an admirer of Darwin, Hume and Schopenhauer the (ambiguously) "progressive" Comte and the work of Fourier Seymour-Smith, [1994: 70–3] has interesting material on this — articles by Björk[91] and Robinson[92] may also be consulted — it isn't clear that Hardy provides a good subject for this kind of critical "recuperation." If, as even the radical re-fashioner of Hardy's image, Peter Widdowson, can conclude that Hardy wasn't a socialist and it would be a "foolish enterprise" to make him appear one (1989: 198), Hardy was clear, if, in retrospect, somewhat apologetically, that his artistic debut was with a novel which was socialistic in character. It seems clear that he withdrew from an overt position in order to get published, suggesting an almost postmodernist situation that meaning as signifying discursive practice, was partly created by publishers and a "social imaginary" created by timid editors and circulating libraries.

Yet, as Hardy puts it elsewhere, "literature is the written expression of revolt against accepted things" (1878).[93] Thus John Goode argues and concludes in Kramer (1990) that if *Jude* cannot sustain a Marxist reading it at least requires a Marxist solution. This sounds as if it is (soundly) based on the remarks by Raymond Williams to the effect that the whole action of *Jude the Obscure* is subversive of the social order which has produced the limiting structures which destroy the protagonists.[94]

The major official organs of Hardy reception, then, still trumpet a relatively naive and pastoral novelist with the balance, still, tipped in favour of the mediocre purveyors of what might be called the middlebrows' Hardy, "warbling his native woodnotes wild," to use the patronizing idiom used by Milton to present the seventeenth century's feeling about Shakespeare.

One might consider, for example, Pettit's introductory remarks in his 1994 collection on how the contributors agree at least on the need to communicate clearly. Such demands usually signal a return to intellectual repressiveness which it is as easy to associate with the traditional intellectual custodianship of Hardy as it is inauthentic for the intellectually and linguistically questing and questioning Hardy himself: this repressiveness about style is a repressiveness of substance (Pettit's own article contains virtually no reading or scholarly points of reference). "All too often," he muses, "the use of unfamiliar jargon and the introduction of abstruse linguistic and critical concepts produce work which seems to speak only to a handful of fellow-specialists and which seems impenetrable to the non-academic reader of literature" (ix). This introductory address keeps the world safe for parochial Hardy experts who converge on Dorchester on the apparent assumption that only from this rural seat are *ex cathedra* pronouncements valid.

It helps lend spurious authority to *in situ* pronouncements, by false analogy with what T. S. Eliot once called "the reassuring science of archeology," there being in fact no "correct" place for discoveries to be made. John Barrell found one way of making the point that geographies of Wessex depend on the individual cartographer, his mental map and new-found lands: "I have never visited Dorset, although I may have passed through it on my way to somewhere else" [1983].[95] Hugh Kenner once remarked that commentators, thanks to the work of critical exegesis, could now tour Eliot territory in chartered buses (1962),[96] and the metaphor catches the ambiguity of the response to Thomas Hardy, where people feel they can in some sense tour "Thomas Hardy country in chartered buses" either as mental voyager or conference buff or by confusion of the roles. Widdowson has written particularly well on Wessex as an always already textualized cultural space in a still very interesting article in the (now defunct) Thomas Hardy Annual[97] (1986), the situation being laconically put by Tim Armstrong when he describes Wessex as "the name of the ancient kingdom which became the designated space of his novels" (1993).[98]

If Wessex is a conceptual space,[99] why is it that people still claim to traverse it, wearing academic gowns as if they were smock frocks? Kevin Moore (1990) correctly reported and developed Hillis Miller's claim that Hardy was imbued with the spirit of "our most marvellous lyrist" (as he called him) who was also a radical *à outrance* and spurned Eton and Oxford. Shelley's Promethean disdain for the Oxonian is an ingredient in *Jude* (1895) for example, and qualifies the idea that the book is written from a perspective of craven underling's *ressentiment*. Intuiting that the world view he inherits as a writer is "structured in dominance," his attitude to the structuring is, in something of Edward Said's sense, "contrapuntal."[100] As I have argued, then, an ideological fault-line separates Hardy from many of his official custodians, who have no quarrel with institutions and ideologies which he subjected to close critical scrutiny.

There is a particularly revealing contribution by Lance St. John Butler which is painful to read as Butler has edited some probing new approaches to Hardy in his time, and his *Alternative Hardy* is still stimulating. Here, though, he steps forward surprisingly as a cultural conservative with an essay which ought to have been called "Hardy's Politics," but evasively (in that willing to wound and yet afraid to strike mode memorably defined by Pope), is entitled "Hardy's Voices." Savaging the "politically correct" yet paradoxically convinced of his own political correctness, he ascribes to Eagleton the belief that "everything is political" (a doubly unfortunate target, as Eagleton rejects the idea in a recent book),[101] and has never, so far as I know, devoted more than obiter dicta to Hardy apart from a short early article,[102] for example in the Walter Benjamin book (1981),[103] the brief introductory remarks to John Goode's richly murky, under-edited work on Hardy in his Blackwell "Re-reading" series (1989),[104] and a sliver in the early *Criticism and Ideology*).[105]

As Butler unwittingly shows (but the unwary reader may not notice), the trouble with attacking the openly political critic is that one is advancing a kind of Toryism while simultaneously disclaiming a political motive. Apolitical, one has, curiously, the answer to anything "political." And indeed, so it proves here. This consists at once in denying any efficacy to that long revolution in the political process which has enabled most people to "get a life"; and in denying that there was anything radical (or, in textual effect "political") about Hardy at all. The article secretes a soft-spoken rage that proceeds from a consciousness of its own perturbed conservatism. His discourse rather confirms the suspicion that behind the benign face of "Hardy studies" is a politics of what Slavoj Zizek calls a "national-organic populist tradition."[106]

According to John Goode, in an early essay of his on Morris,[107] Hardy opposes this in divergent ways — with the authentic communitarian vision of the early regionalism of *Far from the Madding Crowd* and what Goode, citing Scott Fitzgerald, calls "the authority of failure" of Jude in his unhoused, unfree condition. Edward Said ekes out the point very well with reference to Lukacs as well as *Jude* (and Jude) when he points out that "every novelistic hero . . . attempts to restore the lost world of his or her imagination, which in the late nineteenth century novel of disillusionment is an unrealisable dream."[108] He could hardly have put it better if he had singled out a work like *Jude the Obscure* as a specific point of reference.

In effect, Butler's essay, surprising in view of his awareness of experimentalism in literature and new theoretical treatments of it, ascribes its own inadequacy (paraded as superiority) to Hardy himself. Yet the best of recent critique has been able to show that Hardy, however legitimately deferential to his publishers wishes, shadows his textual accommodations of their overanxious hests, has in fact a "political unconscious." Joe Fisher, for example, argues in an interesting book that Hardy is always drawing cruel Swiftian cartoons which he then smudges over in creating his "last effect").[109]

By contrast, Butler's Hardy is the liberal humanist he is himself, although to create him as such he confines himself to official positions enunciated by Hardy in correspondence and so on. For example, he cites an anodyne piece of "consolation" from Marcus Aurelius cited by Hardy ("be not perturbed; for all things are in the nature of the universal"), when the context in his creative writing prepared for such intellectual bromides is hardly an Aurelius-friendly one.

This is an instructive point, though. Donald Davie argues, in response to the fact that Hardy is indeed "writing in fetters," in Blake's idiom, when he is expository (introductions, correspondence, occasional articles etc.) — that "Hardy had no talent for discursive prose,"[110] which sounds plausible but a little mysterious. The fact is that when Hardy writes in what might be called propria persona as a "personage," he exudes a queasy prudentiality which is painful to behold, and indeed it might be said that it is this propria persona which is itself his most laboriously excogitated fiction, something that Peter Widdowson seems to be arguing in his chapter on the *Life* (1989).

It might be argued that it is when such anodynes as the Aurelius quotation turn up in his fiction that they are promptly subject to ironizing and persistent persiflage, with a redoubled alacrity from Hardy's having been so painfully repressed about it in properer contexts. As evidence that Butler does not notice that the whole creative effort of *Tess* (1891) and *Jude* (1895), for example, is indeed strongly deconstructive of the evasively liberal "position" he espouses. A patriarchal note is heard, surely, when he writes that

> the feminist critique of Hardy is fascinating and convincing and puts a big question mark over his attitudes towards women, but when we raise our heads for a moment and consider what Hardy was doing and when he was doing it, it remains obvious that his credentials as a non-sexist somehow remain untouched (40).

But it's the way the point is made which is startling here. The argument here is insouciant, and of course, as Belsey notes in *Critical Practice* (1980) "if what is 'obvious' is also incoherent, non-explanatory or even self-contradictory, it is possible to produce a recognition of the ideological status of what is obvious" (63), written as if to deal with all such soft-spoken liberal bullying. Yet challenging work like Belsey's is constantly side-lined to make room for this recuperative "belle-lettrism." Noting that Hardy formally opposed female suffrage — perhaps "jealous foe" Emma had a hand in this — this is then said to "send a frisson down our politically correct backs," which sounds a bit odd: he can hardly mean his own back, surely? while his audience has been invited to share what he seems to be defining as a political incorrectness which, paradoxically, is in fact "more correct."

Such discussions need the sophistication of a theoretical perspective. One might, for example, question who or what speaks when "Hardy" speaks. Widdowson has some interesting points about this in his chapter on the *Life* (1988: 129–154). Of course, if Butler seems to be offering a particularly depressing idea of what a "Hardy scholar" can be here, it is partly because he previously hosted, with brilliant success, some of the more interesting theoretical writing about Hardy. Even Butler's reference to Bakhtin raises doubts about the uses to which his work has been put, as discussed for example by Tom Cohen in *Cultural Critique* (1996),[111] basically in the hands of brilliant but conservative Slavonic translators who make him appear more reactionary than he is.

There are moments when a sense of "arguments within" this dominant consensus of conference proceedings (to invoke Perry Anderson's useful idea), make the essay more interesting. Butler makes a brief deprecating reference to Rosemarie Morgan, who delivered a paper on Toni Morrison and Hardy investigating analogies between the sex- and class-conscious fiction of the one and the sex- and race-conscious fiction of the other, speaking bodies whose linguistic and sexual deviance puts markers for the articulation of the socially acceptable:[112] in particular, she investigated a homoerotic zone in both writers — corresponding to a reality submerged by socially constructed patriarchal arrangements. These enjoin heterosexuality as the only love which dare speak its name (preferably in church), and here *Desperate Remedies* (1871) and, even more interestingly, *A Laodicean* (1881), in *The Woodlanders* (1887) (Grace and Felice), with trace elements of female liaison even in *The Mayor of Casterbridge*, are the main ports of call (although she does not mention the plainly signposted masculinely homoerotic attraction of Henchard for Farfrae — even if his ardor was hardly reciprocated given Farfrae's strictly Laodicean professionalism).

Here Morgan's arguments come close to those of Fisher in showing the counter-text to the traded text, the narrative lines doomed to be smudged as things become too hot, ideologically speaking, to handle. Her earlier scholarly investment in the idea that freeing female sexuality to express itself in itself constitutes a radical "program" has developed into a subtler critique here. What finally draws Morrison and Hardy together is, she says, that "both give immediacy, bodily presence and authenticity to those who are otherwise marginalised, disenfranchised or, by virtue of the internal politics of he novel, absented in one way or another from public discourse" (142).

This is at once a substantial and a suggestive piece of writing. It has no trouble dismantling the "safety net" approach of Claudius Beatty, who thought that the relation of Miss Aldcliffe to Cytherea in *Desperate Remedies* was purely maternal.[113]

Elsewhere in the (Pettit) volume Peter Levi writes on Barnes and Hardy to some effect, but with a typical and traditional lightness of analytic touch or notice of previous commentators on issues that made these poets at once a highly congruent yet finally non-convergent twain (68–89). Some Victorian commentators are a little snooty about Barnes, and one suspects this disdainful ambience transfers to Hardy's rusticities, and particularly interesting here is Paul Turner's inversion of the requisite *de haut en bas* posture: "those whose appetite is less robust may have to accept relegation to the *profanum vulgus* who cannot fully enjoy his dialect poems."[114]

Gillian Beer provides potential evidence of Hardy's mischief-making creative evasiveness and narrative alibi-creation as the slipperiest of narrative customers, writing on "Hardy and Decadence" (90–102) in an essay which forms a kind of offcut to her longer works[115] on the Victorian Novel, one intelligent conclusion being that

> in reading Hardy's work we often find a triple level of plot generated: the anxiously scheming and predictive plot of the characters' making; the optative plot of the commentary, which often takes the form "Why did nobody" or "had somebody . . . " and the absolute plot of blind interaction and "Nature's laws."[116]

There is also, as Hardy partly intimated in his preface to *The Return of the Native*, the plot imposed from above by publishers as well as the malign narratives which tell of disappointing deities who wreak unwitting havoc.

More entertainingly informative here is Simon Curtis on "Hardy, George Moore and the 'Doll' of English Fiction" (103–114). Despite their well-known enmity, this was much more a matter of Moore's enmity, which could sometimes seem like an enmity with everything that moved — or at least anything that moved an audience more than he could, and the "miching mallecho" of a "back-wounding calumny" which spared nobody his poisonous resentments, or rather *ressentiment*. In fact Moore and Hardy were so highly convergent in their desire to be, as it were, far from the Mudie's crowd, as in Moore's devastating "Literature at Nurse, or Circulating Morals," [1885][117] they might well have been productively friendly.

But Curtis has a revealing tale to tell of the publisher, Vizetelly, who brought out, inter alia, Zola and Maupassant, his risqué but reputable publishing venture ruined by Victorian sanctimony. This would include Tennyson's, railing famously of "troughs of Zola-ism" in "Locksley Hall Sixty Years After."[118] Despite this indignation-inducing tale of rant and cant, sprightly Curtis can still write of Moore as "an unnervingly changeful character to pin down. Postmodernists would have the whale of a time with him, no doubt, though I hope they may leave him alone." Why? Moore had so little attention he might welcome even the mean-minded kind he gave to others.

And postmodernism, whatever (if anything) he means by it here, may have its faults, but once again, it seems as if the scholarly survival of this intelligent academic (not to mention his less intelligent ilk) depended on quashing all new thought, all intellectual development, and with a tone of self-righteousness summoned by the confidence of being surrounded by like-minded reactionaries. But it is not, surely, one of life's littlest ironies to consider that for this reason Hardy himself would have been quite out of sympathy with such a venture as this Hardy appreciation by those who appear to have appointed themselves his foremost literary custodians.

Notes

[1] Donald Davie, *Under Briggflatts: A History of Poetry in Great Britain 1960–1988* (London: Routledge, 1989), 205. In fact Gregory Stevens Cox has an article on "The Hardy Industry," in *The Genius of Thomas Hardy*, ed. Margaret Drabble (London: Weidenfeld and Nicholson, 1976), 170–181, describing the "cult," with its "shrine" and "pilgrims" (181), but also dealing with the commercial aspects of Hardy film and stage adaptations and so on.

[2] Roland Barthes, "Theory of the Text," in *Untying the Text; A Post Structuralist Reader*, ed. Robert Young (London: Routledge, 1981), 41.

[3] Paul de Man, *The Resistance to Theory* (Manchester: Manchester UP, 1986).

[4] Peter Widdowson, *Hardy in History: A Study in Literary Sociology* (London: Routledge, 1989).

[5] John Goode, "Women and the Literary Text," in Juliet Mitchell and Anne Oakley (eds.) *The Rights and Wrongs of Women* (Harmondsworth: Penguin, 1976); "Sue Bridehead and the New Woman," in Mary Jacobus (ed.) *Women Writing and Writing about Women* (Beckenham: Croom Helm, 1979); *Thomas Hardy: the Offensive Truth* (Oxford: Blackwell, 1988); "Hardy and Marxism," in Dale Kramer (ed.), *Critical Essays on Thomas Hardy: the Novels* (Boston: G. K. Hall, 1990), 21–38.

[6] Raymond Williams, *The English Novel from Dickens to Lawrence* (London: Chatto and Windus, 1970); "Wessex and the Border," *The Country and the City* (London: Hogarth Press, 1973), 197–214; with Merryn Williams, "Hardy and Social Class," in Norman Page (ed.) *Thomas Hardy: the Writer and His Background* (London: Bell and Hyman, 1980), 29–40.

[7] Patricia Ingham, "The Evolution of *Jude the Obscure*," *Review of English Studies* 27 (1976): 27–37, 159–69; *Thomas Hardy: A Feminist Reading* (Brighton: Harvester, 1989); "Provisional Narratives: Hardy's Final Trilogy," in Lance St. John Butler (ed.), *Alternative Hardy* (London: Macmillan, 1989).

[8] Roger Ebbatson. *Hardy: The Margin of the Unexpressed* (Sheffield: Sheffied UP, 1993).

[9] George Wotton, *Thomas Hardy: Towards a Materialist Criticism* (Dublin: Gill and Macmillan, 1985).

[10] N. N. Feltes, *Modes of Production of Victorian Novels* (Chicago: Chicago UP, 1986).

[11] Joe Fisher, *The Hidden Hardy* (London: Macmillan, 1992).

[12] Charles Lock, *Thomas Hardy* ('Criticism in Focus') (Bristol: Bristol Classical Press, 1992).

[13] Charles P. C. Pettit, *New Perspectives on Thomas Hardy* (London: Macmillan, 1994).

[14] Charles P. C. Pettit, *Celebrating Thomas Hardy* (London: Macmillan, 1996).

[15] Michael Millgate, *Letters of Emma and Florence Hardy* (Oxford: Clarendon Press, 1996).

[16] James Gibson, *Thomas Hardy. A Literary Life.* (Basingstoke: Macmillan, 1996).

[17] See Margaret R. Higonnet (ed.), "Introduction" to *The Sense of Sex: Feminist Perspectives on Hardy* (Chicago: U of Illinois P, 1993), 11.

[18] See the *Life* (1928), formally ascribed to Florence, but actually (and most appropriately) ghosted by Hardy himself for an account of his first novel, *The Poor Man and the Lady*, which was, he said, "socialistic not to say revolutionary" (73), but was not published; hence this involves a *literal* repression, was *literally* a repression of "Thomas Hardy." (*The Life of Thomas Hardy*, reprinted London:

Studio Books, 1994 [2vols.].) See, for the discussing following Kevin Z. Moore, *The Descent of the Imagination: Postromantic Culture in the Later Novels of Thomas Hardy* (London: New York UP, 1990), J. Hillis Miller, *Thomas Hardy: Distance and Desire* (Cambridge, MA: Harvard UP, 1970), and Harold Bloom, especially *A Map of Misreading* (New York: Oxford UP, 1975).

[19] Robert Gittings, *Young Thomas Hardy* (London: Heinemann, 1975); Martin Seymour-Smith, *Hardy* (London: Bloomsbury, 1994), 509.

[20] Rosemarie Morgan, *Cancelled Words: Rediscovering Thomas Hardy* (London: Routledge, 1992).

[21] Jan Jedrzejewski, *Thomas Hardy and the Church* (London: Macmillan, 1996), 3. He is appreciative but also critical of rival attempts to take Hardy's religious temperature, of Timothy Hands for a too-synchronic approach (in *Thomas Hardy: Distracted Preacher? Hardy's Religious Biography and its Influence on His Novels* [Basingstoke: Macmillan, 1989] and of Deborah L. Collins in *Thomas Hardy and His God: A Liturgy of Unbelief* [Basingstoke: Macmillan, 1990]) for failing to situate him sufficiently "within" the Christianity with which he was, in Wordsworth's idiom, so "inveterately convolved." Jedrzejewski describes Hardy's contrapuntal movements between churchiness without dogma, or even religion, to an emphasis on ethics which involves the Gospel but hardly the church.

[22] Peter Widdowson, *On Thomas Hardy: Late Essays and Earlier* (London: Macmillan, 1998), 9.

[23] Frances Widdowson, *Going Up Into the Next Class: Women and Elementary Teacher Training, 1840–1894* (London: Hutchinson, 1983).

[24] George Watson, *The Literary Critics* (London: Chatto and Windus, 1964).

[25] Donald Davie, "Hardy's Virgilian Purples," *Agenda* (Special Thomas Hardy number) 1972, reprinted in Donald Davie, *The Poet in the Imaginary Museum: Essays of Two Decades* (Manchester: Carcanet, 1977), ed. Barry Alpert, 221–235; Donald Davie. *Thomas Hardy and British Poetry* (London: Routledge. 1973); *Under Briggflats. A History of Poetry in Great Britain 1960–1988* (London: Routledge, 1989).

[26] Harold Bloom, *A Map of Misreading*. New York: Oxford UP, 1975.

[27] J. Hillis Miller, *Thomas Hardy: Distance and Desire* (Cambridge, MA: Harvard UP, 1970; "History as Repetition in Thomas Hardy's Poetry: The Example of 'Wessex Heights,'" in *Victorian Poetry*, Stratford-upon-Avon Studies, 15 (1972): 223–53; "Thomas Hardy, Jacques Derrida and the 'Dislocation of Souls,'" in (eds.) J. H. Smith and W. Kerrigan, *Taking Chances: Derrida, Psychoanalysis and Literature* (Baltimore: Johns Hopkins, 1984), 135–145; "Topography and Tropography in Thomas Hardy's 'In Front of the Landscape,'" in M. J. Valdes and O. Miller (eds.) *Identity of the Literary Text* (Toronto: Toronto UP, 1985), 73–91; also repr. in Richard Machin and Christopher Norris (eds.) *Post-structuralist Readings of English Poetry* (Cambridge: Cambridge UP, 1987); "Prosopopoeia in Hardy and Stevens," in *Alternative Hardy*, ed. Lance St. John Butler (London: Macmillan, 1989), 110–127; and *The Linguistic Moment: From Hardy to Stevens* (Princeton:

Princeton UP, 1985). Four of the essays on Hardy together with an early sketch for a portrait of this "slipperiest" of authors are re-assembled in Miller's *Tropes, Parables, Performatives: Essays on Twentieth Century Literature* (Brighton: Harvester Press, 1991).

[28] Eric Griffiths, *The Printed Voice of Victorian Poetry* (Oxford: the Clarendon Press, 1989), 216–236.

[29] Peter Sacks. *The English Elegy: Studies in the Genre from Spenser to Yeats* (Baltimore: Johns Hopkins UP, 1985).

[30] Dale Kramer, *Thomas Hardy: The Forms of Tragedy* (London: Macmillan, 1975); (ed.) *Critical Approaches to Thomas Hardy* (London: Macmillan, 1979); (ed.) *Critical Essays on Thomas Hardy: The Novels* (Boston: G. K. Hall, 1990).

[31] Peter Casagrande, *Unity in Hardy's Novels:'Repetitive Symmetries'* (London: Macmillan, 1982); *Hardy's Influence on the Modern Novel* (Basingstoke: Macmillan, 1987).

[32] John Goode, "Hardy and Marxism," in *Critical Essays on Thomas Hardy: The Novels*, 16–38; Mary Jacobus, "Hardy's Magian Retrospect," 38–53; Kathleen Blake, "Pure Tess: Hardy on Knowing a Woman"; Philip M. Weinstein, "'The Spirit Unappeased and Peregrine'": *Jude the Obscure*," 228–243.

[33] Dale Kramer, *Tess of the D'Urbervilles* (Cambridge: Cambridge UP, 1991).

[34] William Archer, review of *Wessex Poems* in the *Daily Chronicle*, 21 December 1898.

[35] Edmund Blunden, *Thomas Hardy* (London: Macmillan 1942).

[36] F. R. Leavis, *New Bearings in English Poetry* (London: Chatto and Windus, 1932); "Hardy the Poet," *Southern Review* (1940): 87–98.

[37] R. P. Blackmur, "Hardy's Shorter Poems," *Southern Review*, (1940): 20–48, repr. in *Language as Gesture* (New York: Harcourt, Brace and Co., 1952), 51–79.

[38] Raymond Williams, *The English Novel from Dickens to Lawrence* (London: Chatto and Windus, 1970); *The Country and the City* (London: Chatto and Windus, 1973); (with Merryn Williams) "Hardy and Social Class," Norman Page (ed.) *Thomas Hardy: the Writer and His Background* (London: Bell and Hyman, 1980). Curiously, in the same volume, Norman Page rehearses this persistent note of patronage in a particularly revealing way, given that he writes as a Hardy scholar and something of an official curator of his critical standing. See his "Hardy and the English Language," 150–172.

[39] K. D. M. Snell, "Thomas Hardy, Rural Dorset, and the Family," in *Annals of the Labouring Poor: Social Change and Agrarian England 1660–1900* (Cambridge: Cambridge UP, 1985), 374–410.

[40] Roger Ebbatson, *Hardy: The Margin of the Unexpressed* (Sheffield: Sheffield UP, 1993), 136.

[41] Michael Valdes Moses, *The Novel and the Globalization of Culture* (Oxford: Oxford UP, 1995), 31.

[42] Kevin Z. Moore, *The Descent of the Imagination: Postromantic Culture in the Later Novels of Thomas Hardy* (London: New York UP, 1990).

[43] See Harold Bloom, *The Visionary Company* (Ithaca: Cornell UP, 1961); *The Ringers in the Tower* (Chicago: Chicago UP, 1971).

[44] Northrop Frye, *An Anatomy of Criticism: Four Essays* (Princeton: Princeton UP, 1957); for a temperate presentation of the limitations of Frye's system, see Catherine Belsey, *Critical Practice* (London: Methuen, 1980), 21–29.

[45] Terry Eagleton, "The Idealism of American Criticism," *Against the Grain: Essays 1975–1985* (London: Verso, 1986).

[46] Shaobo Xie, "History and Utopian Desire: Fredric Jameson's Dialectical Tribute to Northrop Frye," *Cultural Critique* no. 34 (Fall, 1996): 115–142.

[47] Marjorie Garson, *Hardy's Fables of Integrity: Woman, Body, Texts* (Oxford: Oxford UP, 1991).

[48] See Michael Millgate *Thomas Hardy: His Career as a Novelist* (London: Bodley Head, 1971); *Thomas Hardy: A Biography* (Oxford: Oxford UP, 1982); *Testamentary Acts: Browning, Tennyson, James, Hardy* (Oxford: Oxford UP, 1992).

[49] John Bayley, *An Essay on Hardy* (Cambridge: Cambridge UP, 1978).

[50] Jan Jedrzejewski, *Thomas Hardy and the Church* (Basingstoke: Macmillan, 1996).

[51] Charles P. C. Pettit, *New Perspectives on Thomas Hardy* (Basingstoke: Macmillan, 1994).

[52] Frank Kermode, *An Appetite for Poetry* (London: Fontana, 1990).

[53] Walter Benjamin, "Goethe's '*Wahlverwandtschaften*,'" cited in Susan Buck-Morss, *The Origin of Negative Dialectics* (Brighton: Harvester, 1977), 246.

[54] Roland Barthes, in *S/Z* tr. Richard Miller (London: Cape, 1975), 15.

[55] Jean Baudrillard, *L'Échange Symbolique et la Mort* (Paris: Gallimard, 1976); and see Mark Poster, "Semiology and Critical Theory: from Marx to Baudrillard," in *The Question of Textuality: Strategies of Reading in Contemporary American Criticism* (Bloomington: Indiana UP, 1982), 284.

[56] Terry Eagleton, "Capitalism, Modernism and Postmodernism," *New Left Review*, 152 (1985), 60–73; rpr. in *Postmodernism: A Reader*, ed. Patricia Waugh (London: Edward Arnold, 1992), 157.

[57] Peter J. Casagrande, "Hardy's Wordsworth: a Record and a Commentary," in *English Literature in Transition* 20, no. 4 (1977): 210–37, especially citing Gosse as exciting Hardy's approval in defining his poetic position as one of "violent reaction against the poetry of egocentric optimism" [from a review entitled "Mr Hardy's Lyrical Poems" in the *Edinburgh Review* of April 1918]; see also Dennis Taylor, "Hardy and Wordsworth," *Victorian Poetry*, 24:4 (Winter, 1986): 441–54.

[58] John Goode, "Hardy and Marxism," in Dale Kramer (ed.) *Critical Essays on Thomas Hardy: the Novels* (Boston: G. K. Hall, 1993), 36.

[59] Isobel Armstrong, *Victorian Poetry: Poetry, Poetics and Politics* (London: Routledge, 1993), 485.

[60] See Norman Page, *Thomas Hardy* (London: Routledge, 1977); Edward Neill, "A Nice Idea (review of Harold Orel's *The Unknown Thomas Hardy)*," *Essays in Criticism*, (April, 1988): 162–6.

[61] Jim Reilly, *Shadowtime: History and Representation in Hardy, Conrad and George Eliot* (London: Routledge, 1993), 2–3.

[62] Valentine Cunningham, *In the Reading Jail: Postmodernity, Texts and History* (Blackwell: Oxford, 1993), 96–127.

[63] Glen Wickens, "Hardy's Inconsistent Spirits and the Philosophical form of *The Dynasts*," in Clements and Grindle, eds., 101–118: 105.

[64] F. R. Leavis, *The Great Tradition* (London: Chatto and Windus, 1948).

[65] F. R. Leavis, *New Bearings in English Poetry* (London: Chatto and Windus, 1932); F. R. Leavis, *Southern Review* 6 (1940): 87–98.

[66] Terence Hawkes, *That Shakespeherian Rag: Essays on a Critical Process* (London: Methuen, 1986).

[67] Anthony Easthope, *Poetry as Discourse* (London: Methuen, 1983); *Poetry and Phantasy* (Cambridge: Cambridge UP, 1989).

[68] Peter Widdowson, *Hardy in History*, 26–28, 74–8.

[69] Catherine Belsey, *Critical Practice* , 11–14; see also "Re-Reading the Great Tradition," in *Re-Reading English* (London: Methuen, 1982), 121–135.

[70] Chris Baldick, *The Social Mission of English Criticism, 1848–1932* (Oxford: Clarendon Press, 1983), 162–234.

[71] Francis Mulhern, *The Moment of 'Scrutiny'* (London: NLB, 1979), passim.

[72] D. H. Lawrence, "Study of Thomas Hardy" (1914), reprinted in *Study of Thomas Hardy and Other Essays*, ed. Bruce Steele. London: Grafton Books, 1986.

[73] Rainer Emig, *Modernism in Poetry: Motivations, Structures and Limits* (London: Longman, 1995).

[74] An early and elementary distinction between Hardy and the typical Victorian novelist is effected when he observes that Hardy is "a realist developing towards allegory . . . an imaginative artist who brought the nineteenth century novel out of its slavery to fact" in "Hardy in Defense of His Art: The Aesthetic of Incongruity," *Sewanee Review*, 6 (1940), reprinted in *Hardy: A Collection of Critical Essays* (Englewood Cliffs, NJ: Prentice-Hall, 1963), 24–45.

[75] See his "Mimesis and Diegesis in Modern Fiction," in *After Bakhtin: Essays on Fiction and Criticism* (London: Routledge, 1990), 37–8.

[76] W. W. Robson, *A Prologue to English Literature* (London: B. T. Batsford, 1986), 190.

[77] Beat Riesen notes the awkwardness of classifications like "major" and "minor," as well as Richard Taylor's failure significantly to challenge settled distinctions of "quality?" in his *The Neglected Hardy: Thomas Hardy's Lesser Novels* (London: Macmillan, 1982). See Beat Riesen, *Thomas Hardy's Minor Novels* (New York: Peter Lang, 1990), 13, 141.

[78] Robert Langbaum, *Thomas Hardy in Our Time* (Basingstoke: Macmillan, 1995).

[79] David Gervais, *Literary Englands: Versions of "Englishness" in Modern Writing* (Cambridge: Cambridge UP, 1993), 57.

[80] Frank Kermode, "T. S. Eliot: the Last Classic," in *An Appetite for Poetry: Essays in Literary Interpretation* (London: Fontana, 1990): 107, citing Philip Larkin's "Wanted: Good Hardy Critic," in *Required Writing: Miscellaneous Pieces 1955–1982* (London: Faber, 1983), 168–74, and Graham Hough, *Image and Experience* (London: Fontana, 1960).

[81] See Ruth Firor, *Folk-Ways in Thomas Hardy* (Philadelphia: U of Pennsylvania P, 1931).

[82] Douglas Brown, *Thomas Hardy* (1954), reprinted Harlow: Longman, 1961.

[83] In Maynard Mack and Ian Gregor (eds.), *Imagined Worlds: Essays in Honour of John Butt* (London: Macmillan, 1968), reprinted in R. P. Draper, *Thomas Hardy: The Tragic Novels* (London: Macmillan, 1975), 79–92.

[84] See John Powell Ward, *Thomas Hardy's Poetry* (Milton Keynes: Open UP, 1993), 93.

[85] See for example the discussion of Hardy by writers like Gittings (the obscure Horace Moule teaches him to write) and Philip Collins in particular on what he takes to be Hardy's sad propensity to fire off what Collins describes as his "popguns of knowledge" in chapter 1. This would be equally accurate to the procedures of Eliot and Pound, but not many writers have taken that tone with them, and if they have, they have not been granted critical respect within the tradition of scholarly reception for those modernist writers who successfully imposed themselves upon (i.e. intimidated) their readers. Like Miss Bates in Jane Austen's *Emma*, Hardy has never been able to "frighten those who might hate him into outward respect."

[86] Donald Davie, "Hardy's Virgilian Purples" *Agenda* X (2–3 [Spring-Summer 1972], repr. *The Poet in the Imaginary Museum* (Manchester: Carcanet, 1977), 221–235.

[87] Alan Durant, "Pound, Modernism and Literary Criticism," in *Futures for English*, ed. Colin McCabe (Manchester: Manchester UP, 1988), 154–166.

[88] Peter Widdowson, *Hardy in History*, 70–2.

[89] Robert Colls and Philip Dodd (eds.) *The Ideology of Englishness: National Identity in the Arts, Politics and Society 1880–1920* (London: Croom Helm, 1986).

[90] Anthony Easthope, *British Post-Structuralism* (London: Routledge, 1988), 11; for the Perry Anderson material, see "Components of the National Culture," *New Left Review* no. 50 (July/August 1968): 26–53.

[91] Lennart A. Björk, "Hardy's Reading," in Norman Page (ed.) *Thomas Hardy: The Writer and His Background* (London: Bell and Hyman, 1980), 102–127.

[92] Roger Robinson, "Hardy and Darwin," in Page, ed.(1980), 128–149. He draws on Peter R. Morton's *"Tess of the D'Urbervilles.* A Neo-Darwinian Reading" in the *Southern Review* [Adelaide] 7 (1974), 38–50 (but finds he makes Hardy a litle too programmatically Darwinian altogether), and F. R. Southerington, *"The Return of the Native*: Thomas Hardy and the Evolution of

Consciousness," in *Thomas Hardy and the Modern World*, ed. F. B. Pinion (Dorchester, 1974), 37–47. Such studies evolved towards works like those of Roger Ebbatson's *The Evolutionary Self: Hardy, Forster and Lawrence* (Brighton: Harvester Press, 1982), and by Gillian Beer noticed and noted elsewhere here.

[93] Thomas Hardy, "Preface" to *The Return of the Native* (1878); see e.g. "New Wessex Ed." (London: Macmillan, 1974)

[94] Raymond Williams, *Politics and Letters: Interviews with New Left Review* (London: Verso, 1981), 222.

[95] John Barrell, "Geographies of Hardy's Wessex," *Journal of Historical Geography* 8 (1982), 347–61, repr. in Peter Widdowson, *Tess of the D'Urbervilles* (London: Macmillan, 1989), 157–171. For Wessex as "dream-country," see W. J. Keith, *Regions of the Imagination: The Development of British Rural Fiction* (Toronto: U of Toronto P, 1988).

[96] Hugh Kenner, *T. S. Eliot: A Collection of Critical Essays* (Englewood Cliffs, Prentice-Hall, 1962), 2.

[97] Peter Widdowson, "Hardy, 'Wessex,' and the Making of a National Culture," *Thomas Hardy Annual*, ed. Norman Page, 4 (1986), 45–69.

[98] Tim Armstrong, "Introduction," to Thomas Hardy, *Selected Poems* (Harlow: Longman, 1993), 3.

[99] In a passing comparison with Goethe and Faulkner, J. Hillis Miller notes Hardy's creation of "an imaginary, internalized landscape," in *Ariadne's Thread: Story Lines* (London: Yale UP, 1992), 179.

[100] See Abdul R. Janmohammed, "Worldliness-Without-World, Homelessness-as-Home: Toward a Definition of the Specular Border Intellectual," in Michael Sprinker (ed.), *The Edward Said Reader* (Oxford: Blackwell, 1992), 97.

[101] Terry Eagleton, *The Illusions of Postmodernism* (Oxford: Blackwell, 1996), 43.

[102] Terry Eagleton, "Thomas Hardy: Nature as Language," *Critical Quarterly*, 13 (1971): 155–62.

[103] Terry Eagleton, *Walter Benjamin: or Towards a Revolutionary Criticism* (London: Verso, 1981).

[104] Terry Eagleton, General Editor's Preface to John Goode, *Thomas Hardy: the Offensive Truth* (Oxford: Blackwell, 1988).

[105] Terry Eagleton, *Criticism and Ideology* (London: Verso, 1976), 94–5, 125–6, 131–2.

[106] Slavoj Zizek, interviewed (with Renata Saleci) by Peter Osborne and Anne Beezer in *A Critical Sense: Interviews with Intellectuals* (London: Routledge, 1996), 28.

[107] John Goode, "William Morris and the Dream of Revolution," in *Literature and Politics in the Nineteenth Century*, ed. John Lucas (London: Methuen, 1971), 231–2; for a comparable sense of "early" and "late" Hardy, see Raymond Williams, "Region and Class in the Novel," in *The Uses of Fiction:*

Essays on the Modern Novel in Honour of Arnold Kettle, edited by Douglas Jefferson and Graham Martin (Milton Keynes: Open UP, 1982), 59–68.

[108] Edward Said, in *Culture and Imperialism* (London: Chatto and Windus, 1993), 189–90.

[109] Joe Fisher, *The Hidden Hardy* (London: Macmillan, 1992).

[110] Donald Davie, *Thomas Hardy and British Poetry*, (London: Routledge, 1973), 6.

[111] Tom Cohen, "The Ideology of Dialogue: the Bakhtin/de Man (Dis)Connection," *Cultural Critique* 33 (Spring, 1996), 41–86.

[112] Rosemarie Morgan "Bodily Transactions: Toni Morrison and Thomas Hardy in Literary Discourse," in *Celebrating Thomas Hardy*, 136–158. Not in itself an original insight. For example, in the course of showing how Hardy is from the outset more set on subverting Mrs Grundy than his deferential manner suggests, James Gibson mentions this incident in "Hardy and His Readers," in *Thomas Hardy: The Writer and His Background*, 193–94, making it clear that more than maternal and filial emotions are in play here.

[113] Claudius [C. J. P.] Beatty, "Introduction" to *Desperate Remedies* (London: Macmillan ["New Wessex Ed."], 1975.

[114] Paul Turner, *Victorian Poetry, Drama and Miscellaneous Prose 1832–1890* (Oxford: Clarendon Press, 1989), 162. Hardy himself apparently rates only one more passing reference in this authoritative reference work.

[115] See Gillian Beer, *Darwin's Plots: Evolutionary Narrative in Darwin, George Eliot, and Nineteenth-Century Fiction* (London: Routledge and Kegan Paul, 1983).

[116] In Gillian Beer, "Finding a Scale for the Human: Plot and Writing in Hardy's Novels," in *Critical Essays on Thomas Hardy*, ed. Dale Kramer (1990), 57.

[117] Cited as "Literature at Nurse" (London: Vizetelly, 1885) by Curtis (in Pettit, 1996), 114.

[118] "Locksley Hall Sixty Years After" (1886). See Alfred Tennyson, *Poetical Works* (London: Oxford UP, 1953), 524.

3: Smock-Frock'd Boor, *Bricoleur*, or Engineer? Hardy's Poetry Assayed

ONE OF THE MOST INFLUENTIAL OF RECENT efforts to take Hardy's strange poetic reputation in hand was that of Donald Davie, himself a poet. Davie saluted Hardy's "scientific humanism" and noted his poetic "engineering" as that of a poetically self-made man, creating a savoury combination of a poetic Samuel Smiles and a poetic Isambard Kingdom Brunel conducting himself with technical assurance and brio but limited and imperiously mechanical poetic aims.[1] Perhaps it's the "visibly ideological" nature of the performance by Davie here which makes it still so arresting, and "smaller and clearer as the years go by". In a once-famous essay, "Shakespeare and the Stoicism of Seneca," T. S. Eliot complained (or at least explained) that the many writers about him re-made Shakespeare in their own images. Coleridge's "smack of Hamlet," which read off a Hamlet invested with his own qualities as he construed them perhaps also indicates how common this sort of thing may be.

There is more than a smack of Davie in Davie's Hardy, and his treatment may include a smack at as well as of himself as a (somewhat refractory) member of "The Movement," the post-war English poetic revival, conducted partly against the excesses of Dylan Thomas (although he was also a man used to noticing such things as Hardy's poems with approval). It would probably be conceded that, if there was a poetic "programme" here, it included elements of bluff philistinism and some reactionary posturing, admittedly more evident at moments in fellow "members" like Philip Larkin and Kingsley Amis than Davie himself. They investigated Pound-free ways to "make it new," beginning in trendiness, ending in confused conservatism.[2]

And Larkin too was eager to claim kin with Hardy, and did so in a famous moment in his introduction to the second edition of his early collection *The North Ship* (1965), in which Hardy-hailing is made cognate with a rejection of Yeats, whose "Celtic fever," it is claimed, had "ruined many a better talent"[3] (although critics have seen Yeatsian qualities in Larkin, including Merle Browne, who saw Yeatsian gaieties allegedly absent from Hardy,[4] while James Booth and Edward Neill have isolated an Oxonian literariness, a pondered, assaying and "builded rhyme" effect alien to Hardy.[5] Larkin returned to the theme in "Wanted: Good Hardy Critic," an article in the *Critical Quarterly* (1966), also reprinted in *Required Writing* (1983) in which he trumpeted the assurance that he would not wish Hardy's *Col-lected Poems* shorter by one poem (174), responding, presumably, to the "severely pruning" orthodoxies of Leavis and Empson. (There's also a short piece on "The Poetry of Hardy" here [175–6], originally a Radio 4 broad-cast reprinted in *The Listener* [1968], which sets the tone of critical un-strenuousness ["Judging? our critics will do that for us"] by this home-grown Villiers de l'Isle-Adam of Hardyists.)

It may be that Yeats's imperious imaginative impositions alienated a Larkin more responsive to Hardy's imaginative willingness to be imposed upon, imprinted, as in "Afterwards," for example. In this respect, Seamus Heaney's attempt to involve the poem with Wallace Stevens's idea of the imagination's pressing back against pressure, or as Stevens puts it, "vio-lence" from without, is less than happy here.)[6] Yet it should be noted that he too pays a fine if glancing tribute to Hardy, citing the poem and de-scribing it as "bewitching."

In this respect, if in no other, Larkin was like J. Hillis Miller, who noted that even the most comprehensive and tidy selection, by the admirable T. R. M. Creighton[7] was inclined to edit out not only distinguished poems but a sweet disorder of address,[8] a rambling rural randomness redolent of Hardy's response to David Hume. Hume dissolved the human (or at least Humean) subject to a wan wistlessness quite in line with poststructuralism and the American deconstruction of which Hillis was of course a leading exponent (so that for him Hardy becomes a kind of poetic deconstructor). An earlier critic, Mark Van Doren, also found selection impossible: "Too many of Hardy's poems . . . are not 'good' . . . I agree[:] but I am always changing my mind as to which those are. I never tire of opening those old doors that resist me a little, and my conclusion is that the building as a whole should be left just as it lies"[9] (surely a lovely sentence, in both senses, apart from the fact that buildings cannot lie.)

With even less resistance, Dylan Thomas declared that he "liked all his poems,"[10] while more cannily, but unmistakably including himself in the camp of the inclusive, Dennis Taylor observes that "the great poems illumi-nate all the poems; and all the poems contribute to the great poems."[11] It is evident, too, that Tom Paulin is also of this party, since though he often gently reprehends, he points out how the weak poem may be a contributor to the general process of understanding Hardy's idiosyncratic modalities, in pointing out for example that "Green Slates," if "trite," offers a "useful de-scription of the way his memory operates")[12] which might feed into an un-derstanding of less perfunctory poetic effects.

Like Miller and Van Doren, Larkin found the attention of editors oti-ose, just as Peter Widdowson, following an article by Trevor Johnson in *Victorian Poetry* (1979), found the anthologist's Hardy unduly constricting.[13] The verdict was that pressures informing such selection turned all to favour and to prettiness, or pettiness, so that certain poems of a thoroughly reassuring nature kept being recycled, not only in a wearying but also ideologically tendentious way. An anthology, after all, is a bunch of flowers, and if, as Donald Davie snarled, an anthology poem may be defined as a poem that offends nobody, so much the worse for anthologies and for Hardy. The occasional stinking weed should be *de rigueur*. (The severe *diktat* includes looking askance at "The Oxen," a poem it's surely a little hard not to feel some affection for. One might do worse than be a peruser of anthologies.) But in any case, and as Davie's comment suggests, the murkily motivated tendentiousness that Widdowson finds among the anthologizing community has a different (if in a way equally depressing) explanation.

Though it might seem logical for crusading but still crusty ex-Wykhamist William Empson to grumble that "a working selection from Hardy's mass of bad poetry is much needed,"[14] Empson fails to specify here what there is of positive value in Hardy's poetry for him to make this a desideratum. In other words, although Empson may mean well, he scarcely sounds sympathetic. He might have done well to read, for example, a little article in *Victorian Newsletter* by David Thatcher[15] which indicates how Hardy's "Afterwards" is in certain respects a more attractive poem than the self-elegizing portion of Gray's "Elegy" from which it takes its textual inception (that being, of course, a poem about which Empson wrote so well).[16] Thatcher argues that in this poem Hardy overcomes a deep-seated tendency to poetic egotism in self-memorializing by a cunning irregularity of relationship to a poetic tradition which Hardy often quietly evokes to recede from (remembering T. S. Eliot's characterisation of his version of free verse), or which he seems virtually to re-invent.

And just as Stinsford, Hardy's very own churchyard was Gray's gravely animated Stoke Poges in his imagination, the Gray poem may be assumed to have meant much to him. Yet, as Peter Sacks puts it, when Hardy re-enters the mode of elegy, for example,

> Hardy's departure from convention [compared with earlier elegists] is at first sight so radical as to place him and his poems in a strange, unhoused condition [and in] isolation with respect to the genre [as pursued by Spenser, Milton, Gray, Shelley and Swinburne].[17]

The gruff critical patronage of Empson (et al. — and there are so many of them) is even more comprehensively dismissed in Jahan Ramazani's acute portrayal of the disconcerting sophistication and reluctant modernity of Hardy's procedures. He observes how his elegies "announce" some of their own difficulties as [they] stumble into the new century, including God's

death, the withdrawal of nature's consolatory powers, the apparent absurdity of elegaic expectation, and the disappearance of the individual from the
mystic pad of history."[18] His elegies are, inter alia, elegies for the elegy itself.

The Empsonian idea that Hardy simply produced a mass of inferior
verse some of which somehow, against the grain and the odds, secretes an
(antithetical) distinction is refuted by such sprightly assayings. But the
Larkin, Mark Van Doren, Dylan Thomas, Dennis Taylor and J. Hillis Miller
claim for a kind of all-round poetic distinction and appropriate forms and
levels of poetic success cannot be sustained, as Hardy's finer poems themselves chafe and jar against his more perfunctory verses, even if different
readers define this fineness differently. Or at least, we may say, Hardy seems
to have achieved something of an *aporia* here — his poetry "asks"/"does
not ask" to be "selected." As the "hempen homespun" of English poetry,
he perhaps, perhaps paradoxically, raises profounder questions as to what
sort of thing poetry is (or, as Derrida, a little pretentiously, puts it, "*Che
cos'e la poesia?*")[19] than other poets.

If we transpose this into a practical problem — with theoretical coefficients? — I would not preclude the possibility that a good "Selected Poems" has simply not been achieved, and an article might rather piquantly be
entitled: "Wanted: Good Hardy Editor" (and *editors* are, necessarily, *critics*,
perhaps finally the most influential of critics). This might be provocative,
with such distinguished editorial names in the field, but David Wright includes, for example, "News for her Mother," "The Jubilee of a Magazine,"
and fusty stuff from The Dynasts.[20] Samuel Hynes includes: "Cynic's Epi-
taph," "Inscriptions for a Peal of Eight Bells" and "The Lodging-House
Fuchsias";[21] Harry Thomas's is a particularly attractive selection, but do we
need "Horses Aboard," or "The Weary Walker," for example?[22] T. R. M.
Creighton includes, for example, "A Refusal" ("Said the Dean of Westmin-
ster/Mine is the best minster . . . "); James Gibson, in his short selection
includes: "A Jingle on the Times" and "To Shakespeare,"[23] while even Tim
Armstrong, who has spent so much time winnowing Hardy critique for his
Longman selection, has "Sapphic Fragment," "A Young Man's Epigram on
Existence," "The Statue of Liberty" and "Nothing Matters Much."[24]

These are all poor poems, and if they contribute to the total effect of a
"Selected Poems," a selected poems might always have had its effect con-
tributed to more by more distinguished examples. Of course, a poem is not
the equivalent of a phoneme here as the smallest unit of "poetic meaning,"
and, as John Lucas reminds us, "even slight or poor poems may be mo-
mentarily redeemed by a visual image of piercing or arresting accuracy"[25] —
or some other feature which might merit more sophisticated characterizing.
Perhaps one of Hardy's mishaps is that his editors have, in a sense, been his
most influential critics. (As a connoisseur of things of ill-omen, Hardy

might have seen the shape of things to come in his own selection for Macmillan, *Chosen Poems*, which was quickly scrapped and replaced by an inferior selection by G. M. Young [1940]).[26]

In fact it was the Yeats/Hardy binarising which probably led into the "naturalising" of the poetry of Hardy as a kind of rallying-point (or rallying-cry) for an anti-modernist position. This has done much damage, and obscures the fact that Hardy is, in his odd way, an extremely experimental writer, announcing a programme of Shelleyan radicality, Darwinian subversiveness and Humean agnosticism while simultaneously drowning in cultural nostalgia. At the same time he seems quite eager to enter the Tennysonian realm of Palgrave's *Anthology*, and to announce, a bit dismayingly perhaps, that any little old song will do for him — the opening of a famous poem characteristically redeemed by his original glosses on the idea and particularly that touching conclusion requiring only "the homeliest of heartstirrings."

Dylan Thomas offers an apparently benign but potentially damaging version of the same "binary," since, according to Vernon Watkins, he liked Hardy best of modern poets, but considered Yeats the "greatest,"[27] an idea rather endearingly savaged by Martin Seymour-Smith in his bluffly biographical polemics.[28] Donald Davie has claimed that even apparently favourable judgements on Hardy are "shot through with protectiveness, even condescension" (1973: 5), and there is even a touch of that in the reported attitude of Robert Graves, whose *Oxford Lectures* were something of an abattoir of modern poetic reputations, since Hardy was "the one poet he loved unreservedly."[29]

The point then is not to do as Geoffrey Grigson understandably did — indignantly to reverse Larkin's binarism and give the honors, or all honor, to Yeats, "preferring," as he puts it, "fanatic indignation, declaimed in the bright sunshine, to murmurs in the gloom"[30] — but to deconstruct Larkin's either/or, to refuse his terms of opposition. Bernard Bergonzi, for example, reluctantly accepts the Grigson diagnosis, still claiming "greatness" for Hardy on his own ground, but the problem is that Hardy is simply allowed to occupy any of the ground — being Yeats it must surely be "high" ground — not previously annexed by Yeats here: "Yeats is a poet of rhetoric, of music, of extremity or absurdity; in a special sense, 'poetic.' Hardy is down to earth, plain, cautious, ironic, unambitious, democratic in sympathy, unrhetorical; 'prosaic' even."[31]

Grigson as a polemicizing figure was once to be reckoned with (although he never really achieved academic recognition as an authority: Leavisites abounded; there were no Grigsonians). But he also had a kind of "back to thatched cottages" program which made his defection from Hardy significant. Was "Hardy" really the reassuringly rustic product Grigson had formerly assumed he was?

He returned to the theme in a book intended mainly as a celebration or *Festschrift*, where critique is muted, somewhat mollified but still plaintive: "Those who begin as devotees of Hardy's verse . . . sometimes end by finding all of this too much . . . as if Hardy represents mortality creeping on the dung of earth (the phrase comes from a play he admired, *The Broken Heart*, by John Ford) . . . . "[32] (The comparison is a little off-key as well as off-the-cuff, as [in a sense] befits the compilation itself.)

Davie, though ostensibly a supporter, also describes with relish what he takes to be Hardy's limitations en route to describing those of his supposed poetic beneficiaries, or the followers of Hardy who may for whatever reason be said to be loosely cognate with him. But the looseness of his governing idea is also suggested by what seems to be a plumping-up chapter on the then voguish epic in prose by J. R. R. Tolkien, *The Lord of the Rings* (1954–55). The link with Hardy here seems tenuous; indeed it seems fair to say that Hardy would have found this ideological *confrère* of C. S. Lewis antipathetic, and gives more colour to the suspicion that Hardy might have challenged his advocate in terms of the allies found for him and the characteristics ascribed to him.

But Davie also dramatises his own "schizophrenia" by writing of a thoroughly modernist Hardy solemnly adjusting nuances of Dante and Virgil in a celebrated essay in a number of *Agenda* (1972) guest-edited by himself and devoted to Hardy,[33] though he swiftly returned in *Thomas Hardy and British Poetry* to the Hardy "used as a stick to beat modernists" as Theodore Weiss contemptuously put it.[34] "Schizophrenia" sounds hyperbolic, but Tom Paulin, discussing the positivism which almost paradoxically underlies Hardy's poetic vision, speaks only to one side of his Hardy brief when he claims that "for Donald Davie, Hardy's poems never get beyond this 'quantifiable reality,' a reality that is about as inspiring as a dual carriageway on a grey afternoon" (105). Davie's discussion of Hardy is not quite so constrained or constraining, although his summing-up is vulnerably close to being targeted by Paulin's slightly polemic point:

> . . . his poems, instead of transforming and displacing qualifiable reality or the reality of common sense, are on the contrary just so many glosses on that reality, which is conceived of as unchallengably "given" and final (*Thomas Hardy and British Poetry* [62]).

The statement is plainly at odds with the presentation of the metaphysical Hardy of the "Virgilian Purples" essay, an unacknowledged sea-change which disconcerts.

But Paulin is making room for himself here, as he considers how Hardy's apparent positivism, or reductive, scientific perspective, is nourished by epiphanies, voices from beyond, eidetic imagery and all the other signifying agents suggesting a broader philosophical perspective. Yet, though as he says, romantic poetry develops from empiricism, the subjectivity it bears with it simultaneously annihilates it, so that the philosophical confusions such literary impressionism brings is the breeding ground of the poetry itself. In fact, far from announcing a philosophical program, Hardy's poems live in the flickering and shuttling between subjective and objective poles, the extremities more dramatically intuited and presented by Yeats.

Perhaps Paulin, excellent in much, might still consider re-reading "After a Romantic Day" to remind himself of what Hardy could (so to speak) do with a dual carriageway. Donald Davie has a chapter on "Hardy Self-Excelling" which shows him occasionally blundering into a transcendence of drabness. Also as Paulin has just been discussing the delightful and rather mystically positivistic "Voices from things Growing in a Churchyard" (103–105), this seems extremely unfair (to this Hardy a graveyard is more fun than a funfair, never mind a dual carriageway). This reductiveness includes unfairness even to the Davie of *Thomas Hardy and British Poetry*. As it is, the Davie of the "Virgilian Purples" essay has a Hardy not only as raptly and rampantly intertextual as T. S. Eliot, but also an elegist whose secure metaphysical underpinnings cause Davie to turn with what he alarmingly calls "a sort of fury" (1977: 233) on J. Hillis Miller, the immediate cause being his insufficiently appreciative response to the "time of such quality" in "At Castle Boterel," — although much also turns on one's view of the perhaps in itself not particularly controversial claim (by Hardy) that the Emma of "Beeny Cliff" is "elsewhere." In this case, as T. H. Huxley's coinage of the word "agnostic" might have been neologised for Hardy's case, this "fury" of Davie's seems excessive. He cashes out as a metaphysical positivity the idea that Emma is "elsewhere," when the word relishes its own inspecificity.

Indeed, Melanie Sexton goes much further than Miller firstly in (meekly) following H. A. T. Johnson's claim that the elegies are (perhaps the first) "written out of total unbelief,"[35] so that, in the poem, "figuring" is not a metaphysical phenomenon but something connected, like memory, with the physical brain."[36] Davie's reversion to an acceptance at least of the critical reproduction of the "simple" Hardy is confirmed by a later short review essay,[37] and one wonders if this entails simplicities of belief (or unbelief) which don't call for complex Virgilian analogies of an afterlife, but equally don't entail turning with "fury" on J. Hillis Miller.

In any case, Davie's simple Hardy is immediately seen to be *sous rature* if we consider Tim Armstrong's consideration of "The Convergence of the

Twain." The point partly is that Hardy was anticipated by both by those who anticipated (textually or otherwise) the Titanic disaster, including minor poet Thaxter. So Hardy is already complexly mediating various theories, from the cosmic to the technical, about how the disaster was to be interpreted, even what might be held to be "good in the way of belief" in embarking on any such interpretation. For example, as Armstrong puts it, the language about the intimate welding is "ambiguous with respect to agency"[38] and thus resumes many of his speculations about teleologies or the lack of them.

Paul Zietlow, arguing against J. O. Bailey's claims that Hardy's first poems echo Darwin, Huxley, Spencer Mill, then move through Schopenhaurian (or Von Hartmannian) paces and evolve towards Evolutionary Meliorism. He finds a tentativeness that finds even this lightly and intermittently pursued poetic program to be inapposite to his sense that, for Hardy, we live in the flicker, not the structure, and that "human consciousness is a profound mystery; its depths are sources of impulses which can never be thoroughly comprehended or controlled."[39]

As he so nicely puts it (and his book-length study by comparison spends too much time on paraphrase exercises which leave insufficient room for such glancingly apposite apercus, "much of the energy in Hardy's poetry is devoted to an affirmation of uncertainty" (116). This does not mean that Hardy is anti-intellectual, merely that he is a poet. Art, though "among the ideologies," never advances one; but an art with no ideology on its hands is shadow-boxing indeed.

The idea is that Hardy works from emotion to fitfully intuited congruence with philosophical concepts. But the converse is also true, and strategically important in the combating of false but received ideas about poetic autobiography and the man who just writes from life. Testifying to the fact that Hardy's "naked emotion" elegies are controlled by a temporally situated philosophical mind-set, violated, as it were, by an idea to excellent effect (and affect), we might also cite Philip Davis: "In a book which Hardy read as an introduction to the philosophy of Schopenhauer, James Sully, a disciple of George Eliot, had written of his age: 'We have resolved to measure the value of the world by human feeling' [and] implicit [in this] were [the] assumptions that the world exists for human emotional purpose or it has no purpose . . . a romantic legacy which leads to stark pessimism and the conclusion that 'reminiscence is less an endowment than a disease'" (369). Hardy might, as Davis might have suggested, used such ideas as "regulative concepts," in Kant's idiom, (or even an epigraph) to the "Emma" poems of 1912–3 even if the "private" emotions seem to leave no room for the "meddling intellect."[40]

In other words, even the nakedly domestic action of Hardy's "Poems 1912–13" may be informed by "philosophical" considerations. W. B. Yeats said that A. E. Housman's *Shropshire Lad* "deserved its fame, but a mile further and all had been marsh." His reflections on how "all that is personal soon rots; it must be packed in ice or salt" seem prophylactic about this, and make for a good critique of all those approaches to poems 1912–13 in particular which seem to suggest that all is indeed "marsh" and a good thing too. To fall back on ideas of raw emotion and biographical conjecture here is to fall back into a familiar world of critical patronage and special pleading where Hardy is concerned. The apparent forms of tribute are themselves forms of patronage. It may be, too, that, though the philosophical informs the domestic space of "Poems 1912–13," critics have been too ready to make these the central focus because they so conveniently elide the political, consideration of which makes Hardy scholars unhappy. John Goode is suggestive when he points out of the "In Tenebris" poems that Hardy is arguing that "the negations of delight are forms of mystification. Though Hardy was not explicitly revolutionary, he hopes that such a feeling 'disturbs the order here.'"[41]

Even a critic like Robert Langbaum, apparently committed to giving Hardy's poetry its due, resurrects T. S. Eliot's version of a Victorian parlour game — is Hardy major or minor? The argument tendentiously involves the novels as the major partner here, and thus crush the poetry into a minor status that remains unproven, especially as he concludes the discussion with an appreciative but perfunctory comparison of "Proud Songsters" with Browning's "Parleying with Gerard de Lairesse," an early Pound title for a poem which reduces Shelley to whimsy. Hardy's poem is much more moving, its lightness of touch does not preclude the *gravitas* of a paradoxically Darwinian mysticism. But the major/minor division is already question-begging and passe.[42]

Indeed, in connection with this "life's like that" Hardy, Weiss seems to have his suspicions about the particular use or abuse of Hardy he specifies confirmed by Irving Howe, when he writes that "reading Eliot . . . one may say, 'ah, here in fulfilment is the sensibility that formed us'. Reading Hardy one say, "but this is how life is, has always been, and probably will remain"[43] (a response made firmly in line with the dutifully nonplussed treatment of the poetry of Hardy in his earlier book: when faced with poems like "During Wind and Rain" one feels only the "grating inadequacy of verbal analysis,"[44] a characteristic injunction to the critic not to open but to shut up shop here. And if the compliment to Eliot is, to put it mildly, excessive (cf., for instance, A. Walton Litz's collection of 1974 entitled *Eliot in His Time*, even if this tome has itself succumbed in turn to time's unflinching rigour), the backhandedness of the compliment to Hardy is characteristic.

Baffled by the terms and conditions on which Hardy seems to offer himself as a poet, critics from Lytton Strachey to Katherine Anne Porter have vied with each other in backhanded compliments which "make strange" the usual criteria brought to bear on poems. This is significant, since, as Kenneth Marsden reports, early responses to Hardy, even when the gestures were appreciative, were (un)usually inchoate and (in both senses, it would seem) "mystified,"[45] and appropriately sophisticated critical responses to Hardy were slow to develop, giving some colour to Dennis Taylor's fundamental claim in his third book about Hardy, using criteria advanced by Eliot in "Tradition and the Individual Talent," that Hardy is the least "recuperable" of poets for tradition, and that this in itself is the source of his unique distinction ("Hardy's literary language never seems to arrive at the stage of standardization"),[46] exploring the idea that "Hardy's awkwardness continues to be harshly judged, or weakly defended. In fact, it stands as a continuing challenge to the standard idiom, and continues to symbolise that challenge" (58).

Even a sophisticated responsiveness, in this case a broadly Leavisian context in a volume suggestively bookended by Henry James and T. S. Eliot, can produce the idea that Hardy is gauche when he approaches London, can be uncouth, "crassly eccentric" in the line "So you've lost a sprucer spouse than I." And Henry Gifford, despite his promising name, even finds the changes of tone in "Channel Firing" "disconcerting."[47] But what a tribute to the poet that he should manage to disconcert such a reader, or rather, the kind of reader Gifford has for the moment constituted himself as. And when he calls two lines from "The Pedigree" "too heavily brocaded," one should ask "too heavily brocaded for what proves to have been intended, or rather, too heavily brocaded for whom? (apart that is, for him)."

An older critic in a recent book seems to protest Taylor's claims in its own claim to the effect that "exaggerated claims have been made for Hardy's original contributions to the language,"[48] but concedes that "his great strength lies in his power of combining words in unexpected ways" (76). Such an idea, not in itself controversial, could be used to challenge the various back handed compliments and abusive epithets fashioned to figure forth the language of his poetry. In a sophisticated argument, Taylor's point would appear to be that Hardy's writing involves *avant la lettre* hesitations, or power to induce these in the reader, over what exactly constituted both "dialect" and "tribe" in Eliot's sophisticatedly Mallarméan, but ultimately conservative and hegemonic concern to "purify the dialect of the tribe." This instability in mode of address corresponds to hesitations on Hardy's part over whom he is supposed to be addressing. Thus his homespun ef-

fects, so often misprized, finally testify, over a range of work, to genuine literary experiment.

This argument can then be used to challenge the assumptions, often rehearsed, which may be represented by Graham Hough, who claimed that
the "lesson" of Eliot "makes difficulties with an obviously great poet like
Hardy, whose control of diction is obviously uncertain,"[49] given that the
idea of greatness is itself being controlled by ideas like "control of diction."
Similarly, Douglas Brown, referring to another well-scanned moment in
Four Quartets, when he claims that "that complete consort" [dancing to-
gether] Hardy seldom achieved,"[50] which may be challenged on its own
terms, or mined by the consideration that a greater poetic good may be
served by an exploration of linguistic dissonances, disharmonies or non-
convergencies. Is it really Hardy or Eliot who is the problem here? The
paradoxes of Eliot's pseudo-modernism might be examined, and indeed
ways of responding to the later Eliot have become increasingly unpredict-
able. Valentine Cunningham has even referred to the steep decline in his
reputation as a fait accompli.[51] (This is worth mentioning here because
Eliot's efforts, however perfunctory, to quash Hardy look increasingly suspect.)

Although Samuel Hynes claimed that Hardy offered a more traditional
sense of tradition than Eliot,[52] Hardy's tradition, offspring of a *miglior fab-
bro*, a better, or at least craftier craftsman than he was given credit for (by
Yeats, for example),[53] may prove to have something in common with Eliot's
disintegrating Hegelian fantasies about Minds of Europe. His patrimony of
folklore proves at last to be a rather "folkloric" patrimony, product, it may
be, of an "abyssal chimeristic engineering."[54] This "engineering" offers, in
its quite weeting way, to become postmodernist *avant la lettre*.

It was rather naughty of Philip Larkin to quote Lytton Strachey's verdict
that "the gloom is not even relieved by elegance of diction"[55] as if this were
some kind of critical *coup de grace*. But Strachey is working his way by critical detour to establish that while the cold correctness of the then Poet Laureate, Robert Bridges, by-passed sensibilities, Hardy, despite his "ugly and
cumbrous expressions, clumsy metres, and flat, prosaic turns of speech"
(196) has found the secret of "touching our marrow-bones."[56] As usual,
though, he does get in a few kicks *en route* to his actually stultified conclusion: he knows not why, nevertheless it is so. But outdoing even this in
back-handed compliments is Katherine Anne Porter asking "What could be
duller? What could be more laboured? . . .? Except for this in my memory: . . . I have seen it, I was there."[57] (A friendlier way of putting this might
be J. P. Ward's sense of the "strange loosely-strung feel of the poems"
which "[allow] Hardy to avoid any sense of the too-accomplished.")[58] G.
M. Young, writing as a Hardy exponent in introducing his chosen poems

seems to find it hard to warm to his theme as he confesses that his chosen poet was "writing . . . with a stilted and self-conscious clumsiness" (xiv). Leavis, of course, was an inimitable master of what might be called the whiplash compliment, or Booby-trap commendation:

> There is something extremely personal about the gauche unshrinking mismarriages . . . of his diction, in which, with naif aplomb, he takes as they come the romantic-poetical, the prosaic banal, the stilted literary, the colloquial, the archaistic, the erudite, the technical, the dialect word, the brand-new Hardy coinage (1940: 92)

Perhaps Leavis's idea of the personal encouraged the rush to impersonality. (Or perhaps he had already reached the stage of wee smacks at the disapppointingly conventional T. S. Eliot, eyeless in Bloomsbury.) Leavis may have taken his cue from the statement by William Archer about Hardy "seeing the words of the dictionary as all on one plane, so to speak," as quoted by Edmund Blunden.[59] Thence to a whole tradition of ambiguous gifts of "praise" for Hardy. Characteristic moments of apologia becoming apology occur, for example, in Norman Page ("bizarre linguistic contortions"),[60] Cicely Havely ("he seems to have imagined that the language was still as flexible as it was in the time of Shakespeare" with consequent habits of using "words in unorthodox ways" which "gives his poetry a tinge of perverse awkwardness.")[61]

Even for Desmond Hawkins, who writes in that warmly commendatory, if unexacting manner of the professional Hardyist, "he invents English-style words as a foreigner might,"[62] perhaps the supreme insult for someone who (in both senses) followed William Barnes. But the slippery nature of the case is shown by his contempt for the phrasing in "Her warble flung its woo/In his ear" (200), as Hardy's excellencies emerge from oddities. Such pronouncements may partly emerge from the tendentiousness of Samuel Hynes's opinings to the effect that "Hardy was left without a poetic vehicle adequate to his needs. He spent his life trying to build another out of old parts,"[63] which is at least suggestive, although it's at least equally suggestive that this doyen of Hardy poetry exponents exacts a full look at the worst with such relish.

Hardy thus moves from being an engineer to bricoleur[64]: it may be felt, then, that the more disconcerting the materials are to these decorous critics the more likely the poem is to be successful. Paul Zietlow, in a workmanlike discussion, has shown how, in propelling his language towards "a cruder, tougher diction and syntax," itself a rather crude way of putting it, he contrives to give "a bite of strangeness,"[65] which will permit us to imagine the reader both biting and being bitten. Moving towards actual analysis of how this happens, Norman Page, in a better (if still slightly patronizing) discussion shows how Hardy advances beyond Barnes by his interest in a more general sense of experimentation which does not form part of a rigidly defined program, and which does not cut him off from the wider resources of the language, including Latinate and polysyllabic "loan-words" as well as the "thew and sinew" style of diction Hopkins so oddly located in Dryden[66] which Barnes himself in fact pursued *à outrance*.

Ultimately, it may be felt, Hardy is simply not recuperable for a certain concept of critical decorum, as critics like Tom Paulin and Dennis Taylor have duly noted. The latter may also claim to be the doyen of all Hardy commentators, at least on the poetry, as a Hardy-intoxicated man who copies out all of his (occasionally comic) pronouncements with greater gusto than any other critic has dared to. Taylor's three immensely erudite books on Hardy (1981, 1988, 1993) certainly make him an authority, on Hardy and other things as well. This includes a well-documented sense of a constant movement towards a tacitly accepted notion of linguistic propriety (some might say a linguistic hegemony) which Hardy challenges. Particularly in the most recent, *Hardy's Literary Language and the New Philology*, he is learnedly eloquent on the wealth of implication to be found in the new ways of investigating language which Hardy was involved in and responded to so deftly and creatively; he notes how one runs into interesting problems of authorship and authority when Hardy, amusingly eager in some ways to honour the linguistic proprieties, consults the OED and finds himself listed as the licensed and licensing user in question.[67] (But Hardy also has the habit of attempting to by-pass language altogether, asserting that a certain scene "was" a poem before his inditings commenced, which is more problematizing than the imputed interest in philologies would allow for.)

Taylor's first book on Hardy showed a particular interest in Hardy's lyrics of the interrupted consciousness, his exploration of experiences which disrupt, disarm or, as bracketed by the poem itself, annul temporality. Connections are drawn between Hardy's procedures and those of romantic lyricists, romantic aesthetics, the Gothic Revival, pastoralism, and so on. The book is a great blow for Hardy, but hard to get through, bitty, and many of the poems listed in the index turn out to appear in lists which merely assign them taxonomically to one of the writer's categories. Unfortunately, the book it is most keenly bidding to overtake or exorcise, Hynes, with his severely limiting, and perhaps limited view of Hardy, is concise and economical. But there may also be a price for putting Hardy so completely at the centre of a world-wide literary web. The specialist view — Taylor's 1966 dissertation was on Hardy's poetry, which he has mined since — lead up to an "imploded," inward-looking world. His work never fully accepted as delivering Hardy from the various charges laid at his door, the relative lack of scholarly and critical authority achieved by the matchless scholarly labour here derives somewhat paradoxically from the attempt to make Hardy uniquely authoritative.

Overall, Dennis Taylor's stance seems to indicate that a scholarly pocket has been turned inside out, and that he has moved from discussing "what is good in or about Hardy" to tacitly suggesting that "good is what Hardy does." Hence by becoming an authority one comes to lack authority, losing, it may be, the balance and perspective of the truly critical intelligence. But in view of the entrenched nescience and negativity of the Hardy commentators and the failure to evolve adequate criteria for critical reception we may say that it is good to have such an expert in the field. The implication is, we might say, that if Leavis could observe that if certain Victorian poets did not respond to his method of investigation that was a reflection on them rather than the method, failure to respond to what Hardy is doing may be a reflection on the assumptions or the procedures brought to bear rather than "the poetry itself."[68]

A revealing move in Davie's continually interesting but misprizing discussion is to separate that "modest journeyman" Hardy forever practising plain chants at humble "village hall" poetic rehearsals from that "self-excelling" Hardy who, working in his unweeting way, backs onstage to give compelling performances which are overheard rather than heard, in his favourite J. S. Mill's idiom, and which the awareness of an audience would only serve to annul or to stultify.

This, indeed, is part of what John Bayley seems to be saying in his magisterial but also rather mystical *Essay on Hardy*.[69] Even a good poem, Davie claims, [like "Overlooking the River Stour"] shows touches of the technocrat, full of a "content" that's been shoehorned into place a little too vigorously as it more obviously is in "Lines to a Movement in Mozart's E-Flat Symphony." (It is possible to find ambiguity here, a teasing artistic brinkmanship over whether the form is "bullying" the content in the way suggested by Davie: the reader is constantly "asked" to adjudicate but finds a constant indeterminacy in her/his own response.)

Unfortunately this argument serves to perpetuate, if in a paradoxical way, some popular myths about Hardy as writer. It should be conceded even by the devoutest Davian that John Lucas responded well to the book in one of his best extended reviews, "Thomas Hardy, Donald Davie, England and the English,"[70] particularly as this wasn't merely the response of a "leftie" to a "rightie." Certainly it did conduct quite a rigorous and by no means wholly unsympathetic inquisition into how Davie's attitude to Hardy had "strangely mingled" with his own "damn you, England" feelings of distaste for Harold Wilson's small unpleasant (is)land. He also disentangled the confused impulses which made Hardy something of a stalking-horse for

Davie himself. However, he also re-examined the poetry in the light or darkness of Davie's thrawn and cranky asseverations. In the process what came up, we might say, was the feeling that Davie engineers Hardy imperiously into the place he wants him to occupy (which is partly that of an Aunt Sally, but with the sort of ambiguity of feeling and treatment that Maggie Tulliver reserved for her doll in *The Mill on the Floss*).

A basic irrationality stems from Davie's attempt to associate Hardy's grindingly engineered exactitudes (books of prosody and rhyming dictionaries to hand) with that land of unlikeness, the slapdash "younger men's" poetry, some of which Larkin was eventually to countenance for his *Oxford Book of Twentieth Century English Verse* (1973). This compilation, incidentally, may be felt to be at least as eccentric as Yeats's much-execrated Oxford Anthology (although only Eliot gets more fully presented than Hardy here). As the slightly feline Michael Alexander puts it: "if, as Davie says, Hardy's example has been so important to recent English poetry, the intellectual and emotional shortcomings of that poetry are not to be found in Hardy, despite his positivism and liberalism, for in his poetry these are subverted by something far more deeply interfused,"[71] which might be described as bullying the reader into accepting something not susceptible to definition, understanding or reference. Given the reference to "liberalism" which enters into combination with Wordsworth here, might the answer be "mystical 'Toryism'," especially as he is eager earlier in the essay to stress that Hardy is no "Tolpuddle curmudgeon" (51)?

All the same, when John Wain claims that "Hardy is just as much a religious poet as Hopkins,"[72] this does not seem outrageous. In fact Wain means simply Hardy's negative metaphysics, yet most readers would leap to the conclusion that include his tenderness, his empathy, as well as the feeling in Hardy of a self fielded, however hesitantly, as a kind of god-substitute at that precise moment in the nineteenth century when Nietzsche was born as a text, God became the fading grin (or unrisible rictus) of Carroll's Cheshire Cat, and Hardy shuffles forward, somewhat reluctantly, as a kind of anti-Jehovah's witness.

From Davie one gathers that although Hardy is now a highly conscious and conscientious "poetic operative," this is mainly when he isn't doing so well. In this account he duly returns to unconsciousness to achieve his best effects, which are then, in Wallace Stevens's phrasing, not so much "balances that he achieves" as "balances that happen" (with Hardy himself as the incarnation of his own immanent will urging himself on to stirring stuff in a suitably "unweeting way," as he might put it).

Once, we might say, autodidactic Hardy garbled his native wood-notes wild, evoking a tradition of critical patronage and back-handed compliments from James and Stevenson to Woolf and Leavis. Now a nice switch of metaphors gives us Engineer Hardy with pistons pounding and girders swaying, but critical patronage is still in place. But Davie at least sticks to his script, that's to say Hardy's. Hardy critics find it difficult to do this, and indeed the great irony of the biographical autoroute is that it leads away from, not into, what his texts are up to.

For example, Peter Robinson tries to rescue Hardy from Davie by pointing out, if murkily, that Hardy's rhetorical overinsistences and "jamming" effects somehow include apologetics for the postures they bring with them and thus a measure of "choice after full knowledge" which eludes Davie's statutes of "limitation." But he slides off into a biographical overinsistence on Hardy's textual dependence on the Emma of *Some Recollections*, so that the piece is smudged and made incoherent by its biographer-like gestures.[73] (To be fair, David Gewanter gets some purchase with the idea that "After a Journey," for instance, contains "Hardy's concession that (Emma's) "'Some Recollections' governs and controls his efforts at retrieval and creation," though here too the anchoring in biography is limiting. In fact the central *aperçu*, that "try as he might, Hardy cannot quite regain his lover outside 'Some Recollections,'"[74] may be read as an allegory of the succumbing of biography to textuality.

My conjecture about this is that the biographical tradition in Hardy studies has become by so much the dominant one that Robinson felt he had to simulate the role of biographer in order either to obtain critical credentials, or critical purchase. While Hardy may, in his curious mixture of the confessional and the reticent, be encouraging this tendency, it should be resisted, and even if, as George Macbeth suggests, "Hardy is part of the late nineteenth century autobiographical tradition"[75] which he so obviously deplores, criticism itself should transpose into an appropriate sense of Hardy's cunning irregularities of poetic architecture and "old linguistic furniture," rather than read off the text as merely the cry of its occasion.

A curious feature of Davie's argument ("Hardy Self-Excelling" is a chapter title) is that Hardy is most himself when least accomplished, so that his best performances contradict what he essentially is. It's a measure of the critical harshness (and ineptitude) with which Hardy has been treated and greeted that where other writers are defined by their virtues and their best performances, Hardy is characterised by his vices and his more hammy, humdrum or apparently perfunctory ones.

Curiously, this resumes Leavis's mainly pejorative descriptions of Hardy[76] and his tendentious attempt to salvage a few arbitrarily selected poems in his earlier foray into Hardy's poetic landscape: "A Broken Appointment," for example, is a slightly absurd exercise in high, self-pitying rhetoric; it never deviates into the strenuous polyphonic collisions which stir and urge everything into his burly idiosyncrasies, what Arthur Macdowall describes as a linguistic "amalgam."[77] As Kenneth Marsden, a sympathetic and underestimated critic puts it, "the really unsatisfactory work is not the odd, strained, gnarled, 'mixed' poems, but those whose technical accomplishment covers hollowness."[78]

Hardy here is embarrassingly present in, as it were, *propria persona*, a self-consciously "High" Victorian of "troubadour abasement in love"[79] to use a critical phrase invented to convey the basis of Pound's critical attitude to Yeats. It seems that only the absence of Hardy as personage produces the dramatic clashes of perspective characteristic of the self-communings of his "interior theatre." In this case, then, it may be said that the death of the author is the birth of the author.

With reference to the novel, it is immediately obvious that an ideological fault-line divides Leavis the admirer of the prose and politics of James and George Eliot, and Hardy, with his critical negation and political volatility. These lead to instabilities of tone and register noted by critics like Wotton and Widdowson. In a comparable or cognate way Leavis as a critic of Hardy's poetry and an early proponent of Eliot's modernism turns a deaf ear to Hardy's subversively Darwinian Victorian experiments as he sets up, in *New Bearings in English Poetry* (1932) a "vicious" (in Derrida's sense) binarism dividing Eliot and Hardy and with initial plausibility consigns Hardy to unsophisticated and olde-worlde charmlessness, as a rooted Victorian rustic with inveterate, limiting assumptions and cripplingly parochial proclivities and preoccupations.[80]

Constructing this constricting little diptych, Leavis ignores "the ache of modernism" announced as a part of Hardy's own poetic- programme and a pressing preoccupation in poems as dissimilar as "Afternoon Service in Mellstock," "The Self-Unseeing" and "Wessex Heights," as well as the sense of the slipperiness of his subject-position in a poem like "So Various." He is, at least at this point (in 1932) blind to Eliot's limitations (not to mention his own), but also to the fact that Lawrence, around whom he conducted a rather ungainly rain-dance, owed Hardy everything. No Hardy, no Lawrence — and he completely failed to negotiate this point, which applies to the poetry as well as the novels. Not that poems and novels are separable here: for example, is *Jude the Obscure* conceivable without Shelley, and "Epipsychidion" in particular? Lawrence himself combs through Hardy's work looking for "aristocrats,"[81] a reading against the grain in an unhelpful way if a barrage of recent critique heavily revising towards a sense of Hardy's sturdily "anti-hegemonic" gait is to be trusted.[82] "Doubting Lawrence" here has to do with doubts about the still suspect ideologies of modernism, so that, finally, the Hardy "used as a stick to beat modernists" might have a certain attraction.

Indeed, although Hardy has often been put into the ring with modernism, modernism was not necessarily disposed to fight. Eliot, for example, was sniffy, but then he was about so very much — Victorian poetry, Romantic poetry, but also the tradition of writing in English (as opposed to French) more generally, if we note his occasional remarks in letters to American correspondents as well as *obiter dicta* in printed reviews. The later, disillusioned Leavis amusingly accused him of a deadly Francophilia contracted at Harvard,[83] although early foreign trips from a Mid-West (which as late as Emerson could be pronounced relatively bookless) to the mesmeric cultural conditions of Paris may also have united to turn his head. For us, now, it is not so easy simply to follow Eliot's program and denigrate Hardy in consequence (what was insulting was less the denigration itself, at once holistic and perfunctory, as the plain insinuation that Hardy was not worth much of anyone's time).

The hugeness of Eliot's cultural moment is indicated by the essay on Hardy's poetry by Delmore Schwartz, in which he spends most of his time wrestling with Eliot's sad lucubrations on poetry and belief, given that, as Schwartz seems to be saying, Hardy has "radiant particulars," in Stevens' idiom, which form patterns according to the mighty working of beliefs one isn't supposed to wish to touch with a bargepole. We should "enjoy his poetry for what it is in its utmost concreteness [but] keep his beliefs *in* his poetry, and our own beliefs outside."[84] But Hardy was, in any case, already asking, "what am I to believe?" like Wallace Stevens, and his "beliefs," even his unbeliefs, both tentative, were not so poisonous, we might feel, as those, finally, of Eliot. Weigh "Afterwards" and "The Oxen" in the scale with *After Strange Gods*, for example, and we are equipped to observe how odd and how pathetic the attractive Delmore's essay is.

What we feel now is perhaps still prompted by a sharp observation in a relatively obscure context by Tom Paulin to the effect, rather piquantly, that "Hardy, like Donne, could find no substitute for sense experience, and it is Eliot's effort in *Four Quartets* to discover that transcendental substitute which would take him beyond time and experience. Because of his commitment to this search and because of its accompanying detestation of sense experience — not just sex, but all human experience — Eliot is a much more negative poet than Hardy."[85]

But does "Eliot" mean "modernism" here? Pound, so much more receptive and paradoxically congenial in these matters, complained for example that "Eliot don't *see* . . . Hardy"[86] (1950: 198), for example (meaning Hardy as poet, that is). We may assume that, as one of the most strenuous readers of Browning, most strenuous of poets (see James Langenbach's *Stone Cottage* for interesting details of this), he was inclined to take Hardy on board in Christopher Ricks's terms of "the poet who owed so much to

Browning."[87] This modifies Harold Bloom's account of Hardy as "Shelley's ephebe"[88] (although he seems to be proving that Hardy makes Shelley sound like *his* ephebe. ("Ephebe" is a rather affected term borrowed from Wallace Stevens, who glosses it as "the figure of the youth as virile poet.") But since, as Bloom nicely puts it "all Hardy's words are Winter Words," although only his last collection is called that, Hardy becomes the Zeus or Jehovah here, making himself, and in this respect at least defying temporality, into Shelley's crusty antecedent.

But although it looks as if J. Hillis Miller's view of Shelley as the immanent will that stirs and urges everything in Hardy's poetic (and novelistic) world will need to be modified to include Hardy's complex negotiations with his fellow Victorian poets, there seem to be objections to this. Maurice Bowra, although a polyglot who wrote easily about Lermontov and Hölderlin, has a chapter on Hardy which is warmly sympathetic without condescension. It would be perfectly respectable to accept his claim that Hardy is not like any of the poets he has been twinned with, despite his own praise for them, so that he is self-condemned to an involuntarily obdurate individualism. As Bowra puts it:

> . . . as a poet, he is a singular figure. The poets whom he most loved, Scott, Shelley, Keats, and Swinburne, left no trace on his work. Even Crabbe . . . belongs to a different world and shows no points of resemblance to what is most characteristic in Hardy. It is usual to say that he owed something to the Dorset poet William Barnes [but he didn't] . . . he was not a true peasant like Burns . . . too familiar with nature to cherish any Wordsworthian ideals about it . . . [and did] not wish to write poetry like that of Keats . . . [89] [and so on]

This might invoke Harold Bloom's argument about intertextuality, misunderstood as a neon glow of verbal reminiscence wearing its precursor on its sleeve,[90] and certainly Victorian studies writers have made something of Hardy's debts, allegiances and affiliations to Meredith, Swinburne, Browning, Barnes, Wordsworth, Shelley, Patmore, Arnold. However, it is still possible to see these as being a bit dubious in the light of Hardy's dazzling poetic slalomings, or at least to feel that his really great poetic purchases are on Shelley and Wordsworth. He announces a Shelleyan programme and negates it in the small print, while he "deconstructs" (while still in a manner "inveterately convolved" with) that aspect of Wordsworth which was proving such a "succedaneum and a prop" to Victorian pietism.

As David Perkins puts it in the course of his argument about Hardy's isolation which paradoxically proceeds from a sense of solidarity and a sensitivity to web-like connectivities with the world of woe, "[when] he summons Nature directly to the bar of judgement, it is almost as though Hardy were trying to turn the tables on Wordsworth, whom he so closely parallels in other ways — in brooding sensitivity, in sympathy with the homely and concrete, in open recognition of the isolation of man from the larger course of things and in the yearning to overcome it.[91] Opposition is true friendship, it seems, and Wordsworth is finally an "other oneself" (in Michel Serres's phrasing). More generally, John Holloway offers a kind of amateur-night distinction of Hardy-style poems and those of the others who inherited high romantic rhetoric: "in his work we find not an ambitious and aspiring style, but the informal and unassuming. Even in his unhappy poems he often writes with a strange kind of unlaboured jauntiness . . . His finest lyrics are the heroic achievements of a poet whose role was that of an anti-hero."[92]

Robert McCarthy, in an article drawing on that of David Perkins, evokes Heidegger and J. Hillis Miller and cites Lance Butler on the idea that "Hardy speaks to us today as Shakespeare does and Beckett does"[93] in an exploration of consciousness which secretes an "undeniable modernity" in order to lodge a militant corollary to the effect that "so many of his contemporaries have ceased to speak to us at all."[94] (Spender queried the modernity, cued by the ever-prejudiced Eliot, but is over-responsive to the technical innovations of modernism as a necessary and sufficient sign of innovative contemporaneity.)[95] But G. S. Fraser seems to nod agreement, finding in modernism proper the "quick light incisive talk of intellectuals in a capital,"[96] too ready, it seems, to recreate the Pound-Eliot tandem (as Davie called it) in the image of his beloved Augustans.

Indeed, Hardy is not usually the gainer in these comparative exercises. As a not untypical writer on Hardy, James Richardson, for example, has a chapter on Browning in which he calls Browning "a more interested and interesting person than Hardy,[97] and seems altogether more taken with him, which suggests that he should perhaps have been writing a book on Browning. He does have some instructive remarks on what kebabs them together linguistically ("for Browning and Hardy, language is a highly volatile substance, which vaporizes without constant stretching, cramping, and roughing up . . . their poems are artifacts — they assert their madeness, their physicality [78–9]) and on the common debt to Shelley.

However, Browning is more interestingly indebted to Shelley, his language is also more interesting, and the whole tone of the comparison is suggested by the suggestion that "all in all, the attempt to find the common ground of Browning's sprightly, muscular and rapid intelligence and Hardy's ponderous and vague intuition must at first seem an exercise in the improbable" (32). In a 133-page book stuffed with long quotations, he forgets Hardy completely from page 33 to page 57. Exacting a full look at the worst, he cites negligible poems like "How She Went to Ireland," for example (yet the poem itself returns, strategically placed in Margaret Mahar's misty argument for Hardy's abandonment of a particular teleology associated with the novel in his embracing of the eternal returns and formal recyclings of poetry.[98]

The idea is much better handled in Terri Witek's quasi-Deleuzian demonstration that "the repetitions in his poems, modern in sensibility, traditional in form, demonstrate the incremental power of the past to haunt the present with repetitions based in difference," and convince the enchanted reader that even Hardy's triolets, or, even, especially his triolets, are Nietzschean.)[99] Richardson perhaps takes his tone from Hynes (although Leavis and Blackmur may have had a hand in this), and cites him to give a tentative sense of Hardy's development, often denied: "the bad early poems are bad Shakespeare or bad Swinburne; the bad late poems are bad Hardy" (131). Four occurrences of the word "bad," mysteriously deployed, hold open the possibility of goodness in a way that's typical of Hardy critics in their blindingly negative theologies; goodness in Hardy must presumably ooze or squelch like ketchup from some generally unnutritious hot dog.

Untouched by the Shakespearean consideration that in levelling at Hardy's excesses they may be reckoning up their own, Hardy's self-appointed custodians spend a suspicious amount of energy chalking up his faults, even declaring him chock-full of faults, the Jamesian idiom, and showing long videos of his poetical pratfalls. (As one critic points out, discussion of Yeats don't usually begin with a catalogue of his failings — what Martin Dodsworth has called his "awful bombastic frankness," for example.) His "Shelleyan" and Darwinian sides would not appeal to Leavis, and similar bearings are the cause of Blackmur's outraged, Eliotian accusations, with the charge of his having an "absolutist, doctrinaire, totalitarian frame of mind."[100] Derived from Eliot's compliment to James, that he had a mind so fine that no idea could violate it, Blackmur makes haste to violate Hardy with this idea. Eliot writes about Hardy like the "creature of clerical cut" he describes in his own poems.

C. Day Lewis demands citation here. He certainly proved his devotion to Hardy in what for Hardy must be the supreme gesture — he had himself buried at Stinsford. He nobly describes Eliot's "frigid and unctuous phrases" and quotes "To an Unborn Pauper Child," not a poem that would move him much.[101] Blackmur, who tries to expand Eliotic remarks in the best modern way of Elioto-Jamesian patronage seems almost hysterically inapposite. In this respect, Davie's revisionary account of Hardy's excellences from an almost excessively Eliotic perspective in "Hardy's Virgilian Purples" in particular seems to have been a necessary realignment (although his account occludes the reference to the Thomas Gray poem which also obsessed Hardy with its "purple light of love," as well as the fact that Hardy uses the word purple to mean "purple" as well as "[romantically] bright)."

And Tim Armstrong has an interesting footnote to all this, adding scholarly details and showing us that the ashes of an old flame are also commemorated in "Where the Picnic Was.")[102]

Richardson is a good example of that strong tendency in critique of Hardy's poetry memorably referred to by Kenneth Marsden when he points out that Hardy seems to be the sort of poet of whom to whom one can apply the old adage that "he had no enemies; but all his friends disliked him."[103] And Richardson is snappish in tendency, though, as usual, he seems to take his eye off the object to make his points, and when he observes that "'hardy' is a word which describes the poet and his poems" (115), one feels he never spoke an untruer word for this poet of tremulous stay, as assiduous in evading the implications of his surname as Lawrence *Sterne* was in fleeing from his, apparently.

His final verdict on Hardy as achieving a "difficult sanity" (p.132) recalls the early I. A. Richards whose utilitarian grounding of poetry in a more general scheme of value, or values, has perhaps been undervalued, and Richards himself wrote perceptively on Hardy as late as 1979 as a man whose strenuous pithy phrasings and engineered collisions of diction were inevitably a high-risk strategy.[104] (Leavis's apparently more watertight investments in intrinsic value became an impermeable membrane rather stretched to create a chauvinist drum which came to drown out the subtler language of his earlier achievements.)

Richardson did, however, a decade later, write a book on other Victorian poets, and seems finally to qualify as an expert on Victorian poetry rather than as a specialist Hardian. In general, it has been a decided problem that Victorian poetry scholars have problems reconciling Hardy with their other subjects or projects in the area. Ross C. Murfin has shown something of the impact of Swinburne,[105] while Cornelia Cook traces the debt to George Meredith[106] and Rod Edmond has interesting remarks about the relationship to Patmore, which shows Hardy as being influenced by as well rather than being cognate with him,[107] quite comparable to Griffiths's brief notations of influence. He argues that Patmore is the simpler of the two elegists. Peter Casagrande[108] and Dennis Taylor[109] have made graphs of his grafts or implants from Wordsworth, who survived to become a Victorian property, against which he develops antibodies, and to whom, again, his relationship is complexly antithetical; he wrestles with the "problem" of Wordsworth, and emerges, in Harold Bloom's favourite idiom, as a *strong* poet — as Trevor Johnson, for example, notes, even in *Wessex Poems* "there are only faint, intermittent traces of that overt, if usually unwitting, indebtedness most poets display."[110]

In fact Bloom is interesting here, since, for him, although he is far from being a professional Hardyan, the two strong poets of the twentieth century

are Hardy and Stevens. The thesis is briefly enunciated, but follows from
the earlier claim that Hardy is one of the few poets who achieves not only a
clinamen or poetic swerving from precursors, but a *kenosis*, or poetry of dis-
continuity.[111] Although Bloom's terminology has not, on the whole, caught
on, and it may be suspected that they are part of a repertoire of anxious
mannerisms developed in his struggle with his strong precursors, Northrop
Frye and T. S. Eliot, the account remains suggestive.

Casagrande notes that the discussion of indebtednesses to Wordsworth
has a history and that the influential books of Rutland and Weber were dis-
proportionately repressive with respect to Wordsworth's imprint on Hardy,
rather as if they were anxious to find him an anxiety of influence which, according to Bloom, he had creditably transcended.[112] Trevor Johnson argues
for the imprint of Wyatt, Donne and Herbert as part of an un-Tennysonian
emphasis on poetical strenuousness uncongenial to editors like the Ten-
nyson-puppet Palgrave and his soul-brother and follower, Sir Arthur
Quiller-Couch.[113]

These intertextualities are potentially illuminating, although we might
also consider, as mediating the sound of sense and the sense of sound and
informing the poignancies of that self-excelling Hardy who, the estimate of
any other poet in question would simply be "Hardy," Tom Paulin's claim
that "Hardy's extraordinary sensitivity to the speaking voice must have been
nurtured in the depths of a rural folk culture"(92). Even if Hardy proved to
be something of an inventor of folk culture for our time, to recall Eliot's
ironic compliments to the Pound of *Cathay*, that would still be something
to reckon with: yet to a "sort-of-Marxist" critic like Widdowson Hardy is
only of interest when he transcends his pseudo-folkish matrix and reaches
the bourgeois stage in both senses.[114]

Although it was Pound himself who remarked, with his intermittently
endearing pretentiousness: "Ich stamm aus Browning. Pourquoi nier son
pere" (1950: 218), Hardy was the man who shared, in Tom Paulin's pawky
idiom, "certain squitchy sounds" (1986: 4) unavailable to Tennyson, a
Tennyson Hopkins, whose professionally prescribed faith made it, as it
were, impossible not to believe in six impossible things before breakfast, was
at least able to indulge in doubt about Tennyson, that's to say about his
"poetic," existence.[115]

Completely similar in his arrogant and much ruder dismissal of Tennyson, Pound was quite humble (and finally moving) about Hardy as well
as Browning, and seems to have been moved to create a strangely overdetermined sense of poetic oedipality to tunnel free from the anxiety of influence, especially as Walt Whitman was another poetic father he was forced to
acknowledge. But the very downrightness of his apodictic overinsistencies
issues in a certain mysticism.

Firstly, Pound (36) who in the *Guide to Kulchur* (New York: New Directions, 1970) asks, "when we, if we live long enough, come to estimate the "poetry of the period," against Hardy's 600 pages we will put what?"[116] (285), he is challenging as ever, but we are to assume the question is rhetorical. His criteria, apparently grounded in his enunciations, turn out to be knock-down arguments disguised as soberly consensual facts, for example in his reference to "the harvest of having written twenty novels first" (April 1937; 1950: 294.) (Curiously, in another *obiter dictum* on the matter, Eliot will not even concede that Hardy's novel-writing was beneficial to him as a poet,[117] while as one of life's little ironies, Hardy was inclined to give the honour, or the honours to Eliot's poetry over that of Pound.)[118] Pound's further comment, in another letter, is that "I do not believe there are more than two roads:

1. the old man's road (vide Tom. Hardy) — CONTENT, the INSIDES, the subject matter.

2. Music. (30.10.1934; 1950: 248-9)

One is left, here, somehow, in Adorno's idiom, with two torn halves of a ticket that do not unite to form a whole.

Pound, though, is suggestive as well as, finally, rather touching in his references to Hardy, and there is also one to Ford Madox Ford which is all that, claiming that "Hardy gets through despite his funny way of writing verse. Have just had a poem from him, full of every sort of inversion verbal, but so DAMN straight in thought" (26 May 1921) while he also claims, six years after Hardy's death, in 1934: "Nobody has taught me anything about writing since Thomas Hardy died" (1950: 264). He also praises Hardy in the appendix to an anthology he edited with Marcella Spann.[119]

Curiously, then, we have a Hardy which "modernism" does not find inherently uncongenial, which a major "Movement" poet can acclaim while simultaneously complaining about features which alienate him from his own "Movement" (so the performance might finally recall the desire not to belong to any club which would have oneself as a member). Hardy is also hailed as virtually a fellow-deconstructor by an American deconstructor, loved by Bardic Dylan Thomas and quite un-Bardic Auden alike.[120] More specific, and specifically academic critics can also come to appreciate, those of them, at least, who have avoided strangling by that insidious creeper growth, the "ivy-wife" of biographical explication which dominates comprehensive commentaries still cited as guides (by J. O. Bailey[121] and F. B. Pinion, for example).[122]

Such biographical explanations, which J. Hillis Miller has called "wonderfully appeasing to the mind,"[123] accept a philistine substitution of a (textually constructed) life for a carefully constructed artistic statement, also a text. But specialists in Victorian Studies and even Victorian poetry still tend to bypass Hardy. The kind of language used to figure forth the achievements of the others does not seem to be so successful with Hardy, and Owen Schur's interesting book founders on its persistent attempts to run Hardy and Tennyson together and also to suggest that Hardy is a contributor to the Country House poem tradition, (with absurd references to Maynard Mack, Pope, Penshurst, "Upon Appleton House," Horatian Epistles, etc.), absurd because non-congruent, as Hardy's Good Places are not great. It might be claimed that Hardy re-writes this kind of poetry to compel respect for the humbler circumstances he enjoyed or endured, but this would have to be flagged as a primary issue, and nothing is gained from smudging the account in the way Schur does. Finally, though, he returns upon his own argument like Arnold's Edmund Burke and becomes a good critic: "Hardy writes poems that allude to the country-house tradition, but in ways that disrupt the country-house ideal,"[124] while adding that "these disruptions involve issues of poetics and the structure of representation in the poems" (202).

What has impeded recognition of Hardy is a certain skewing in Victorian Studies itself. Significant here for example is Paul Turner's rather unpleasant inversion of the requisite *de haut en bas* posture in discussing the work of William Barnes, the Dorset poet poetically congruent with Hardy: "those whose appetite is less robust may have to accept relegation to the *profanum vulgus* who cannot fully enjoy his dialect poems."[125] This performs the unusual feat of making snobs of those who relish dialect, and Hardy himself, who wrote a rarely appreciative review of Barnes, rates only one more passing reference in this authoritative tome, so presumably is involved in this critical disdain by implication. It's a silence which many Victorian experts are prone to, and although many of these literary historians are falsely reckoned as critical intelligences anyway, it seems a dismaying confirmation of Dennis Taylor's well-urged claim that there is something specially defiant and uncompromising about the whole Hardy project.

From this point of view, a rather startling but finally gratifying recent intervention was that by Eric Griffiths in *The Printed Voice of Victorian Poetry*, which sounds like literary history but is informed by an admirable sticklerishness over the examination of those verbal contraptions called poems, not exactly surprising as Christopher Ricks suggested and "helped him finish" the book. Here, though the discussion is brief, and surrounded by both Brownings, by Carlyle and Coventry Patmore, who crowd in supportively. Hardy for once is not being diminished by a comparative exercise free from critical patronage no less than that special pleading which has a habit of singling out the converted. For example, in place of Richardson's use of Browning as a crusty baguette to beat (Mother's Pride?) Hardy with, Griffiths give us the informative, critically alert but essentially non-partisan:

> Hardy inherited this dramatic skill with the stanza from Browning, though he developed its potential in more calculatedly grim directions.[126]

His discussion shows a nice touch with "A Church Romance," noting "the wonderful, quiet dexterity of the style," the more so because Griffiths is not a Hardy-devoted specialist (indeed his section on him is much too short) and hence need not be suspected of blinkered partiality, but also because Hardy has run the gauntlet of critics, some of whom claim to be enthusiastic well-wishers in the very act of striking a blow, and compose a series of scholarly nightmares of dumbly domineering reception.

His discussion of the Emma poems of 1912–13 brings Carlyle extracts and analogies with Patmore to bear. These are distinguished widowers who speak to their bereavements with less exquisitely contrapuntal, though still moving and distinguished, affect. Indeed, as Griffiths points out, "The Going" re-writes Patmore's "Departure." This is itself a genuine poem, though the opening line ("It was not like your great and gracious ways") shows its problem — a slight suggestion of an Edwardian walrus moustache, making the line sound like a Gielgud voice opportunity. Griffiths' remark that in the Patmore, even the small phrase, "my dear" is left by Hardy to tremble between the sardonic and the plangent, where Patmore polishes it up, reverently, into "my Dear" (224–5) initiates a comparison between writers that does not demean Hardy. His way with "Lament" is even more felicitous, and that "Bright-hatted . . . " trembles, among many other things, with rage (228) one can well believe, and though I am still not quite sure how he knows this, it sounds about right. Having identified Christopher Ricks as "onlie begetter" of this sterling contribution, it is interesting to see him weighing in with a "Note on Hardy's 'A Spellbound Palace,'" itself a bit spellbinding, the startling claim being that it is the beneficiary of Eliot's "Sweeney Erect" (published five years earlier) (with the implication that swaggering Henrys are congruent with Erect Sweeneys as much as this one is with that Ozymandias who also turns up in the discussion.)[127]

But what it also effects is that indeed its close reading shows that Hardy's work too is so responsive to the sort of reading people rather expect when the subject is Geoffrey Hill that Hardy even begins to sound a little like him as well. One may question whether this is a typical Hardy poem, one may question whether Griffiths has not slightly exposed himself given the inadequate space he renders unto Hardy, comparatively speaking. One might also wonder whether the close reading doesn't obscure the legitimately exploring sense of how Hardy, offering "art among the ideologies," isn't unsettling many of the truisms of Victorian poetry critique in a way that should be investigated, but their testimonies ring truer from not being the vacant chaff well meant for grain of the typical Hardy buff.

This sort of thing is not of course unique. For example, W. David Shaw, though more perfunctorily, shows what can be done (in "Without Ceremony") and points out how "Hardy uses two-way syntax to leave the speaker poised between the shock of death and a mere style of disappearing," correlating his audaciously homely imagery with that of Emily Dickinson, marshalling a respect that means intensely and means good.[128] A good article by Patricia O'Neill, again a Victorian Studies specialist but not a professional Hardy custodian, is very intelligently à propos. Touched by currents of theory, it communicates well without traducing intellectual complexity and a sophisticated awareness of language. It senses that Hardy sensed that things had changed, that, in early Eliot's praise for Wagner, he had "an acute sense of his own age" and what "the age demanded" was "a poetic language that would be attuned to the exigencies of a newly scientific and technologically minded human society."[129] All this caused Hardy to desert metaphor for metonymy, so that "one might say that Hardy's use of metonymy shows how words earn their figurative meanings" (135). Comparing "Neutral Tones" with its major precursor text, Shelley's "Lines: When the Lamp lies shattered . . . " she argues that the metonymic approach to language can "recall to the metaphysicist's symbolic words the experience from which his conceptions took flight (139). She cites Hugh Bredin on the idea that metonymy relies "upon those relations between objects that are habitually known and accepted" (140), without wishing to disparage metonymy for that as Bredin seems to wish to. "Old Furniture" is a natural port of call here, as his is the famous and cognate statement that battered tankard human associations of things, which may include even humble ones like the "battered tankard" (there's a Heideggerian feeling about this) are more valuable than landscapes in all their grandeur. All rather suggestively stated so as to encourage further enquiry.

I found this a highly congenial essay. It deploys the linguistic opposition of metaphor and metonymy as elaborated by Jakobson. But it also "does what it describes" by keeping the reader in the homely familiar world of Hardy's poetry, and its conclusion is quite enticing (143). If Hardy revises the romantics' interest in an ideal language, he does so in order to promote one that can subvert the abstract and literal, the dehumanizing uses of language in a technological society.

That was a long paragraph on a short article. But the article itself was both cogent and suggestive. One of the problems in handling the critical reception of such as Hardy is that much critical material is inferior, and even, sometimes one might feel *especially* when it achieves book form. For example, a recent book-length study of the poetry by Brian Green might seem to call for comment, and its bibliography is helpful. But here is an example of its critical manner, as he sets the scene:

> Recent critics have revealed a great feature of his pastoralism that is stronger, more integral than the rural-urban contrast — or any other element of conventional pastoral, if it comes to that, be it honest simplicity, nostalgia for a Golden Age, criticism of modern life, or creation of a world remote in time and space. That feature is realism. for instance, although Hardy depicts sheep and shepherds inhabiting a beautiful rural scene, neither animals nor people have a perpetual summer fling. Carefully selected realistic details invariably qualify the nostalgic vision he evokes.[130]

Or again: "Hardy is a clear-headed traveller from an antique countryside, a flawed Eden, bringing fresh, first-hand impressions of Nature and orally transmitted lore of immemorial, elementary human woe" (17). Even if it might be thought creditable to be "against theory," is this really what really what Hardy supporters want to rehabilitate? That, it seems to me, in its texture, is undistinguished undergraduate writing, and it is part of the persistent patronage of Hardy in Britain that this particular tone of untrained impressionism should be thought appropriate to his critical reception.

In fact Brian Green is much more successful in giving a sense of Hardy's achievement in his article on the "*In Tenebris*" poems, in which the speaker oscillates in defiance and abasement in defining his alienation.[131]

Licking this chapter into shape has not been easy, since, as William W. Morgan remarks, such work as appears on Hardy's poetry is "curiously miscellaneous and not a little cacophonous."[132] Although there is a poetic Hardy modernists can approve of, a Hardy the "Movement" marked as their own, a deconstructor's Hardy, a Hardy poets as diverse as Auden and Dylan Thomas could claim as original, and nobly exegetical (American) incursions into Wessex deploying post-structuralist insights, Victorian Studies perspectives on Hardy are swayed by dyed-in-the-wool Hardyists who, in a sense, take Hardy as read. Taking a Hardy of their own figuring on trust, they refract it, repeat the ceremony of conferring canonicity with *confrères*, exercising a cultivated tunnel vision.

But even where it gestures towards advanced and theoretical writing, such critical receptiveness is often implicitly anti-intellectual. Yet it remains true that the positivities of Hardy critique tend to be vaguely gesturing, vacant chaff well-meant for grain. On the other hand, when "loony hooters," in Empson's idiom, rush to negative judgement, their particularities are perceived as a series of damaging blows that keep people away from a challenging body of work which, in Stevens's phrasing, by setting out apparently neither "to console, nor sanctify, but plainly to propound," is able to do something of the former as well as, perhaps, more of the latter than a poet like Stevens, though often exquisite, could often manage.

Notes

[1] Donald Davie, *Thomas Hardy and British Poetry* (London: Routledge, 1973), 13–40.

[2] See Blake Morrison. *The Movement: English Poetry and Fiction of the 1950s* (Oxford: Oxford UP, 1980), 132: "Here they come — tramp, tramp, tramp — all those characters you thought were discredited . . . or (if you are like me) had never heard of — Barbusse, Sartre, Camus, Kierkegaard . . . [from a review by Kingsley Amis of Colin Wilson's *The Outsider*]. But James Booth, in *Philip Larkin: Writer* (London: Harvester Press, 1992) points out that Larkin's interviews persona at least is a bluff, slightly invented version of himself, or possibly his father Sidney, so a sophisticated response to his *pour epater*-style comments is very much in order; I would extend the idea to his critical writing.

[3] Reproduced in *Required Writing: Miscellaneous Pieces 1955–1982* (London: Faber and Faber, 1983), 29–30.

[4] Merle E. Browne, *Double Lyric: Divisiveness and Communal Creativity in Recent English Poetry* (London: Routledge and Kegan Paul, 1980), 78.

[5] James Booth, *Philip Larkin: Writer* (London: Harvester Press, 1992); Edward Neill, "Modernism and Englishness: Reflections on Larkin and Auden." *Essays and Studies* edited by Beatrice White (London: John Murray, 1983), 79–93.

[6] J. Hillis Miller, *The Linguistic Moment: From Wordsworth to Stevens* (Princeton: Princeton UP, 1985), 286.

[7] T. R. M. Creighton, *Poems of Thomas Hardy: A New Selection* (London: Macmillan, 1974).

[8] Seamus Heaney, *The Redress of Poetry: Oxford Lectures* (London: Faber and Faber, 1995), xvi, 190.

[9] Mark Van Doren, *Autobiography* (New York: Harcourt, Brace, 1958), 167–8.

[10] Dylan Thomas, in "An Introduction to Thomas Hardy," *An Evening with Dylan Thomas* (Caedmon Records, 1963).

[11] Dennis Taylor, *Hardy's Poetry, 1860–1928*, 2nd. ed. (London: Macmillan, 1989), 38.

[12] Tom Paulin, *Thomas Hardy: The Poetry of Perception* 2nd ed. (London: Macmillan, 1986), 105.

[13] Trevor Johnson, "'Pre-Critical Innocence' and the Anthologist's Hardy," *Victorian Poetry*, 17 (1979): 9–29; and see Peter Widdowson, *Hardy in History: A Study in Literary Sociology* (London: Routledge, 1989), 95–96.

[14] In a review of G. M. Young's edition of a *Selected Poems* of Hardy (*New Statesman* 14 September 1940). Reprinted in *Argufying: Essays on Literature*

and Culture, ed. John Haffenden (London: Chatto and Windus, 1987), 421. His severity with Hardy is emphasized in a commentary on Hardy's "Hap" mounted in a review of Wayne Booth's *A Rhetoric of Irony* also reprinted in *Argufying* (178–183). One might note how it qualifies itself when he says that the poem is "badly written" — "so badly that it cannot be admired at all, except for a kind of hammered-out sincerity" (181). The concessive last phrase undercuts the round condemnation, and makes you want to go in quest of this "hammered-out sincerity." Also downright and equivocal at the same time in its own way is Trevor Johnson's "'Thoroughfares of Stones': Hardy's 'Other' Love Poetry," in *New Perspectives on Thomas Hardy*, ed. Charles P. C. Pettit (London: Macmillan, 1994), 59.

[15] David Thatcher, "Another Look at Hardy's 'Afterwards,'" *Victorian Newsletter* 38 (1970): 14–18.

[16] William Empson, *Some Versions of Pastoral* (London: Chatto and Windus, 1935), 4–5.

[17] Peter Sacks, "Hardy: 'A Singer Asleep' and *Poems of 1912–13*," in *The English Elegy* (Baltimore: Johns Hopkins UP, 1985), 234.

[18] Jahan Ramazani, "Hardy's Elegies for an Era: 'By the Century's Deathbed,'" *Victorian Poetry*, 29 (1991): 133.

[19] See *A Derrida Reader: Between the Blinds* (London: Harvester Wheatsheaf, 1991), 221–237.

[20] See David Wright (ed.), *Thomas Hardy: Selected Poetry* (London: Penguin, 1978).

[21] See Samuel Hynes (ed.) *Thomas Hardy: Selected Poetry* (Oxford: Oxford UP, 1996).

[22] See Harry Thomas (ed.) *Thomas Hardy: Selected Poems* (London: Penguin, 1993).

[23] See James Gibson (ed.) *Thomas Hardy: Selected Short Stories and Poems* (London: Dent [Everyman], 1992).

[24] See Tim Armstrong (ed.), *Thomas Hardy: Selected Poems* (London: Longman, 1993).

[25] John Lucas, "Thomas Hardy: Voices and Visions," *Modern English Poetry from Hardy to Hughes: A Critical Survey* (London: B. T. Batsford, 1986), 23. Lucas thinks that the limitations of Hardy are to to with "the causes of [the] discontinuities out of which much of his poetry is made," and that "as a result," they are "presented as fact" and "cannot be argued with" (49).

[26] G. M. Young (ed.) *Thomas Hardy: Selected Poems* (London: Macmillan, 1940).

[27] See, e.g. Dylan Thomas, *Letters to Vernon Watkins*, ed. Vernon Watkins (London: Dent, 1957), 17.

[28] Martin Seymour-Smith, *Hardy* (London: Bloomsbury, 1994): " . . . poetry itself is not an expression of vanity and egotism. That is one of the differences between Hardy and Yeats, who has seemed to so many critics to have been more "sophisticated" and "modern" and "important." There is poetry in Yeats,

but also much more vanity and egoism. That is why so many readers have ultimately turned back to Hardy" (573). That this is bluffly journalistic is partly signalled by the fact that the words in quotation marks are not citing anyone in particular. But they have a certain point.

[29] See Robert Graves, *Oxford Addresses on Poetry* (London: Oxford UP, 1962), ch. 1–3; and Martin Seymour Smith, *Robert Graves: His Life and Work* (London: Hutchinson, 1982), 87.

[30] Geoffrey Grigson, *The Contrary View: Glimpses of Fudge and Gold* (London: Macmillan, 1974), 194–195 (in "The Poet Who Did not Care for Life," 183–195).

[31] Bernard Bergonzi (ed.), *Poetry 1870 to 1914* (London: Longman, 1980), 118–9.

[32] Geoffrey Grigson, "The Poems," in *The Genius of Thomas Hardy.* Edited by Margaret Drabble (London: Weidenfeld and Nicholson, 1977), 93.

[33] Donald Davie, "Hardy's Virgilian Purples," *Agenda* 10 (1972): 2–3, 138–56; reprinted in *The Poet in the Imaginary Museum*, ed. Barry Alpert (Manchester: Carcanet, 1977), 221–235.

[34] Theodor Weiss, "The Many-Sidedness of Modernism," *Times Literary Supplement*, 1 February 1980: 124–5; also Robert Langbaum, "The Issue of Hardy's Poetry," in *Thomas Hardy in Our Time* (London: Macmillan, 1995), 27.

[35] H. A. T. Johnson, "'Despite Time's Derision: (Donne, Hardy and the 1913 Poems)," *Thomas Hardy Yearbook* 7 (1977): 9.

[36] Melanie Sexton, "Phantoms of His Own Figuring: The Movement towards Recovery in Hardy's Poems," *Victorian Poetry*, 29 (1991): 209–226.

[37] Donald Davie, *Under Briggflatts: A History of Poetry in Great Britain 1960–1988* (Manchester: Carcanet, 1989), 204–7.

[38] Tim Armstrong, "Hardy, Thaxter and History as Coincidence in 'The Convergence of the Twain," *Victorian Poetry*, 30 (1992): 35.

[39] Paul Zietlow, "The Tentative Mode of Hardy's Poems," in *Victorian Poetry* 5 (1967): 113–126.

[40] Philip Davis, *Memory and Writing from Wordsworth to Lawrence* (Liverpool: Liverpool UP, 1983), 368.

[41] John Goode, *Thomas Hardy: the Offensive Truth* (Oxford: Blackwell, 1988), 13.

[42] Robert Langbaum, "The Issue of Hardy's Poetry," in *Thomas Hardy in Our Time* (London: Macmillan, 1995), 27–63.

[43] Irving Howe, "Hardy the Obscure," *New York Times Book Review* (7 May 1978): 11.

[44] Irving Howe, *Thomas Hardy* (London: Weidenfeld and Nicholson, 1968), 164.

[45] See Kenneth Marsden, *The Poems of Thomas Hardy: A Critical Introduction* (London: Athlone Press, 1969), 1–2.

[46] See Dennis Taylor, *Hardy's Literary Language and the New Philology* (Oxford: Clarendon Press, 1993), 2. For Taylor, Hardy, in the wake of the OED, "illustrates a new consciousness of the English language" (172).

[47] Henry Gifford, "Hardy in his Later Poems," in *From James to Eliot* ("New Pelican Guide to English Literature"), ed. Boris Ford (London: Penguin, 1983), 166–179.

[48] Raymond Chapman, *The Language of Thomas Hardy* (London: Macmillan, 1990), 76.

[49] Graham Hough, *Image and Experience* (London: Fontana, 1960), 80.

[50] Douglas Brown, *Thomas Hardy* (Oxford: Blackwell, 1954). 2nd. ed. 1961: 168.

[51] Valentine Cunningham, *In the Reading Gaol: Postmodernity, Texts and History* (Oxford: Blackwell, 1993).

[52] Samuel Hynes, "The Hardy Tradition in Modern English Poetry," in *Thomas Hardy: The Writer and His Background* (London: Bell and Hyman, 1980), 173–191.

[53] See W. B. Yeats, *Oxford Book of Modern Verse 1892–1935* (London: Oxford UP, 1936).

[54] Nicholas Royle, *After Derrida* (Manchester: Manchester UP, 1995), 6.

[55] As cited by Larkin in *Required Writing*, 29.

[56] The review ("Mr. Hardy's New Poems," *The New Statesman* [Dec. 19, 1914]) was republished by Strachey in *Characters and Commentaries* (London: Chatto and Windus, 1933), 195–201: "All the taste, all the scholarship, all the art of the Poet Laureate . . . end in . . . something that is irremediably remote and cold; while the flat, undistinguished poetry of Mr. Hardy has found out the secret of touching our marrow-bones" (198).

[57] Katherine Anne Porter, cited in Ralph W. V. Elliott, *Thomas Hardy's English* (Oxford: Basil Blackwell, 1984), 16. Retrieved from her "On a Criticism of Thomas Hardy," in *The Days Before* (New York: Harcourt Brace, 1952), 23–35.

[58] See J. Powell Ward, *The English Line: Poetry of the Unpoetic from Wordsworth to Larkin* (London: Macmillan, 1991), 123. This book is radically unsure of what it's trying to do, or at least it ought to be. One is tempted to say that if, as he puts it "blindness, greyness and colourless scenes and writing are endemic in English-line poetry" (114), they are even more "endemic" in English-line criticism.

[59] William Archer, in the *Daily Chronicle*, 21 Dec., 1898; cited in Edmund Blunden, *Thomas Hardy* (London: Macmillan, 1941), 104.

[60] Norman Page, *Thomas Hardy*. (London: Routledge, 1977), 155.

[61] Cicely Havely, *Thomas Hardy* (Milton Keynes: Open UP, 1975), 43.

[62] Desmond Hawkins, *Hardy: Novelist and Poet* (London: Macmillan, 1981), 200.

[63] Samuel Hynes, *The Pattern of Hardy's Poetry* (Chapel Hill: U of North Carolina P, 1961), 88.

[64] See J. P. Ward, *Thomas Hardy's Poetry* (Milton Keynes: Open UP, 1993), 93.

[65] Paul Zietlow, *Moments of Vision: the Poetry of Thomas Hardy* (Cambridge, MA: Harvard UP, 1974), 30–1.

[66] Norman Page, "Hardy and the English Language," in *Thomas Hardy: The Writer and His Background* (London: Bell and Hyman, 1980), 151–172.

[67] See, for example, Dennis Taylor, *Hardy's Literary Language and Victorian Philology*, 381–386.

[68] F. R. Leavis, *Revaluation* (London: Chatto and Windus, 1936).

[69] John Bayley, *An Essay on Hardy* (Cambridge: Cambridge UP, 1978).

[70] John Lucas, "Thomas Hardy, Donald Davie, England and the English," in the *Thomas Hardy Annual* 1 (1982), 134–151.

[71] Michael Alexander, "Hardy Among the Poets," in Lance St. John Butler (ed.), *Thomas Hardy After Fifty Years* (London: Macmillan, 1977), 49–63 (63).

[72] John Wain, *Professing Poetry* (London: Macmillan, 1977), 353.

[73] Peter Robinson, "In Another's Words: Thomas Hardy's Poetry," *English* 31 (1982): 221–46.

[74] David Gewanter, "'Undervoicings of Loss' in Hardy's Elegies to his Wife," *Victorian Poetry* 29 (1991), 193–207: 199. His summarizing phrasing to the effect that "in a sense, these elegies place slivers of Victorian lyric inside modern geriatric wisdom," is appealing.

[75] G. Macbeth, ed. *The Penguin Book of Victorian Verse* (Harmondsworth: Penguin, 1969), 33.

[76] In the *Southern Review* (1940), 87–98 ("Hardy the Poet").

[77] Arthur Macdowall, *Thomas Hardy: A Critical Study* (London: Macmillan, 1931), 205.

[78] Kenneth Marsden, "Hardy's Vocabulary," in *The Poems of Thomas Hardy*, 161.

[79] See James Langenbach, *Stone Cottage: Pound, Yeats and Modernism* (New York: Oxford UP, 1988).

[80] F. R. Leavis, *New Bearings in English Poetry* (London: Chatto and Windus, 1932), 52–56.

[81] See D. H. Lawrence, *A Study of Thomas Hardy and Other Essays* (Cambridge: Cambridge UP, 1985).

[82] See, for example, George Wotton, *Thomas Hardy: Towards a Materialist Criticism* (Dublin: Gill and Macmillan, 1985).

[83] F. R. Leavis, *Thought, Words and Creativity* (London: Chatto and Windus, 1976), 16.

[84] Delmore Schwartz, "Poetry and Belief in Thomas Hardy," in *The Southern Review*, 6 (1940); repr. in A. J. Guerard (ed.) *Hardy: A Collection of Critical Essays* (Englewood Cliffs, NJ: Prentice-Hall, 1963), 123–134: 134.

[85] In "Time and Sense Experience: Hardy and T. S. Eliot," *Budmouth Essays on Thomas Hardy*, ed. F. B. Pinion (Dorchester: The Thomas Hardy Society Ltd., 1976), 192–204: 196.

[86] See the *Selected Letters of Ezra Pound,* ed. D. D. Paige (London: Faber and Faber, 1950), 198.

[87] Christopher Ricks *New Oxford Book of Victorian Verse* (Oxford: Oxford UP, 1987), xxxi.

[88] Harold Bloom, *A Map of Misreading,* 9, 19.

[89] See C. M. Bowra, *Inspiration and Poetry* (London: Macmillan, 1955), 225.

[90] Bloom, *Map of Misreading,* 6.

[91] David Perkins, "Hardy and the Poetry of Isolation," ELH 26 (1959): 256.

[92] John Holloway, "No Answerer I," in *The Proud Knowledge: Poetry, Insight and the Self 1620–1920* (London: Routledge and Kegan Paul, 1977), 233–253: 233.

[93] Lance St. John Butler, "How It is for Thomas Hardy," *Thomas Hardy After Fifty Years* (London: Macmillan, 1977), 119.

[94] Robert McCarthy, "Hardy and 'The Lonely Burden of Consciousness': The Poet's Flirtation with the Void," *English Literature in Transition,* 23 (1980), 89–98: 90.

[95] Stephen Spender, *Journals 1939–1985* (London: Faber and Faber, 1986), 473.

[96] G. S. Fraser, *The Modern Writer and His World* (Harmondsworth: Penguin, 1964), 203.

[97] James Richardson, *Thomas Hardy: The Poetry of Necessity* (London: Chicago UP, 1977), 31–2.

[98] Margaret Mahar, "Hardy's Poetry of Renunciation," ELH 45, no. 2 (1978), repr. in H. Bloom (ed.) *Thomas Hardy* (1987), 155–173.

[99] Terri Witek, "Repetition in a Land of Unlikeness: What 'Life Will not be Balked of' in Thomas Hardy's Poetry," *Victorian Poetry* 28 (1990), 119–128: 128.

[100] R. P. Blackmur, "The Shorter Poems of Thomas Hardy," in the *Southern Review* (Summer, 1940): 44; reprinted in *Language as Gesture* (New York: Harcourt, Brace, 1952), 51–79.

[101] Lewis, C. Day, "The Lyrical Poetry of Thomas Hardy," *Proceedings of the British Academy* 37 (1951): 155–174. Reprinted in James Gibson and Trevor Johnson (eds.), *Thomas Hardy: Poems. A Collection of Critical Essays* (London: Macmillan, 1979), 147–60.

[102] Tim Armstrong, "Hardy's Dantean Purples," *Thomas Hardy Journal* 7 (May, 1991): 47–54.

[103] Kenneth Marsden, *The Poems of Thomas Hardy,* 2.

[104] I. A. Richards, "Some Notes on Thomas Hardy's Verse Forms," *Victorian Poetry* 17 (1979): 1–17.

[105] Ross C. Murfin, "New Words: Swinburne and the Poetry of Thomas Hardy," in *Swinburne, Hardy, Lawrence and the Burden of Belief* (London: U of Chicago P, 1978), repr. H. Bloom (ed.) *Thomas Hardy* ("Modern Critical Views") New York: Chelsea House, 1987), 137–153.

[106] Cornelia Cook, "Thomas Hardy and George Meredith," in Clements, P. and J. Grindle, *The Poetry of Thomas Hardy* (London: Macmillan, 1980), 83–100.

[107] Rod Edmond, "Death Sequences: Hardy, Patmore and the New Domestic Elegy," *Victorian Poetry* 19 (1981): 151–65.

[108] Peter J. Casagrande, "Hardy's Wordsworth: A Record and a Commentary," *English Literature in Transition* 20, no. 4 (1977): 210–37.

[109] Dennis Taylor, "Hardy and Wordsworth," *Victorian Poetry* 24 (1986): 441–54.

[110] Trevor Johnson, "'Ancestral Voices': Hardy and the English Poetic Tradition," *Victorian Poetry* 29 (1991): 49.

[111] Harold Bloom, *The Anxiety of Influence: A Theory of Poetry* (New York: Oxford UP, 1973), 42.

[112] Peter Casagrande, "Hardy's Wordsworth": 210–211; W. R. Rutland, *Thomas Hardy: A Study of his Writings and their Background* (Oxford: Blackwell, 1938), 15–16, etc.; Carl J. Weber, *Hardy of Wessex* (New York: Columbia UP, 1940) [2nd ed. 1962], 15–16, 90–1, etc.

[113] Trevor Johnson, "'Ancestral Voices'": 52–57; references to *The Golden Treasury*, ed. Francis T. Palgrave (Oxford: Oxford UP, 1964); and Arthur Quiller-Couch (ed.) *The Oxford Book of English Verse* (Oxford: Oxford UP, 1900).

[114] Peter Widdowson, *Hardy in History: A Study in Literary Sociology* (London: Routledge, 1989), 199.

[115] See *Further Letters of G. M. Hopkins,* ed. C. C. Abbott (London: Oxford UP, 1938); discussed in Christopher Ricks, *Essays in Appreciation* (Oxford: Clarendon Press, 1996), 328.

[116] See *Guide to Kulchur* (New York: New Directions, 1970), 285.

[117] See T. S. Eliot, *A Choice of Kipling's Verse* (London: Faber and Faber, 1941), 5.

[118] See Trevor Johnson, *A Critical Introduction to the Poems of Thomas Hardy* (London: Macmillan, 1991), 7.

[119] See the Appendix to *From Confucius to Cummings,* ed. Ezra Pound and Marcella Spann (New York: New Directions, 1964), 326–7. Further praise is found in Pound's *ABC of Reading* (London: Faber and Faber, 1951), 193.

[120] See W. H. Auden, "A Literary Transference," *Southern Review* 6 (1940–41), 78–86; repr. in *Hardy: A Collection of Critical Essays,* ed. Albert J. Guerard (Englewood Cliffs, NJ: Prentice-Hall, 1987), 135–142.

[121] J. O. Bailey, *The Poetry of Thomas Hardy: A Handbook and Commentary* (Chapel Hill: U of North Carolina P, 1970).

[122] F. B. Pinion, *A Commentary on the Poems of Thomas Hardy* (London: Macmilan, 1976).

[123] J. Hillis Miller, *The Linguistic Moment: From Wordsworth to Stevens* (Princeton: Princeton UP, 1985), 286.

[124] Owen Schur, "A Dwelling's Character: from Pastoral to the Country House in Hardy," in *Victorian Pastoral: Tennyson, Hardy and the Subversion of Forms* (Columbus: Ohio State UP, 1989), 200–218: 200.

[125] Paul Turner, *Victorian Poetry, Drama and Miscellaneous Prose 1832–1890* (Oxford: Clarendon Press, 1989), 162.

[126] Eric Griffiths, *The Printed Voice of Victorian Poetry* (Oxford: Clarendon Press, 1989), 216–236.

[127] Christopher Ricks, "A Note on Hardy's 'A Spellbound Palace,'" in *Essays in Appreciation* (Oxford: Clarendon Press, 1996), 235–244.

[128] W. David Shaw, *The Lucid Veil: Poetic Truth in the Victorian Age* (London: Athlone Press, 1987), 73–74.

[129] Patricia O'Neill, "Thomas Hardy: Poetics of a Postromantic," *Victorian Poetry* 27 (1989), 129–156: 139.

[130] Brian Green, *Hardy's Lyrics: Pearls of Pity* (London: Macmillan, 1996), 15.

[131] Brian Green, "Darkness Visible: Defiance, Derision and Despair in Hardy's 'In Tenebris'" Poems," *The Thomas Hardy Journal,* 6 (1990): 126–146.

[132] William W. Morgan, "Thomas Hardy" in *Victorian Poetry* 28 (1990): 201; the remarks in question were intended to apply to the critical reception of the work as a whole over a limited period.

4: *Jude the Obscure*: The "Untimely Text"

THAT *NONPAREIL* AMONG FRENCH INTELLECTUALS Gilles Deleuze startlingly entered Hardy's critical lists to announce that his characters were "collections de sensations intensives,"[1] which at least gets them out of the frame in which they can be pelted with critical missiles by the proponents of realism. This doesn't involve treating his "people" as people, but nor does it entail treating his texts as texts. Similarly, even Geoffrey Thurley's claim that Hardy's "people" are "dominated by their psycho-physical constitution"[2] declines to enter into the full condition of textuality. But what is a text?

Indeed. One man's text is another man's happening, apparently. In a recent Deleuzian study, John Hughes reads *Jude* as an untimely book in the Nietzschean sense of one "acting counter to [its] time and thereby acting on [its] time."[3] As he puts it, "*Jude* is a novel which has always had the status of a kind of violent, destructive and unassimilable event, and its own bizarre, bleak and agonizing happenings, its effects of overdetermination, repetition, tragedy, and parody continue to provoke critical comment and to confound readers with undiminished intensity across a hundred years"(86).

This is a kind of postmodernist summary of Guerard's much earlier and still influential argument for a recognition of Hardy's modernity. This is patronizing only in that Hardy always suffers in comparison with full-blown modernists who came later, and he can claim that the outcry over *Jude* in particular was the "fury of outraged optimism, mobilized by the moralistic and optimistic middle classes against one who questioned the 'integrity of God in his Heaven and of human nature in its earthly prison, or of society as a noble experiment.'"[4] The compliment over the capacity to create outrage is severely qualified by the imputation of "traditional" means of presentation, For a comparable effort to keep Hardy safe for traditionalists, see Christine Brooke-Rose, arguing against Boumelha and Lodge "who both treat Hardy as highly innovative."[5]

Informally, in the relaxed, untheorized manner of the *Hudson Review*, Paul Pickrel suggests a certain distance from High Victorian forms of mimesis in asserting that to a degree unmatched by any other Hardy novel, *Jude* "has a temperamental affinity with northern Expressionism; Edvard Munch would have been its perfect illustrator."[6] Corroboratively, P. N. Furbank not only draws an analogy with late-century ["expressionist"] composers

like Mahler and Richard Strauss, but suggests that he relates to them as the
great names of the Victorian novel do to classical age composers like Beethoven.[7] This is imprecise but suggestive, and serves to release Hardy, tem-
porarily at least, from a besetting critical patronage his official critical
reception seems, on the whole, quite happy to abet.)

Joe Fisher, while implicitly agreeing with all this, also brings together
formal and generic considerations with intimations of subversiveness. Developing, if unwittingly, Deborah Collins' argument that *Jude* we have an
"inverted Bildungsroman"[8] which succumbs to the ache of modernism, for
him *Jude the Obscure* is "in many ways a self-consciously complete inversion
of Victorian novelistic practice."[9] He might have strengthened (or perhaps
he feared he might actually weaken) his hand here with some actual examples: "Nineteenth Century English fiction seems often to adopt a
Bildungsroman into an ameliorative parable, dealing often with a young
male bourgeois protagonist thrust by circumstance into an alien working-
class or petty-bourgeois world. There he becomes *déclassé*, it seems, and by
strength of character finds his way through a quasi-Gothic "chateau" of
previously unmapped class and cultural experience to a lost inheritance of
authority and money . . ." (174).

But all this is lost on, and to, Jude, in his "wild, Polonial novel."[10] This
is how R. P. Draper rather fetchingly puts it in his critical argument that the
novel exhilaratingly smudges the ley-lines of literary taxonomies but also
commits a number of ideological infringements painful for the mind which
dwells among late-Victorian doxa to contemplate.

One of the critics who has perhaps best caught the spirit of the novel's
excess, the way its semantic exuberancies exceed its programmatic intentions, is Paul Pickrel, particularly in his point that it may allegorize wi[l]der
heterodoxies than it formally manages, in a young man's ethos which may
for example recognise the homoerotic suggestiveness of Sue as a Ganymede
figure dressed in Jude's clothes after her contretemps with Wiltshire's larg-
est waterway. (The "Ganymede" idea is confirmed by Kathleen Blake[11] in
an argument about *Jude* summarized below.)

But one might wonder, finally, if Pickrel's foray into myth-making with
Jude as an embodiment of "Phaethon" doesn't finally trap him into a conservative critical position which implicitly falsifies *Jude*'s undoubted provocativeness? A roster of intelligent critics agree that whether as avant-gardiste
or as subversive text, then, *Jude* is a novel which inevitably ruffles feathers as
it points towards a future in which its "para-doxa" or opposition to received
ideas will have helped to bring about a world of rather kindlier aspect than
would have been possible without it.

In his remarks on the reception of the text John Goode shows how the
original critical reception for *Jude* follows precisely the "untimely text"

contour which Hughes, in his reference to Nietzsche, was able to impute to the novel. He, however, emphasises the impassioned advocacies which such a recognition can foster rather than the denigrations which so swiftly followed its original appearance. He points out that "if the Bishop of Wakefield publicly burnt the novel and Mrs Oliphant [in a review in Blackwood's Magazine] took it as evidence of Hardy's membership of an 'anti-marriage league', a whole group of reviewers wrote about it with a passionate commitment."[12]

The commitment itself may, at least in part, derive from critical abuse as a reactive phenomenon — as an aspect of what Peter Widdowson calls "critiography."[13] This is particularly so, as Michael Millgate puts it, because "much of the comment was gratuitously and often grossly offensive."[14] Yet this favourable reception hardly suggests that Hardy was altogether "standing up to be shot at," as he plaintively put it, or at least not without an answering volley from some crack shots clustered about their culture hero.

Indeed, if we look at the originals, questions might immediately be raised about the real significance of Hardy's abandoning of the novel genre. The *Illustrated London News* hailed *Jude* as "manifestly a work of genius;"[15] for Havelock Ellis, in a subtle probing, Jude was "one of the greatest novels of this century;"[16] D. F. Hannigan observed that "but for the miserable priggery of this tail-end of the nineteenth century, the first part of *Jude the Obscure* would be held up by the critics as one of the most touching records in all literature;"[17] for Richard le Galliene "*Jude* remains the most powerful and moving picture of human life which Mr. Hardy has given us."[18] W. D. Howells was equally enthusiastic ("I find myself defending the book on the ethical side when I meant chiefly to praise it for what seems to me its artistic excellence,"[19] and finally H. G. Wells hailed the work as not only great in itself, but all the greater for (as he implied) having spurred critics to greater silliness than usual. But just as Wells reduced Joyce's *Portrait* to one of "a catholic upbringing," he made Jude patly representative and interestingly tendentious. *Jude* is, essentially, "the voice of the educated proletarian, speaking more distinctly than it has spoken before in English literature."[20]

As if in "proleptic" response to the abusiveness which may have had a role to play in the silencing of Hardy as a novelist, they effectively embraced the text more as a cause than as the object of a professional judgement. These responses, then, serve to confirm Hughes' initial Nietzschean diagnosis, although they also serve to make the novel seem like a bit of a tract. As a representation of a representative man, this problem novel is in this way deproblematized as representation.

Indeed in a sense it's hardly possible to be too *literal* about what *Jude*/Jude is "about." The epigraph of the novel — "the letter killeth" —

which has occasioned so much critical comment — pulls the reader's attention towards textuality and that pursuit of signs which so much preoccupies
the main characters themselves, partly a matter of what Ramon Saldivar
maintains in his critical argument "the importance of writing, signs, inscriptions and marks in the lives of [the] characters."[21] But although this tilts its
emphasis towards word(l)iness rather than worldliness, romanticism rather
than radicalism, semiotics rather than socialism, we should suspect a reading
which robs the text of the "miching mallecho" intentions: "you mean mischief," as the elder Macmillan remarked in a letter announcing the rejection
of his first novel.

Hardy typically, in fact, announces himself after the manner of Shelley's
Milton, as "a bold inquirer into morals and religion"[22] — before retiring
into what Shakespeare might have called his "shelly cave" — which is, precisely, not a very Shelleyan one. And Christminster itself was originally
glimpsed as a "mirage," a "thither" of romantic aspiration, the empty token
of an internalised quest romance (the relevance of the Bloomian phrase was
noticed by Hassett),[23] embraced with the passion of a lover. As Marjorie
Garson argues, Christminster, Sue and Phillotson are each virtually metonymic each of the other.[24] In this argument, the "object" is identified by
difference and deferral, by being as Browningesquely evasive as the Victorian heart desires rather than by intrinsic properties, as Sue, Christminster
and Phillotson can hardly be said to be highly congruent — "while the one
eludes must the other pursue." For Garson, then, Jude is in fact only possessed by what eludes his possession. For Jude at any rate, reality, it seems,
is composed mainly of the signs that tell of it. Such an argument presumes
that Jude is the nomadic consciousness of late romanticism, a déclassé version of Arnold's Shelley beating his luminous wings in the void in vain,
compared indeed (and not vainly) by Ward Hellstrom to the Scholar-Gipsy
of Arnold's own poem.[25] Garson and Hellstrom would converge on the
idea of Jude's impracticality, ensnarement by a "beautiful soul" idealism
which brackets practical or political consideration.

But as Kevin Moore points out in now wild, now magisterial analyses
which take flight from a Bloomian poetics of intertextuality, it is the effete-
ness of Arnoldian versions of Romanticism as a "simulacrum" or enfeebled
rump of that quite radical mixture (brewed in the years leading up to the
Revolutionary Decade) which is itself seen to be "under erasure" rather
than the inappropriateness of Jude's own forms of responsiveness. As he
puts it (and he deserves to be cited at length, particularly as the dominant
strain of Hardy critique is surprisingly conservative): "Jude's quest for culture within a domain of institutions and representations dominated by Arnoldian culture renders him a ghost of Shelley's program, like Hamlet's
father, to challenge the inactivity and bad consciousness of the son, whom

Hardy casts as Matthew Arnold . . . in his attempt to achieve [his "romantic quester's"] goal he will find that flexibility is what culture preaches but does not practice, that in fact, his city of light is a dark and stony place of institutional power."[26]

He then muddies the waters a little by wrong-footing Jude himself as one "locked in Blake's 'Crystal Cabinet' of glorifying self-delusion" (224), but critics pursuing a Bloomian program often enact a "clinamen" or creative swerve away from the radicality which is the raison d'etre of the romanticism they at once uphold and traduce. So perhaps we should rather be surprised by such traces of subversiveness as survive unscathed in his pursuit of an intertextuality which strangely mingles Nietzsche and Freud in order to airbrush the text's politically questing, interrogative moments, Shelleyan and perhaps utopian as they might seem.

Michael Steig also pursues informative arguments within the psychoanalytic tradition, showing in detail the Shelleyan mould for Sue in "The Revolt of Islam," the Freudian implications of Shelleyan and Hardyan women, and the Lawrentian versions and inversions of Hardy and Shelley, particularly in Sons and Lovers,[27] while Phyllis Bartlett offers a cognate explication in seeing Sue as "Hardy's full-length, mature study of the Shelleyan woman . . . as he imagined she would disintegrate under the stress of child-bearing, poverty and social custom."[28]

To be fair, Terry Eagleton also reckons up Jude's understandable limitations in arguing that Jude's fault or flaw is his being "too ready to be appropriated, too uncritically willing to be the adopted son of the deathly lineage of Christminster"[29] in a lively introduction which seems sturdily convinced that poor Jude is almost real enough to be knocking, however feebly, at his own oaken Oxonian door. But in implying that Jude is unaware that "the cultural ideal is parasitic on working energies it ignores and represses" (65), he represses the way in which the text sees to it that these and other de(con)structive notions do surface, if fitfully, in a consciousness which is indeed subject to severe "hegemonisation."

In this account Jude, if not a real man, is at least a representation of a representative one, in spite of Hardy's own eagerness to raise doubts that "there ever was such a person,"[30] and despite (or perhaps due to) the fact that critics have hastened to explain the novel by identifying Jude with a "bio-graphized" Hardy: and certainly Ian Gregor,[31] John Bayley[32] and William Morgan have pursued critical arguments which appear to confirm the association.[33] In this way, it has often been remarked that the narrator is largely in cahoots with Jude, and critical energies have consequently been heavily invested in condemning Sue for her effect on him. Jacobus[34] notes the fiercely critical accounts of Sue advanced by Hyde,[35] Heilman,[36] Millgate (1971: 319–21) and Gregor (1974: 207–33), and bases her own re-

reading on Lawrence's moving "return upon himself" to achieve a moment
of empathy with the Sue he had so eloquently excoriated.

Lawrence's reading is already a kind of re-writing of his "potently impotent predecessor" (as John Maynard puts it in his study of how in *Jude*,
Hardy brings the Victorian twinning of religious and sexual discourse, so
pronounced in Patmore and Kingsley for example, to a juddering halt.)[37] In
depicting a Hardy whose pyrrhic triumph is to set forth on a quest for a
language which will directly enunciate desire itself, he has already brought
Hardy, who in fact elides the direct representation of the sexuality he so un-
remittingly assumes or implies as completely as the great Jane Austen herself) into the folds of his own creative processing. Indeed Lawrence himself
seems to have turned the novel into a dry run for *Women in Love* and *The
Rainbow*. Wayne Burns makes the point that critics have been deflected
from Sue's "sexiness" by the "strong misreading" of Lawrence[38] which un-
derrates Hardy's own ambivalence about this, derived from Shelley's ambivalence about the need at once to sublimate and satiate sexual passion in
his powerfully confused "Epipsychidion."

Lawrence, indeed, berated the destructiveness of Sue's besetting mind-
driven delusions and cold, moon-like apartness; but then pleaded Sue's
uniqueness as one outrageously trampled on by the generic restraints of society ("Sue had a being, special and beautiful . . . Why must man be so ut-
terly irreverent . . . Why must she feel ashamed if she is specialized?").[39] This
gives Jacobus's memorable article its cue. But, like Lawrence's, Jacobus's
account is theoretically unadventurous, using criteria like "true to life"
(120) to indicate those glancing effects which deflect a sense of his person-
ages as mere chess pieces moving in accordance with the rules of Hardy's
narrative enclosures, marching to the sombre tones of his determined and
determining purposes.

Rosemarie Morgan also provides a subtler language for Sue's behaviour
and predicament without venturing into the problems of representation in
themselves, fascinatingly offering parallels between Sue's defensive psycho-
logical strategies: her shufflings, appeasements and accommodations and
those the woman's movement and the suffragettists in particular performed
in their feinting confrontations with patriarchy.[40] Rita S. Kranidis notes a
certain quasi-Freudian testiness about Hardy or his narrator which mingles
emancipatory overtures with a critique of feminism as a kind of cultural
imaginary. But she preserves a measure of sympathy for Hardy himself in
the face of Sue the enigma.[41] But while she imagines her point is buttressed
by Ann Ardis's observation that Hardy "refuses to let the New Woman
challenge his own monologic discourse,"[42] both arguments merely take
their eye off the narrative itself to make simplifying historicist points. Radi-

cal in their intention of exposing Jude's radicality, these studies are theoretically conservative in remaining within paradigms of character study.

As Eagleton points out in the introduction mentioned above, "Hardy, through his presentation of Sue, is evoking movements and forces which can't be exhaustively described or evaluated at a simply personal level" (68), in a judgement which is sustained rather than subverted by the fact that Sue emerges from poems by Shelley and Browning by way of Hardy's eager imaginations of this "type of woman who has always had an attraction for me." This "type," Gittings argues, is of the 1870s not the 1890s, a nervous, Comtean young miss rather than a woman with an aggressively "feminist" program.[43] But Rosemarie Morgan, without actually mentioning Gittings, refutes the idea, suggesting that Sue's mother might just have fitted the bill, and also rejecting Laurence Lerner's claim that she is a New Woman of the Nineties[44] and Constance Rover's insinuations that she is a neo-Malthusian[45] (if she is, she certainly knows how to delegate), and entering a general plea for the non-proliferation of "stereotypic labels" to define Sue (1988: 186).[46]

An unhappier claim, ruined more by its tone than its overt content, is Lance Butler's to the effect that "Sue's unhappy type was one of several stages in the development of women from undereducated sex-objects trussed up in inconvenient clothing to betrousered equals with educational opportunities."[47] This manages, at least to my ear, to secrete a certain patriarchal *ressentiment* despite its apparently neutral tones, and returns us to the problem of Sue's uniqueness as a textual event which challenges facilely historicist readings. Even Eagleton, from whom one would expect sophisticatedly liberal judgements seems a little disconcerted by the forms that Sue's "uniqueness" take.

Michael Steig notes Norman Holland's sardonic points about inferences made about the unconscious (that is, unrepresented) life of imaginary people, of what Wallace Stevens called "men [but also women] made out of words."[48] But Steig then applies Reichian typology to Sue considered as a hysterical character[49] — all of which might invoke Foucault's mordant remarks about "psychologism," which entails a conservative mind-set, as well as doubts about characters who merely live in books. Maria Dibattista, for example, whose argument seizes on Jude's self-analysis or diagnosis as he accuses himself of an "erotolepsy" [it's a Hardy coinage], fails to note that the novel is deconstructive towards such scientific seizures in noting, for instance the "commonplace" nature of Jude's sexual kindlings, and is thus closer to Foucault than her quite suggestive and lively argumentation would suggest.[50]

For example, for the defence of Sue, Garson notes the oddity and self- and-Sue destructiveness of Jude's behaviour on his return to Christminster

(1991: 167). It might have helped them in their plight, if not their plot, if Sue *had* turned a little hysterical just then, what with Jude haranguing crowds in the rain and leaving her, pregnant, to negotiate with petty-bourgeois landladies and the like. In a brilliantly sympathetic analysis and diegesis partly based on the work of Lloyd Fernando,[51] Kathleen Blake, in the article mentioned above describes Sue's dazzlingly contrapuntal effects as "a free woman but a repressive personality, sophisticated but infantile, passionate but sexless, independent but needing men, unconventional but conventional, a feminist but a flirt" (83) and so on; I'd suggest that any suggestion of historical conditioning is mediated by the intervenient conditioning of Hardy's imperial plot-machinating, although questions might still be asked about what moved him to make them, apart from Proustian theories that he was a kind of linguistic master mason,[52] enabling a kind of repetition of the father by other means.

Blake is a dab hand at showing how other critics get into pickles, and it's interesting to note Goode's point that critics may find it hard to get critical purchase as the text is always already "there" where critics hope to occupy a site with its own metadiscursive "interferon." Its tendency to discuss itself renders it, as he puts it, not fit for consumption (1988: 140). The characters, he points out, narrate their predicament and comment on their narratives and their own reactions in pre-emptive moves which would appear to guarantee critical frustration. In fact we can well imagine Sue answering her perter critics, possibly even challenging her advocates, for example when Jean Brooks gives her a death wish, what Auden would call "Brunnhilde's *Sehnsucht* for the dark,"[53] or when A. O. J. Cockshut raises the question of linkage, noting grimly that Sue has to choose between being a flirt and a feminist, opining, with the slightly mincing nuances of old Oxbridge, that "the attempt to turn Hardy into a feminist is altogether vain."[54]

With a liberal hand, Blake herself notes that, as she excitingly puts it, "she needs to keep alive in herself a sexuality in danger of being disciplined all the way down to the source"(94), and it might not seem overly patriarchal even now to murmur mildly that this, in its results, seems rather hard on her menfolk. Vincent Newey, more pragmatically psychologistic, seems to articulate part of what in Sue will always raise eyebrows (even if she no longer raises hackles) when he points out that in placing herself (at last "literally") in Phillotson's hands she "constructs a field of force in which she becomes the object of her own compulsion to effect suffering. Her masochism is her sadism introverted."[55] If psychologistic and still critical of Sue this is at least genuine critique.

More Foucauldian in tone, presumably by accident, is Enstice's point, in a book which is happily forced to desert its ruling concept at times, that Sue "emerges very clearly as the victim of the body in which she is trapped, and the mores of the society which guards the body."[56] (Indeed: "Habeas Corpus" might make an interesting alternative title for *Jude*, as the predicament of Jude and Sue is equally somatic and semantic). In this connection, attention might be drawn, quite piquantly, to the strong critical itch to punish Sue at least as well as she seems able to do so for herself, a category which includes quite modern critics who have not the excuse of a besetting Victorianism. According to Desmond Hawkins, for example, a typical doyen among those Hardy-Society-style scholars who perambulate the globe talking of trivial things about Hardy, Sue is "just about the nastiest little bitch in English Literature." With slightly patriarchal bluster he proceeds to observe that "a cynic might be pardoned for suggesting that she aimed to replace the register office with the clip joint."[57] To concede that one is a "cynic" is perhaps to confirm that one is not quite the ideal reader of *Jude*.

Perhaps that's roughly what Yelverton Tyrell meant when, reviewing *Jude* in 1896, and wearing the regulation linguistic straitjacket, he describes Sue as "an incurably morbid organism."[58] Yet Hawkins's no-nonsense, "pull-yourself-together" approach is at least bi-partisan, as he observes of Jude that "in his self-pity he appears to be wishing, as at times as we may all at some time wish, that our social institutions could achieve the impossible task of protecting the fool from his folly" (155). His critique, by a specialist Hardy expert, shows a mismatching of critic to artistic intention which is quite typical of dominant areas of Hardy critique, a marriage of contraries which is at least as infelicitous (in both the ordinary and the Austinian senses) as those so poignantly memorialized by Hardy and his relentless biographers.

To be fair, the fairer, if slightly bluff and militantly untheorized John Lucas also confesses (1980) to finding Sue "irritating."[59] William Blake points out that Locke and Newton may at least be useful in distilling Error in a particularly potent form which can then be aerosolled away by imaginative poetic practice. So the remedy for Lucas's at once too literal-minded and not literal-minded enough bluffnesses is to be found in the theory that has given us a more sophisticated sense of what representation actually entails, of how it meshes with hegemony and ideology. Childers notes the initial cue for irritation with Hardy's presentation of women,[60] citing Katharine M. Rogers's all too successful trawl for signs that, according to them, according to Hardy, "women are irrational, irresponsible, vain and inconstant."[61] There are, though, contraindications from the start, and even from *Desperate Remedies* to *Far from the Madding Crowd* there is a running intimation that language in particular has been given to man [*sic*] to promote patriarchal thoughts.

It is worthy the noting though, that not everyone agrees that he is as staunchly gynophile as later critics like Morgan (1988) suggest. Lascelles

Abercrombie, who influenced Lawrence, finds him, in his treatment of women "subtle, a little cruel, not as tolerant as it seems,"[62] and we may feel that Lawrence intensified rather than extirpated the wrongs of women that Abercrombie might have found more generously indulged by his and Hardy's most productive student. Indeed, Childers points out difficulies for feminists like Gail Cunningham (1978),[63] Nina Auerbach,[64] Katharine M. Rogers and Mary Ellmann,[65] all of whom struggle to understand Hardy's pattern of appearing to embrace the myths about women he also defies (Childers: 320). Childers can conclude that instead of pointing to readily available evidence of misogyny, many feminists are now concerned with identifying conditions of representation that are psychologically, culturally, and economically overdetermined (321). Sue is, inter alia, a study in such overdetermination.

But if Sue has been dogged by a pack of male critics hysterically alleging hysteria, at least there is a pronounced recognition of the historicization of hysteria's overdetermined symptoms, given the predominance of such discourses, sanctioned by sanctity, as countenance the behaviour of what Arabella (in the mode of enthusiastic recommendation) describes as "a stone-deaf taskmaster."

Critique of *Jude*, then, may be divided into that which attempts to characterise what the text is assumed to be representing, and that which sees the idea of representation as itself problematised — that the text is, in fact, about representation, or representations. It is possible to claim that the latter form of response is deeper, but tends to be politically compromised, attempts to marginalize what in *Jude* is never quite sidelined as a "case to answer," as Goode argues, if elliptically, in his chapter on Jude in his book and his later essay in a Dale Kramer collection (1990), in which he roundly asserts that *Jude* poses a problem to which there is only a Marxist solution.[66] Like Widdowson, he does not have to concede that Hardy himself is "about" subversion, but the results of his critical endeavour seem to establish Hardy's textual potential for just such *miching mallecho*. Although Widdowson claims that he "does not intend to overbid his hand by constructing Hardy as a closet revolutionary as "the discourses of his writing are determinate enough to make any such enterprise a foolish one" (1989: 198), this is a curiously lame and impotent conclusion, since his retrieval of a "more spirited" Hardy (1989: 226) from the results of his "critiography" (1989: 10–11) seems designed to suggest just this, with the rider that Hardy was partly involved in "living out the fiction of his own class position."

Nevertheless, it may be argued, as Joe Fisher does, that Hardy, characteristically, produces a "cartoon of Swiftian brutality," then covers this with a "traded text" through which the original counter-text may, palimpsest-like, (1992: 174–192), be glimpsed, fleetingly but memorably as a Dracula through the drawing-room window. It may then be suggested that *Jude* is the point at which he abandons the novel because the counter-text is beginning to surface, like some textual Kraken (as in the Tennyson poem), to die on the surface. Fisher's book is brilliantly suggestive, but he simultaneously pursues a folkloric quest for "Wild Men" and the like which is less happy, even, here, giving Jude himself trace elements of this *outré* and irrelevant figure. His radical tune is a great melody against the dominant strain of Hardy critique, which read off a rural nostalgia as the occasion of a neo-Burkian philosophy which does not correspond to Hardy's final creative intention (intention being less an origin than a product, as Derrida suggested). A famous Althusserian point about formally Royalist Balzac reminded us that the political effect of his *oeuvre* does not correspond with the position of the novelist in, as it were, propria persona. In a similar fashion, Hardy is, if not on double business bound, writing better than he knows. Indeed, this is just as well, as his discursive self issues in inveterate self-contradiction. (Donald Davie mystifies the point by saying that Hardy has no talent for discursive prose.)[67]

For example, although Rosemarie Morgan refers to Hardy's becoming "openly iconoclastic,"[68] especially in the matter of dialect, Jude and Sue speak in an almost mincingly proper way, while the touches of dialect that inform the conversation of Phillotson and Gillingham contrast the aspiring pair in question with the provinciality of these men in a way that favours Sue and Jude, while claiming for them a formally "below stairs" class position.

However, it must be said that socialist credentials are not always the key to incisive critique. Widdowson, Moore and Fisher, for example, get real purchase, but George Wotton's earlier version of a radical Hardy is unsatisfactory. He pays tribute to Macherey for dissolving his sleep of Leavisite dogmatism, talks much of the integration of being and consciousness, fails to mention Sue, embarks on some surprisingly old-fashioned paraphrase, in a suggestive, highly intelligent, but finally unincisive critical mixture.[69] We shall simply have to call him a "precursor text" as he has provided inspiration for later critique which uncovered a Hardy at work to undo the Grundian straitjacket and the "framing" effect of the class position offered by the "readerly imaginary" constructed (for example) by Mudie of circulating library fame, and Leslie Stephen, the hero turned villain of Hardy's critical reception.[70]

The most profound explorer of Hardy's tensions, contradictions and mixed feelings is, in a way, Marjorie Garson. However, in her anxiety not to prove that Hardy is "politically correct" as Wotton, Fisher, Widdowson wish to do in their various and often impressively sophisticated ways, she empties her well up examination of him of the political altogether.[71] On the one hand, her scholarly but traditional mentor at Toronto, Michael Millgate, and her conservative and anti-theoretical D. Phil. supervisor John Bayley combine with an unclearly "subversive" use of Lacan.

Note, for example, Bayley's (on the face of it) rather complacent point that the "ordained" [sic] members of Oxford simply "take the place for granted" (1977: 213). With assumptions like this, much may be elided. Silent but hardly dissentient on such subjects, Garson enlists Lacan to make Hardy say the roughly the same thing in novels as different as *Under the Greenwood Tree* and *Jude*, examining how (male) somatic anxieties are awakened by thoughts of what someone in *Under the Greenwood Tree* calls "united 'ooman," and the claim that women seem to work together to enfeeble, undo, dissever, or "castrate" the protagonists.

Thus, she argues, in *Jude*, Arabella, Drusilla and Sue (with Widow Edlin as first reserve) perform like three witches to undo Jude — or, in Robert Lowell's phrasing, "the plot is hexed." *Jude* is brilliantly suggestive in conveying, if not what Tennyson called the abysmal deeps of personality, the relay of subject positions subject to unremitting ideological pressure. Garson brilliantly contrasts the pert theoreticalness and opportunistic bricolage of Sue's untimely utterances as they are sprayed at Jude's mode of phenomenological reverence (164–165). But Garson's brilliantly suggestive chapter is finally evasive about the social and political realities which Sue and Jude confront, Hardy said he was confronting, and subsequent critics seem to have confirmed he was confronting (156 e.g.).

"Political correctness" is a phrase which in its very accusations of pre-emption attempts to pre-empt discussion of the right wing reprehensibilities it uses as a stalking-horse. It is difficult in fact to define apart from a consideration of its own unequivocally right wing attempt to see that illiberal and reprehensible opinions go unchallenged. And indeed what a (Nietzschean) "untimely text" like *Jude* does is in fact to achieve "political correctness" by sticking its neck out — as Goode (in a chapter I shall return to) well describes how *Jude* "asks for it" and gets it (but also raises questions which, as he puts it in his ringing conclusion, "call for a reply" [1988: 170]).

This is possibly because, as Irving Howe argues, fortified by his new knowledge of Ibsen, by the *furore* over the Parnell case, and his reading in Schopenhauer, "[Hardy] had threatened his readers not merely in their opinions but in their deepest unspoken values."[72] It is odd to accuse Hardy of "persecution mania" as biographical "supporters" like Millgate virtually do, when he *was* somewhat persecuted. It is also interesting to recall Clodd's "no largeness of soul" verdict on Hardy, so often echoed, when it is obvious that Hardy was (culture) hero enough to "stand up to be shot at" in his own understandably resentful idiom. If, as Casagrande reports, as reported by Davie,[73] Hardy worried about his inability to rehearse as a cultural Coriolanus, the provocative performances (and performatives) of his late novels seem to offer sufficient appeasements for any lingering doubts about pusillanimity, and John Goode is surely right to entitle his chapter on *Jude* in his book on Hardy "Hardy's Fist," and to point out that Bishop How was right to burn his copy of the novel from fear of cultural pollution. In this his action was rather like that of Sir Thomas Bertram, that dubious agent of probity in *Mansfield Park*, last seen burning every copy of *Lovers' Vows* he could find.

Perhaps this is worth mentioning specifically as "Lovers' Vows" is a most suggestive alternative title for *Jude*. Critics like Goetz and Saldivar demonstrate this as they explore the relation of the letter to the spirit in the novel's kaleidoscopic treatment of "elective affinities," the appeal from "law" to "nature," mentioned by Hardy when he cites Diderot on this in relation to marriage contracts (played off against "lovers' vows"), is not an easy one to negotiate.[74] It is possible to reach a deep appreciation of the meaning of Jude (and *Jude*) from a perusal of these nimble-witted critics, interesting indeed to observe that the whole thing is threading a way through its own aporiae to contrapuntal effect. On the other hand, its potential for mischief is missed by the conservative recuperativeness they find at work in the very capillaries of the text itself. On the other hand, this may involve distortion by omission. What critics say is partial, and their own *non-dits* may be as significant as those of the texts they examine.

For example, if, as Goetz notes, the final "felicity" (in J. L. Austin's sense of performative appositeness) of Sue's remarriage to Phillotson, he may be felt to underplay the "infelicity" in the ordinarily sense of deep unhappiness which attends the formal correctness he indicates. As such, Goetz's is a sophisticated version of Hassett's study of compromised romanticism in *Jude*,[75] fruit of those T. S. Eliot years which quashed romanticism in the interests of reactionary mischief. This may be felt to have been, in retrospect, a kind of intensification of its traducing by the recuperative bourgeois ferocity of late Victorian appropriations of its rhetoric to conservative ends. But for us the sense of romanticism as *pharmakon* has moved closer to cure than poison. It might seem that *Jude* is indeed a more conservative text than Goode would claim, but its outspokenness, its undoubted sense of itself as an untimely text, validate the idea that it was indeed "interrogative," if not "radical." *Jude* also, from the first, attracted passionate denigration — and support.

However, as Seymour-Smith points out, not only did Hardy have overtly ideological foes, he had what might be described as "enemies within" in the form of such as the all-too-aptly named Gosse,[76] the great infiltrator who carefully observed the proprieties (despite his private pruriences), and ended his days as librarian to the House of Lords (while Hardy was being abused — simultaneously for provocativeness and timorousness). Although he was understood to be writing primarily as a friend and ally, his account of Hardy's "grimy" last novel offered sufficient appeasements to the "respectable" reader to ensure his own career would go unscathed. Indeed, his carefully reader-oriented questions ("Is it too late to urge Mr. Hardy to struggle against the jarring note of rebellion which seems growing upon him?" [269]) exactly recapitulate the conservative/ recuperative *furore* provoked by Charlotte Bronte, in the "hunger, rebellion and rage" anxiety which provided a litmus test of touchstone for the Arnoldian culture too hugely in hock to an elite and reactionary clerisy.[77]

Tellingly, Gosse is cited with approval by Millgate, one of Hardy's strangely resentful "admirers" in his arguing for *Jude* to be seen as tragedy, which quashes its modern sociological import,[78] as Widdowson notes (1989: 84). This is, indeed, a point which covers much of what he is saying in his justifiably dogged attempt to point out how Hardy's provocative analysis of class are invariably transposed by a traditionally conservative critical reception into the "eternal" or the "metaphysical." The critical result is (implicitly) that the impassioned gestures of protest in a work like *Jude* are processed into a social innocuousness. The point is made elsewhere that Greek tragedy, if not serving the "sociological imagination" is at least transposed into a kind of post-romantic modernity. As John R. Reed reminds us, in Hardy "Greek tragedy now serves modern sensibilities, and its external determinism is now internalized and seen as of man's own making,"[79] which mediates usefully the cultural amputations the sociological approach may perform and the scholarly antiquarianism which merely notes points of contact. By comparison, Bert G. Hornback is too close to Hardy's official explanations of what he is doing, too close to a cosmic view which implies that Hardy is simply *reproducing* the effects of Greek tragedy in his chapter on *Jude*.[80]

Millgate's traditional approach to genre is already problematised in its unawareness that a *novel* (form) as "tragedy" (content) can hardly be at one with tragedy as itself dramatic form. But, more significantly, such an approach also ignores the possibilities explored by John Peck of the *subversion* of the traditional modes Hardy may at unguarded first sight appear to be working in. According to Peck, in an interesting if sketchy essay, Hardy is indeed en route to a kind of participation in the "self-conscious" procedures of modernist writing.[81] Howe had already broached the idea in showing a Hardy who breaches the teleological narrative structure which provides coherent explanations and explications, "abandoning the realistic novel of George Eliot and Thackerey."[82] He describes well Hardy's introverted modern characters in whom we hear the dialogue of the mind with itself, too sicklied o'r with the pale cast of thought, and Jude-Sue's double-helixing relationship, a Shelleyan pair *ab ovo* "linked in seriousness, in desolation, in tormenting kindness, but above all, in an overbred nervousness" (403), yet finally convinced that "to present *Jude* as a distinctively modern novel is an exaggeration" (401).

Similarly, Tony E. Jackson, in his Lacanian account of modernism as realism's "other" points out — no ghost needed to come from the grave to tell us this, you might think — "Joyce writes in a significantly different way than . . . Hardy [does]."[83]

The context for the remark is interesting, however. Peck's own argument works to forestall the patronage which bedevils discussion of Hardy, but like Howe ends by recycling it in making him merely broach that modernism which Joyce and Kafka will consummate, granting Hardy merely a humble vestibule in the Palace of Modernism, unaware that, as Harold Bloom puts it, the shibboleths of High Modernism have themselves hardly gone unchallenged. This point might itself have been made clearer by noting the forms of rehabilitation undergone by post-romanticism itself. These make Hardy a more congenial figure than Eliot for many modern critics, and render the hangdog attitude which is often in evidence here unnecessary. Unlike Peck, then, in saluting its modernity, such critics show how *Jude* need not be apologised for (in the non-Socratic sense): ideologically speaking, it seems at once more pertinently provocative and more "reassuring" than that of modernism, despite the avant-garde innovativeness of modernism's sophisticated procedures.

But Peck is at least well disposed to the work in general (and to *The Mayor of Casterbridge* and *Jude the Obscure* in particular). In fairly stark contrast, Arthur Mizener had already perceived that Hardy was breaking through naturalistic form, but implies that this is not strength but weakness, leaving Hardy stuck on a plateau of platitudes, consisting of thumping narratorly statements, melodramatic presentation and a damaging hesitation between formal and ideological aporiae which mutually undercut the effect of tragedy.[84] In this negative light Hardy's "ache of modernism," ascribed to Tess in *Tess* but a recurrent feature of his own mind and life and looming even larger in *Jude* than in *Tess* itself, is formally imprisoned in his own unwillingness to "desert his naturalistic narrative" and trust to symbols — trusting to luck instead, presumably. The result is then that "confusion of many standards" in which Bernard J. Paris famously found the Hardyan narrator wallowing,[85] a critical moment for the Hardy advocate in which s/he may find the narrator himself precipitating out as a kind of character, his pseudo-authoritative diegesis, in Bakhtinian terms, becoming a kind of mimesis.

This argument is rehearsed in a different style in David Lodge's attempt to come to terms with Bakhtin's achievement in a glancing but suggestive reference to the Hardyan narrator as shuttling nervously between extremes of empathy and Olympian detachment, eager to be caught with his hands clean, as it were.[86] For him, the Hardyan narrator is at once void of responsibility and with a flickering, intermittent awareness of overall significance. The way the semiotic burdens exceed his grasp is finally more significant than his high-handed yet self-parodying, pseudo-authoritative and yet self-deconstructing versions of narratorship. Yet, though seen in this light the narrator himself is little more than an extra character, even an extra, a little string whose subdued notes are forced to make themselves heard amid a crowd of voices, we might still wish that Hardy had approached modernism by a less "bumpy" route.

Mizener, as you would expect, is happy to cite the Jamesian *procédé* as a rebuke to that of Hardy. No doubt the eager exponent of Hardy might rush in with a dossier of anti-Jamesianisms, as Hardy was as eloquent over his limitations as James persistently was about his from the moment of his feline review of *Far from the Madding Crowd* in 1874.[87]

Critical approaches, then, are divided between those which arbitrate over what *Jude* represents and those which realise that the book is in a complex way "about representation" and about "the pursuit of signs." The prime defect of the former is to talk about the characters as if they were real people and ignore the fact of textuality. The defect of the second is that in problematizing representation critics tend to reproduce the very social conservatism the book is disquieted about, dissolving social aspirations and inquisitions as analysed by critics like Williams, Boumelha, Goode, Widdowson, Eagleton, Fisher and Wotton. However, the example of Eagleton shows that there is no logical connection between a sophisticated approach to representation and a conservative viewpoint.

Elizabeth Langland's suggestive claim (in Higonnet, 1993: 32) that "Hardy engaged profound social dislocations in ways that disturbed the stablity of gender classifications," is perhaps not entirely beyond criticism. Like much sophisticated recent critique, it looks a little like a pre-cooked or prefabricated theory looking for a text to hang itself on, not something that the great masters of textuality like Derrida and de Man actually encourage. But she is surely right to claim that in *Jude*, for example, part of its brilliance derives from Hardy's ability to represent Jude's battle with the class and gender self-constructions [she might have written "constrictions"] his culture offers him"[88] (32). Also suggestive is her sense of Hardy's liminality, as he is "poised between centuries (nineteenth and twentieth), between cultures (rural and urban), and between classes (peasantry and middling)"(32), where this between-ness is textually registered, strenuously and stressfully, a salamadrine talent thoroughly immersed in its own deconstructive element. It is even, indignant critics note, curiously empathetic with the crippling ideological malformations and "mind-forged manacles" from which Hardy would appear to be attempting to distance himself.

If the phrasing suggests Althusser's attempt to show how art enacts this particular kind of detachment, that is because the formulation seems particularly a propos for Jude, which is all about interpellation, the hailing or even haling of the "subject" into its "ordained" position — and the resistance to it. It seems unfortunate, then, that the 1970's study by Boumelha, which was conceived under the sign of Althusser, was so very elliptic as a critical performance while remaining rather magnificent as a scholarly-historical one. Recent criticism has become enormously sophisticated, but the threat to its efficacy and acceptance lies in this sense of a paradoxical "engagement which is not one," in a briskly generalising certainty arrived at *avant la lettre* — the letter of the text itself. Here, indeed, so far from intimating that "the letter killeth," as the epigraph to *Jude* has it, it is the letter, precisely, which giveth life.

In this respect, and with reference to the tension between the semantic and the social emphasis in scholarly readings, Philip M. Weinstein offers an unriddling of the semiotics of desire in *Jude*, which seems equally a desire of semiotics. Yet we can accept that the novel magnificently provides "a landscape of signifiers emptied of those meanings they promise,"[89] a remark disposing of the critical patronage which erupts even in so sophisticated a critique as that of Christine Brooke-Rose.

But in indicating at once the landmarks in the novel which "comprise the human institutions and conventions by which the journeying spirit finds itself stymied rather than fulfilled"(120) there is a stasis where a sense of the dialectic should be: that sense of a thwarted utopian impulse of romanticism itself which, advancing under the watchwords of Arnoldian sweetness and light, offers a stony place of dereliction and despair presided over by an arrogant and élitist clerisy. Kevin Moore's insight into all this, soundly based as it is on the whole tradition of Romanticism, for me at least, seems an unavoidable critical encounter which so few have encountered because the leading tradition in Hardy scholarship is parochial and even anti-intellectual. In particular, those critics who criticise Jude for his monstrous unrealism are understandably wrong-headed about his wrong-headedness.

Examining the phenomenology of Hardy's novels, Bruce Johnson points out that "the question behind much of Jude is . . . less whether Oxford itself will open its doors than whether Oxford itself will become another of these failed symbols of organicism and continuity,"[90] whether, to invoke the terms of Janet Burstein's interesting article, his journey from myth isn't always already a journey inspired by a new one.[91] It is not Jude himself who is to be blamed for entering so whole-heartedly into the pursuit of signs he takes for signifieds. Jude is wanting in the sense of being conceived in, or even of, lack. Then he is tried in the balance and found wanting. But it is not his fault. Too many critics have proceeded as if Fawley, his surname, simply indicated "folly." Fawley was also a place where lowly ancestors suffered deprivation and exploitation.

Notes

[1] G. Deleuze, G. *et* C. Parnet. *Dialogues* (1977). As translated by H. Tomlinson and B. Hammerson. London: Athlone Press, 1987.

[2] Geoffrey Thurley, *The Psychology of Hardy's Novels: The Nervous and the Statuesque.* (St Lucia: Queensland UP), 1975), 188.

[3] John Hughes, *Lines of Flight: Reading Deleuze with Hardy, Gissing, Conrad, Woolf* (Sheffield: Sheffield Academic Press, 1997): 86. Compare Walter Allen's argument that *Jude* "is his one attempt to write a novel strictly of his own times," in *The English Novel* (Harmondsworth: Penguin, 1958), 255.

[4] Albert J. Guerard, *Thomas Hardy: The Novels and Stories* (Cambridge, MA: Harvard UP, 1949), 37. Similarly, a "defense" of Hardy which founders in the light of its own scholarly cosmopolitanism, apologia in the Socratic sense becoming apology in the ordinary sense, is Morton Dauwen Zabel's "Hardy in Defense of His Art: The Aesthetic of Incongruity," [1940], reprinted in Albert J. Guerard, ed. *Hardy: A Collection of Critical Essays* (Englewood Cliffs, NJ: Prentice-Hall, 1963), 24–45.

[5] See her "Ill Wit and Sick Tragedy: *Jude the Obscure*," in Lance St. John Butler, *Alternative Hardy* (London: Macmillan, 1989), 50. Curiously, one back-door route to a sense of Hardy's experimentalism might lie in the direction taken by Donald Davidson in his "The Traditional Basis of Thomas Hardy's Fiction," [orig. 1940], repr. in Albert J. Guerard, *Hardy: A Collection of Critical Essays* (Englewood Cliffs, NJ: Prentice-Hall, 1963), 10–23. Introducing ballad-like elements into a Victorian novel would certainly entail some structural shifts and expedients.

[6] Paul Pickrel, "*Jude the Obscure* and the Fall of Phaethon," *Hudson Review*, 39, (1988) (231–50): 240.

[7] P. N. Furbank, "Introduction" to *Tess of the D'Urbervilles* (London: Macmillan ["New Wessex Edition"], 1974); compare Robert Schweik, "The 'Modernity' of Hardy's *Jude the Obscure*," in *A Spacious Vision: Essays on Hardy*, ed. Philip V. Mallett and Ronald P. Draper (Newmill: The Patten Press, 1994), 49–63, in an essay which finds "expressionist" modes in Hardy and which is fertile in musical analogies.

[8] Deborah L. Collins, *Thomas Hardy and His God* (London: Macmillan, 1990), 139. Frank Giordano, Jr. finds, in an earlier study, that *Jude* "begins with the initial assumptions of the form about personal development" but "concludes by reducing the assumptions [of the Bildungsroman] to absurdity."

See his "*Jude the Obscure* and the *Bildungsroman.*" *Studies in the Novel* 4 (1972): 589. This sense of the absurd persists in Barry N. Schwartz's view of Jude as a "little man," a nineteenth century Willie Loman, in "*Jude the Obscure* in the Age of Anxiety," *Studies in English Literature 1500–1900* 10 (1970): 793–804. He pursues a perfectly Lukacsian argument about the novel being a oxymoronic "modern epic" of a world which lacks Homeric ingredients without, apparently, his being aware of Lukacs himself.

[9] Joe Fisher, *The Hidden Hardy* (London: Macmillan, 1992): 175. It's interesting to contrast this view with that of V. S. Naipaul, who finds reading Hardy an exercise in "nostalgia" for a "vanished, ordered world." See "A Novel for Our Time: V. S. Naipaul's *Guerillas*," in Patrick Parrinder's *The Failure of Theory: Essays on Criticism and Contemporary Fiction* (Brighton: Harvester, 1987), 185. In fact much of the critical purchase on Hardy has derived from a sense of his specifically iconoclastic "faculty." Terry Eagleton observes of him that "having 'exploded' the organic forms of fiction, he was forced to disembark" in *Criticism and Ideology* (London: NLB, 1976), 132.

[10] R. P. Draper, in Dale Kramer (ed.) *Critical Essays on Thomas Hardy: The Novels* (Boston: G. K. Hall, 1992): 246. This is probably the best answer to Q. D. Leavis, who finds something "un-English" (a hard word coming from Leavises) in *Jude*'s structural rigidities. See "The Englishness of the English Novel," in *Collected Essays*, Vol 1, ed. G. Singh (Cambridge: Cambridge UP, 1983), 313. Connected, perhaps to Draper's "wild Polonial" claim is Alexander Fischler's observation that "despite or perhaps precisely because of his intense personal involvement in the story, Hardy allowed himself unprecedented detachment in tone and levity in treatment," in "An Affinity for Birds: Kindness in Hardy's *Jude the Obscure*," *Studies in the Novel* 13 (1981): 251.

[11] Kathleen Blake, "Sue Bridehead: 'The Woman of the Feminist Movement,'" *Studies in English Literature*, 18 (1978): 703–26, repr. in Bloom (1987) (81–102): 92.

[12] John Goode, *Thomas Hardy: The Offensive Truth* (Oxford: Basil Blackwell, 1988), 140.

[13] Peter Widdowson, *Hardy in History: A Study in Literary Sociology* (London: Routledge, 1989), 6–7.

[14] Michael Millgate, *Thomas Hardy: His Career as a Novelist* (London: The Bodley Head, 1971), 340.

[15] Unsigned Review, *Illustrated London News* (11 January 1896), cviii, 50; repr. in *Thomas Hardy: The Critical Heritage*, ed. R. G. Cox (London: Routledge and Kegan Paul, 1970): 274–276.

[16] Havelock Ellis, *Savoy Magazine* (October, 1896), vi, 35–49, repr. in *Thomas Hardy: The Critical Heritage*: 300–315.

[17] D. F. Hannigan, *Westminster Review* (January, 1896), cxlv, 136–9, repr. in *Thomas Hardy: The Critical Heritage*: 270–274.

[18] Richard le Gallienne, *Idler* (February, 1896), 114–5, repr. in *Thomas Hardy: The Critical Heritage*: 277–8.

[19] W. D. Howells, *Harper's Weekly* (7 December 1895), repr. *Thomas Hardy: The Critical Heritage*: (253–256): 255.

[20] H. G. Wells, *Saturday Review* (8 February 1896), repr. *Thomas Hardy: The Critical Heritage*: 279–283, but noted by Cox as simply an "Unsigned Review."

[21] Ramon Saldivar, "*Jude the Obscure*: Reading and the Spirit of the Law," *ELH* 50 (1983): 607–25; repr. in Harold Bloom (ed.) *Thomas Hardy's 'Jude the Obscure'* (New York: Chelsea House, 1987), 103–118: 109.

[22] Shelley, "Preface" to *Prometheus Unbound*, in (e.g) *Selected Poems*, ed. Timothy Webb (London: Dent, 1977), 31; it's a Shelleyan posture Hardy emulated, even imitated (before crumpling into something slightly more plaintive).

[23] Michael E. Hassett, "Compromised Romanticism in *Jude the Obscure*," *Nineteenth Century Fiction*, 25 (1971): 432–43. This may be compared with Patricia Ingham's argument that "there is little to suggests that what [Jude] aspires to really exists," in "The Evolution of *Jude the Obscure*," *Review of English Studies* 27 (1976): 169. Curiously, this might seem to commit one to a conservative ideology that Ingham's subsequent work on Hardy would hardly endorse. It seems cognate with the conservatism Goode legitimately sees in David Lodge's "*Jude the Obscure*: Pessimism and Fictional Form," in *Critical Approaches to the fiction of Thomas Hardy*, edited by Dale Kramer (London: Macmillan, 1979): 193–201. For example, he asks, in a perhaps not wholly convincing "rhetorical" question: "But is it true that he and Sue would have been happier in the age of the Open University and the Permissive Society?" That a more Hardy-friendly development of this concept is possible is indicated by Shalom Rachman, who develops Eugene Goodheart's idea that Jude is an emanation of Hardy's anachronistically Romantic temperament in "Thomas Hardy and the Lyrical Novel," *Nineteenth Century Fiction* 12, no. 3 (1957): 215–225. Rachman asserts that the work itself is the tragedy of "the romantic temperament frustrated in all the spheres in which it seeks to fulfil itself," in "Character and Theme in Hardy's *Jude the Obscure*," *English* 22 (Summer, 1973): 45–53.

[24] Marjorie Garson, *Hardy's Fables of Integrity: Woman, Body, Text* (Oxford: Clarendon Press, 1991), 153, 169.

[25] Ward Hellstrom, "Hardy's Scholar-Gipsy," in *The English Novel in the Nineteenth Century*, ed. G. Goodin (Illinois: U of Chicago P, 1972), 196–213; for a further examinaion of the way *Jude* embodies Hardy's sense of being a "child at a conjuring-show," see Emma Clifford, "The Child: The Circus and *Jude*," *Cambridge Journal*, 7 (1954), reprinted in *Jude the Obscure*. Norton Critical Editions, ed. Norman Page (New York: Norton, 1978), 459–65.

[26] Kevin Z. Moore, *The Descent of the Imagination: Postromantic Culture in the Later Novels of Thomas Hardy* (New York: New York UP, 1990), 226.

[27] Michael Steig, *Stories of Reading: Subjectivity and Literary Understanding* (London: Johns Hopkins UP, 1989), 183–201.

[28] Phyllis Bartlett, "'Seraph of Heaven': A Shelleyan Dream in Hardy's Fiction," *PMLA* 70 (1955): 624–35.

[29] Terry Eagleton, "Introduction" to *Jude the Obscure* (London: Macmillan, 1974); repr. in Bloom, ed. (1987, 61–71), and re-titled "The Limits of Art": 67. See also Penelope Vigar, *The Novels of Thomas Hardy: Illusion and Reality* (London: Athlone Press, 1974), who argues that Jude's "dream-world of ideals is seen as either indifferent or absurd" (196).

[30] Florence Hardy, *The Later Years of Thomas Hardy* (London: Macmillan, 1930), 233.

[31] Ian Gregor, *The Great Web: The Form of Hardy's Major Fiction* (London: Faber and Faber, 1974), 1–2.

[32] John Bayley, *An Essay on Hardy* (Cambridge: Cambridge UP, 1978), 195.

[33] William Morgan, "The Novel as Risk and Compromise, Poetry as Safe Haven: Hardy and the Victorian Reading Public," *Victorian Newsletter*, 69 (1986): 1–3.

[34] Mary Jacobus, "Sue the Obscure," *Essays in Criticism*, 25 (1975): 304–28. Compare Michael Steig's claim that Sue is a "coherent" character as she conforms to Reich's characterisation of the "hysterical" character in his "Sue Bridehead," in *Novel: A Forum on Fiction* 1 (1968): 260–6.

[35] W. J. Hyde, "Theoretic and Practical Unconventionality in *Jude the Obscure*," *Nineteenth Century Fiction*, 20 (1965): 155–64.

[36] R. B. Heilman, "Hardy's Sue Bridehead," *Nineteenth Century Fiction* 20 (1966): 307–23.

[37] John Maynard, "Conclusion: Hardy's *Jude*: Disassembling Sexuality and Religion," in *Victorian Discourses on Sexuality and Religion* (Cambridge: Cambridge UP, 1993), 279.

[38] Wayne Burns, "Flesh and Spirit in *Jude the Obscure*," *Recovering Literature* 1 (1972): 26–41. It is interesting to note F. R. Leavis's attempt to make a cult of Lawrence combined with a firm exclusion of Hardy from any canon with which one should wish to be associated, given that Lawrence was so involved with Hardy, or "inveterately convolved" with Hardy. For an argument about the relationship which seems to imply, quite rightly that Hardy is already doing better than (or for) Lawrence some things which Lawrence would claim as his own achievement, see K. W. Salter's "Lawrence, Hardy and 'The Great Tradition,'" in *English* 22 (1973): 60–65.

[39] D. H. Lawrence, "Study of Thomas Hardy," in *Phoenix: The Posthumous Papares of D. H. Lawrence*, ed. E. D. McDonald (New York: Viking, 1936), 398–516: 510.

[40] Rosemarie Morgan, *Women and Sexuality in the Novels of Thomas Hardy* (London: Routledge, 1988), 110–154.

[41] Rita S. Kranidis, *Subversive Discourse: The Cultural Production of Late Victorianm Feminist Novels* (London: Macmillan, 1995), 124–5.

[42] Ann Ardis, *New Women, New Novels: Feminism and Early Modernism* (New Brunswick, NJ: Rutgers UP, 1990), 31.

[43] Robert Gittings, *Young Thomas Hardy* (London: Heinemann, 1975), 93–95.

[44] Lawrence Lerner, *Love and Marriage: Literature and its Social Context* (London: Chatto and Windus, 1979), 170.

[45] Constance Rover, *Love, Morals and the Feminists* (London: Routledge and Kegan Paul, 1970), 132.

[46] Interestingly, and partly composing an answer to Kate Millett's irritation with Sue as, by turns "an enigma, a pathetic creature, a nut, and an iceberg" (in *Sexual Politics* [London: Hart-Davis, 1977], 133), Elizabeth Langland argues that Sue as a character is filtered almost entirely through Jude's perspective. But Sue also *wants* Jude to "construct" her, as in the "Epipsychidion" episode: "say it's me, Jude. Say it's me!" See Elizabeth Langland, "A Perspective of One's Own: Thomas Hardy and the Elusive Sue Bridehead," *Studies in the Novel* 12 (Spring, 1980): 12–28.

[47] Lance St. J. Butler, *Thomas Hardy* (Cambridge: Cambridge UP, 1978), 140.

[48] Michael Steig, "Sue Bridehead," *Novel*, 1 (1968): 260–6.

[49] Norman Holland, *Psychoanalyisis and Shakespeare* (New York: McGraw-Hill, 1966), 296; see also Norman Holland, "*Jude the Obscure*: Hardy's Symbolic Indictment of Christianity," *Nineteenth Century Fiction* 9 (1954): 50–60, where he argues that in *Jude* he takes advantage of the fact that textual people are not people by treating his characters as "nonrealistic symbols for ideas" (50).

[50] Maria Dibattista, *First Love: The Affections of Modern Fiction*, (Chicago: U of Chicago P, 1991), 216.

[51] Lloyd Fernando, *The "New Woman" in the Late Victorian Novel* (London: Pennsylvania State UP, 1977).

[52] Marcel Proust, *A La Recherche du Temps Perdu*, ed. Pierre Clerac and Andre Ferre (Paris: Gallimard, 1954), iii, 376.

[53] Jean R. Brooks, *Thomas Hardy: The Poetic Structure* (London: Elek, 1971), 254–75.

[54] A. O. J. Cockshut, *Man and Woman: A Study of Love and the Novel 1740–1940* (London: Collins, 1977), 129.

[55] Vincent Newey, "Thomas Hardy and the forms of Making: Interpreting *Jude the Obscure*," in *Centering the Self: Subjectivity, Society and Reading from Thomas Gray to Thomas Hardy*, 217.

[56] Andrew Enstice, *Thomas Hardy: Landscapes of the Mind* (London: Macmillan, 1979), 177.

[57] Desmond Hawkins, *Hardy: Novelist and Poet* (London: Macmillan, 1976), 161; and in his *Thomas Hardy* (Darby, PA: Folcroft Library Editions, 1950), he makes the point that "the impact of this madly egocentric little sensation-hunter on Jude is not very savoury" (84). Very much in the "local color" tradition is his anthology *Hardy at Home: The People and Places of His Wessex*. London: Barrie and Jenkins, 1989.

[58] R. Y. Tyrell, *Fortnightly Review* (June, 1896), lxv, n.s.lix, 857–64; repr. in *Thomas Hardy: The Critical Heritage* (London: Routledge and Kegan Paul, 1970), 295.

[59] John Lucas, *The Literature of Change* (Brighton: Harvester, 1977), 188.

[60] Mary Childers, "Thomas Hardy: The Man Who 'Liked' Women," *Criticism*, 23 (1981), 317–34: 317. Childers cites, inter alia, a placid acceptance of what he takes to be Hardy's sexual stereotyping in Randall Williams, *The Wessex Novels of Thomas Hardy: An Appreciative Study* (New York: Dutton, 1924), 83.

[61] Katharine M. Rogers, "Women in Thomas Hardy," *Centennial Review*, 19 (1975): 249–58.

[62] Lascelles Abercrombie, *Thomas Hardy: A Critical Study* (London: Secker, 1912), 160–1. This chimes well with the later argument by Judith Mitchell to the effect that in Hardy's novels "in their representation of women, they function both as indignant condemnations of the ideological atrocities of patriarchy and, — ironically, paradoxically — as formidable examples of such atrocities themselves," in "Hardy's Female Reader," (Higonnet, 1993: 186). But the point might better have been put the other way about, showing how the novels elide or discomfit the patriarchality they seem to evoke without misgiving. For a late-flowering and cheerfully unironic notation of Hardy's apparent "sexism," in his "surprising knowledge of girlish coquetries and mannerisms" and so on: see Albert J. Guerard, "The Women of the Novels," in his *Hardy: A Collection of Critical Essays*, 63.

[63] Gail Cunningham, *The "New Woman" and the Victorian Novel* (New York: Harper and Row, 1978).

[64] Nina Auerbach, "The Rise of the Fallen Woman," *Nineteenth Century Fiction*, 35 (1980): 29–52.

[65] Mary Ellmann, *Thinking about Women* (London: Virago, 1979), 129.

[66] John Goode, "Hardy and Marxism," *Critical Essays on Thomas Hardy: the Novels*, edited by Dale Kramer (Boston: G. K. Hall, 1990), 21–38.

[67] Donald Davie, *Thomas Hardy and British Poetry* (London: Routledge and Kegan Paul, 1973).

[68] Rosemarie Morgan, "Bodily Transactions: Toni Morrison and Thomas Hardy in Literary Discourse," in Charles P. C. Pettit, ed., *Celebrating Thomas Hardy* (London: Macmillan, 1996), 136–158; for further discussion, see Raymond Chapman, "'A True Representation': Speech in the Novels of Thomas Hardy," *Essays and Studies* (1983), edited by Beatrice White, 40–55.

[69] George Wotton, *Thomas Hardy: Towards a Materialist Criticism* (Dublin: Gill and Macmillan, 1985).

[70] Martin Seymour-Smith, *Hardy* (London: Bloomsbury, 1994), 184; Rosemarie Morgan, *Cancelled Words* (London: Routledge, 1992), 136–50.

[71] Marjorie Garson, *Hardy's Fables of Integrity.* " . . . to see him simply as politically correct is to miss the anxieties, ambivalences, and ambiguities, the defensiveness and self-consciousness, which often get expressed in the novels . . . " (3); but it took a long time to produce a "politically correct" Hardy. We may also boggle at the tendentiousness of "politically correct."

[72] Irving Howe, *Thomas Hardy* (London: Macmillan, 1966), 132–146; reprinted as "A Distinctively Modern Novel" in *Jude the Obscure*, ed. Norman

Page (London: W. Norton, 1978), 395–406. Mary Ellen Chase had noted the specifically controversial nature of his cultural productions in relating him to Ibsen, a potential for offending which underlies her own investigations into the shifts and expedients necessary to him as a writer. See *Thomas Hardy from Serial to Novel* (New York: Russell and Russell, 1964), 196. Also giving a sense of contemporaneity and controversy is John Holloway, "Hardy's Major Fiction," in *Hardy: A Collection of Critical Essays*, ed. Albert A. Guerard, 52–62.

[73] Donald Davie, *Under Briggflats: A History of Poetry in Great Britain 1960–1988* (Manchester: Carcanet, 1989): 204–7; Casagrande's article appeared in *The Thomas Hardy Annual* 1 (1983).

[74] W. Goetz, "The Felicity and Infelicity of Marriage in *Jude the Obscure*," *Nineteenth Century Fiction*, 38 (1983): 189–213.

[75] Michael E. Hassett, "Compromised Romanticism in *Jude the Obscure*," *Nineteenth Century Fiction*, 25 (1971): 432–43.

[76] Edmund Gosse, *Cosmopolis* (Jan., 1896), i, 60–9; repr. *Thomas Hardy: the Critical Heritage*: 262–70. Millgate comments sympathetically (sympathetically, that is, to the feline Gosse, not Hardy), that "Gosse, like many another reader since, had found the bleakness of the story excessive and more than a little gratuitous . . . " (1982: 370).

[77] Tellingly for his own cultural program, of culture as a decided cure for anarchy, and also typically in terms of the critical reception of *Jane Eyre*, Matthew Arnold wrote of Charlotte Bronte that "her mind contains nothing but hunger, rebellion and rage." See *The Letters of Matthew Arnold*, ed. George W. E. Russell (London: Macmillan, 1896), 1:34. As I am suggesting, this telltale outrage has its counterpart in the critical response to Hardy's *Jude the Obscure*, which is itself partly a creative response to and critique of Arnold and Arnoldian notions of culture and the function of critique, as Kevin Moore so well observes.

[78] Michael Millgate, "The Tragedy of Unfulfilled Aims," [re-titled] in Bloom (1987): 7–17 from *Thomas Hardy: His Career as a Novelist* (London: The Bodley Head, 1971): 317–335.

[79] John R. Reed, *Victorian Will* (Athens: Ohio UP, 1989), 352. See Frederick R. Karl, ed. *The Mayor of Casterbridge* (Norton Critical Editions) (New York: Norton, 1979), 383. Another useful "mediation" with a most useful and judicious conclusion is found is Laurence Lerner's *Thomas Hardy's 'Mayor of Casterbridge': Tragedy or Social History?* (London: Chatto and Windus, 1975), 100–105.

[80] Bert G. Hornback, *The Metaphor of Chance: Vision and Technique in the works of Thomas Hardy* (Athens, OH: Ohio UP, 1971), 126–139.

[81] John Peck, "Hardy and Joyce: A Basis for Comparison," *Ariel*, 12 (1981): 71–85.

[82] Irving Howe, *Thomas Hardy* (1966); chapter on *Jude* reprinted in *Jude the Obscure*, ed. Norman Page (New York: W. Norton, 1978), 401.

[83] Tony E. Jackson, *The Subject of Modernism: Narrative Alterations in the Fiction of Eliot, Conrad, Woolf and Joyce* (Ann Arbor: U of Michigan P, 1994), 10.

[84] Arthur Mizener, "*Jude the Obscure* as a Tragedy," *The Southern Review* 6 (1940–41): 193–213.

[85] Bernard Paris, "A Confusion of Many Standards: Conflicting Value-Systems in *Tess of the D'Urbervilles*," *Nineteenth Century Fiction*, 24 (1969): 57–79.

[86] David Lodge, *After Bakhtin: Essays on Fiction and Criticism* (London: Routledge, 1990), 37–38. As Lodge puts it: "Hardy hedges his bets, equivocates, qualifies or contradicts his own authorial dicta, uses tortuous formulae to avoid taking responsibility for authorial description and generalisation." An interesting note on the nature of the Hardy nature is provided by A. F. Cassis when he speaks of "the narrator who simulates a spoken story in print," although, as he points out, Hardy also simulates the organ-voice of the well-educated, perhaps even pompous, *écrivain*. Cited in Kristin Brady, *The Short Stories of Thomas Hardy* (New York: St. Martin's Press, 1982), 200.

[87] Henry James, *Nation* (24 December 1874), reprinted in *Thomas Hardy: The Critical Heritage*: 27–31.

[88] Elizabeth Langland, "Becoming a Man in *Jude the Obscure*," in M. Higonnet (ed.), *The Sense of Sex: Feminist Perspectives on Hardy* (Chicago: U of Illinois P, 1993), 32–48: 32.

[89] Philip M. Weinstein, "The Spirit Unappeased and Peregrine: *Jude the Obscure*," in *The Semantics of Desire: Changing Models of Identity from Dickens to Joyce* (Princeton: Princeton UP, 1984); reprinted in Bloom (1987), 119–135.

[90] Bruce Johnson, *True Correspondence: A Phenomenology of Hardy's Novels* (Tallahassee: U of Florida P, 1983), 187.

[91] Janet Burstein, "The Journey Beyond Myth in *Jude the Obscure*," *Texas Studies in Literature and Language* 15 (Fall 1973); repr. in Bloom (ed.) 1987, 19–36.

Works Cited

James, Henry. *Nation* (24 December 1874): 27–31. Reprinted in *Thomas Hardy: The Critical Heritage*. Edited by R. G. Cox. London: Routledge and Kegan Paul, 1970.

Anon. [New York] *Critic* (28 December, 1895).

Howells, W. D. *Harper's Weekly* (7 December, 1895). Reprinted in *Thomas Hardy: The Critical Heritage*, 253–256.

Gilder, Jeanette. *The New York World* (8 December, 1895).

Gosse, Edmund. *Cosmopolis* (Jan., 1896), i: 60–9. Reprinted in *Thomas Hardy: The Critical Heritage*, 262–270.

Oliphant, Mrs M. "The Anti-Marriage League." *Blackwood's Magazine* (Jan., 1896, clix): 135–49. Reprinted in *Thomas Hardy: The Critical Heritage*, 256–62.

Butler, A. J. "Mr Hardy as a Decadent." *National Review* (May, 1896), xxvii: 384–90. Reprinted in *Thomas Hardy: The Critical Heritage*, 284–291.

Hannigan, D. F. *Westminster Review* (January, 1896), cxlv: 136–9. Reprinted in *Thomas Hardy: The Critical Heritage*, 270–274.

Unsigned Review. *Illustrated London News* (11 January, 1896), cviii: 50. Reprinted in *Thomas Hardy: The Critical Heritage*, 274–276.

Le Gallienne, Richard. *Idler* (February, 1896): 114–5. Reprinted in *Thomas Hardy: The Critical Heritage*, 277–8.

Wells, H. G. *Saturday Review* (8 February, 1896). Reprinted in *Thomas Hardy: The Critical Heritage*, 279–283 [but noted by Cox as simply an "Unsigned Review"].

Tyrell, R. Y. *Fortnightly Review* (June, 1896), lxv, n.s.lix: 857–64. Reprinted in *Thomas Hardy: The Critical Heritage*, 291–299.

Ellis, Havelock. *Savoy Magazine* (October, 1896), vi: 35–49. Reprinted in *Thomas Hardy: The Critical Heritage*, 300–315.

Russell, George W. E., ed. *The Letters of Matthew Arnold*. London: Macmillan, 1896.

Archer, William. "Review" of *Wessex Poems*. In the *Daily Chronicle*, 21 December 1898.

Quiller-Couch, Arthur, ed. *The Oxford Book of English Verse*. Oxford: Oxford UP, 1900.

Garwood, Helen. *Thomas Hardy: An Illustration of the Philosophy of Schopenhauer.* Philadelphia: John C. Winston, 1911.

Abercrombie, Lascelles. *Thomas Hardy: A Critical Study.* London: Secker, 1912.

Chesterton, G. K. *The Victorian Age in Literature.* London: Williams and Norgate, 1913.

Lawrence, D. H. "Study of Thomas Hardy" (1914). Reprinted in *Study of Thomas Hardy and Other Essays.* Edited by Bruce Steele. London: Grafton Books, 1986.

Strachey, Lytton. "Mr. Hardy's New Poems." *The New Statesman* (Dec.19, 1914). Reprinted by Strachey in *Characters and Commentaries.* London: Chatto and Windus, 1933. 195–201.

Gosse, Edmund. "Mr. Hardy's Lyrical Poems." *Edinburgh Review*, (April, 1918), ccvii, 272. Reprinted in *Thomas Hardy: the Critical Heritage*, 444–463.

Eliot, T. S. "Tradition and the Individual Talent." In *The Sacred Wood.* London: Methuen, 1920.

Beach, Joseph Warren. *The Technique of Thomas Hardy.* Chicago: Chicago UP, 1922.

Brennecke, Ernest. *Thomas Hardy's Universe: A Study of a Poet's Mind.* London: T. Fisher Unwin, 1924.

Williams, Randall. *The Wessex Novels of Thomas Hardy: An Appreciative Study.* New York: Dutton, 1924.

Brennecke, Ernest. *Thomas Hardy: A Biography.* New York: Greenberg, 1925.

Firor, Ruth. *Folk-Ways in Thomas Hardy.* Philadelphia: U of Philadelphia P, 1931.

Hardy, Florence E. *The Early Life of Thomas Hardy 1840–1891.* London: Macmillan, 1928.

Hardy, Florence E. *The Later Years of Thomas Hardy 1892–1928.* London: Macmillan, 1930.

Macdowell, Arthur. *Thomas Hardy: A Critical Study.* London: Macmillan, 1931.

Leavis, F. R. *New Bearings in English Poetry.* London: Chatto and Windus, 1932.

Eliot, T. S. *After Strange Gods: A Primer of Modern Heresy.* London: Faber and Faber, 1934.

Empson, William. *Some Versions of Pastoral.* London: Chatto and Windus, 1935.

Lawrence, D. H. "Study of Thomas Hardy." *Phoenix: The Posthumous Papers of D. H. Lawrence*, Edited by E. D. McDonald. New York: Viking, 1936. 398–516.

Leavis, F. R. *Revaluation.* London: Chatto and Windus, 1936.

Yeats, W. B. *Oxford Book of Modern Verse 1892–1935.* London: Oxford UP, 1936.

Hopkins, G. M. *Further Letters of G. M. Hopkins.* Edited by C. C. Abbott. London: Oxford UP, 1938.

Rutland, W. R. *Thomas Hardy: A Study of his Writings and their Background*. Oxford: Blackwell, 1938.

Blackmur, R. P. "Hardy's Shorter Poems." *Southern Review* 6 (1940): 20–48. Reprinted in *Language as Gesture*. New York: Harcourt, Brace and Co., 1952. 51–79.

Leavis, F. R. "Hardy the Poet." *Southern Review* 6 (1940): 87–98.

Mizener, Arthur. "*Jude the Obscure* as a Tragedy." *The Southern Review* 6 (1940): 193–213.

Schwartz, Delmore. "Poetry and Belief in Thomas Hardy." *The Southern Review*, 6 (1940). Reprinted in *Hardy: A Collection of Critical Essays*. Edited by A. J. Guerard. Englewood Cliffs, NJ: Prentice-Hall, 1963. 123–34.

Thomas Hardy: Selected Poems. Edited by G. M. Young. London: Macmillan, 1940.

Weber, Carl. *Hardy of Wessex: His Life and Literary Career*. New York: Columbia, 1940.

Eliot, T. S. *A Choice of Kipling's Verse*. London: Faber and Faber, 1941.

Blunden, Edmund. *Thomas Hardy*. London: Macmillan, 1942.

Cecil, David. *Hardy the Novelist*. New York: Bobbs-Merrill, 1946.

Southworth, J. G. *The Poetry of Thomas Hardy*. London: Athlone Press, 1947.

Hawkins, Desmond. *Thomas Hardy*. Darby, PA: Folcroft Library Editions, 1950.

Pound, Ezra. *Selected Letters of Ezra Pound*. Edited by D. D. Paige. London: Faber and Faber, 1950.

De Sola Pinto, Vivian. *Crisis in English Poetry: 1880–1940*. London: Hutchinson, 1951.

Pound, Ezra. *An ABC of Reading*. London: Faber and Faber, 1951.

Deutsch, Babette. *Poetry in Our Time*. London: Cape, 1952.

Porter, Katherine Anne. "On a Criticism of Thomas Hardy." *The Days Before*. New York: Harcourt, Brace, 1952. 23–35.

Tennyson, Alfred. *Poetical Works*. London: Oxford UP, 1953.

Brown, Douglas. *Thomas Hardy*. Oxford: Blackwell, 1954. [2nd. ed., 1961].

Clifford, Emma. "The Child: The Circus and *Jude*." *Cambridge Journal*, 7 (1954). Reprinted in *Jude the Obscure*. ("Norton Critical Editions"). Edited by Norman Page. New York: Norton, 1978.

Hardy, Evelyn. *Thomas Hardy: A Critical Biography*. London: Hogarth Press, 1954.

Holland, Norman. "*Jude the Obscure*: Hardy's Symbolic Indictment of Christianity." *Nineteenth Century Fiction* 9 (1954): 50–60.

Howe, Irving. *Thomas Hardy*. London: Macmillan, 1966. Pages 132–146 reprinted as "A Distinctively Modern Novel" in *Jude the Obscure*. Edited by Norman Page. 395–406. London: W. Norton, 1978.

Purdy, R. L. *Thomas Hardy: A Bibliographical Study*. Oxford: Oxford UP, 1954.

Proust, Marcel. *A La Recherche du Temps Perdu*. Edited by Pierre Clerac and Andre Ferre. Paris: Gallimard, 1954.

Bartlett, Phyllis. "'Seraph of Heaven': A Shelleyan Dream in Hardy's Fiction." *PMLA* 70 (1955): 624–35.

Bowra, C. M. *Inspiration and Poetry*. London: Macmillan, 1955.

Neiman, Gilbert. "Thomas Hardy: Existentialist." *Twentieth Century Literature* 1 (1956): 207–214.

Thomas, Dylan. *Letters to Vernon Watkins*. Edited by Vernon Watkins. London: Dent, 1957.

Frye, Northrop. *An Anatomy of Criticism: Four Essays*. Princeton: Princeton UP, 1957.

Allen, Walter. *The English Novel*. Harmondsworth: Penguin, 1958.

Goodheart, Eugene. "Thomas Hardy and the Lyrical Novel." *Nineteenth Century Fiction* 12, no. 3 (1958): 215–225.

Van Doren, Mark. *Autobiography*. New York: Harcourt, Brace, 1958.

Perkins, David. "Hardy and the Poetry of Isolation." *ELH* 26 (1959): 253–270. Reprinted in *Hardy: A Collection of Critical Essays*. Edited by Albert J. Guerard, 143–159. Englewood Cliffs, NJ: Prentice-Hall, 1963.

Hough, Graham. *Image and Experience*. London: Fontana, 1960.

Bloom, Harold. *The Visionary Company*. Ithaca: Cornell UP, 1961.

Hynes, Samuel. *The Pattern of Hardy's Poetry*. North Carolina: Chapel Hill, 1961.

Graves, Robert. *The White Goddess: Oxford Addresses on Poetry*. London: Oxford UP, 1962.

Kenner, Hugh. *T. S. Eliot: A Collection of Critical Essays*. Englewood Cliffs, NJ: Prentice-Hall, 1962.

Alvarez, A. "*Jude the Obscure*: Afterword." [1961]. Reprinted in *Thomas Hardy: A Collection of Critical Essays*. Edited by A. J. Guerard. Englewood Cliffs, NJ: Prentice-Hall, 1963. 113–122.

Davidson, Donald. "The Traditional Basis of Thomas Hardy's Fiction." Reprinted from *Still Rebels, Still Yankees and Other Essays*. Baton Rouge: The Louisiana State Press, 1957. In *Hardy: A Collection of Critical Essays*. Edited by Albert A. Guerard. Englewood Cliffs, NJ: Prentice-Hall, 1963. 10–23.

Guerard, Albert J. "The Women of the Novels." In *Hardy: A Collection of Critical Essays*. Edited by Albert J. Guerard. Englewood Cliffs, NJ: Prentice-Hall, 1963. 63–70.

Holloway, John. "Hardy's Major Fiction." In *Hardy: A Collection of Critical Essays*, ed. Albert A. Guerard. Englewood Cliffs, NJ: Prentice-Hall, 1963. 52–62.

Stewart, J. I. M. "Hardy." *Eight Modern Authors*. Oxford: Clarendon Press, 1963. 19–70.

Thomas, Dylan. "An Introduction to Thomas Hardy." *An Evening with Dylan Thomas*. London: Caedmon Records, 1963.

Zabel, Morton Dauwen. "Hardy in Defense of His Art: The Aesthetic of Incongruity." *Southern Review* 6 (1940). Reprinted in *Hardy: A Collection of Critical Essays*. Englewood Cliffs, NJ: Prentice-Hall, 1963. 24–45.

Chase, Mary Ellen. *Thomas Hardy from Serial to Novel*. New York: Russell and Russell, 1964.

Fraser, G. S. *The Modern Writer and His World*. Harmondsworth: Penguin, 1964.

Palgrave, Francis T., ed. *The Golden Treasury*. Oxford: Oxford UP, 1964.

Pound, Ezra and Marcella Spann, eds. *From Confucius to Cummings*. New York: New Directions, 1964.

Watson, George. *The Literary Critics: A Study of English Descriptive Criticism*. London: Woburn Press, 1964.

Hyde, W. J. "Theoretic and Practical Unconventionality in *Jude the Obscure*." *Nineteenth Century Fiction* 20 (1965): 155–64.

Deacon, Lois and Terry Coleman. *Providence and Mr Hardy*. London: Hutchinson, 1966.

Heilman, R. B. "Hardy's Sue Bridehead." *Nineteenth Century Fiction* 20 (1966): 307–23.

Holland, Norman. *Psychoanalysis and Shakespeare*. New York: McGraw-Hill, 1966.

Howe, Irving. *Thomas Hardy*. London: Macmillan, 1966.

Kettle, Arnold. *An Introduction to the English Novel*. 2nd. ed. London: Hutchinson, 1967.

Zietlow, Paul. "The Tentative Mode of Hardy's Poems." *Victorian Poetry* 5 (1967): 113–126.

Anderson, Perry. "Components of the National Culture." *New Left Review* 50 (July/August 1968): 26–53.

Barber, D. F., ed. *Concerning Thomas Hardy: A Composite Portrait from Memory*. London: Charles Skilton, 1968.

Howe, Irving. *Thomas Hardy*. London: Weidenfeld and Nicholson, 1968.

Lerner, Laurence and John Holmstrom. *Thomas Hardy and His Readers: A Selection of Contemporary Reviews*. New York: Barnes and Noble, 1968.

Steig, Michael. "Sue Bridehead." *Novel: A Forum on Fiction* 1 (1968): 260–6.

Daiches, David. *Some Late Victorian Attitudes*. New York: Norton, 1969.

Macbeth, G., ed. *The Penguin Book of Victorian Verse*. Harmondsworth: Penguin, 1969.

Marsden, Kenneth. *The Poems of Thomas Hardy: A Critical Introduction*. London: Athlone Press, 1969.

Paris, Bernard J. "A Confusion of Many Standards: Conflicting Value-Systems in *Tess of the D'Urbervilles*." *Nineteenth Century Fiction* 24 (1969): 57–79.

Bailey, J. O. *The Poetry of Thomas Hardy. A Handbook and Commentary*. Chapel Hill: North Carolina, 1970.

Benvenuto, Richard. "Modes of Perception: The Will to Live in *Jude the Obscure*." *Studies in the Novel* 2 (1970): 31–41.

Herbert, Lucille. "Hardy's Views in *Tess of the D'Urbervillles*," in *ELH: A Journal of English Literary History* 37 (1970): 77–94.

May, Charles E. "Thomas Hardy and the Poetry of the Absurd." *Texas Studies in Literature and Language* 12 (1970): 63–73.

Miller, J. Hillis. *Thomas Hardy: Distance and Desire*. Cambridge, MA: Harvard UP, 1970.

Pound, Ezra. *Guide to Kulchur*. New York: New Directions, 1970.

Rover, Constance. *Love, Morals and the Feminists*. London: Routledge and Kegan Paul, 1970.

Schwartz, Barry N. "*Jude the Obscure* in the Age of Anxiety." *Studies in English Literature 1500–1900* 10 (1970): 793–804.

Thatcher, David. "Another Look at Hardy's 'Afterwards.'" *Victorian Newsletter* 38 (1970): 14–18.

Thwaite, Anthony. "The Poetry of Philip Larkin." In *The Survival of Poetry: A Contemporary Survey*. Edited by Martin Dodsworth. London: Faber and Faber, 1970. 37–55.

Williams, Raymond. *The English Novel from Dickens to Lawrence*. London: Chatto and Windus, 1970.

Bloom, Harold. *The Ringers in the Tower*. Chicago: Chicago UP, 1971.

Brooks, Jean R. *Thomas Hardy: The Poetic Structure*. London: Elek, 1971.

Eagleton, Terry. "Thomas Hardy: Nature as Language." *Critical Quarterly* 13 (1971): 155–62.

Goode, John. "William Morris and the Dream of Revolution." *Literature and Politics in the Nineteenth Century*. Edited by John Lucas. London: Methuen, 1971. 221–78.

Hornback, Bert G. *The Metaphor of Chance: Vision and Technique in the Works of Thomas Hardy*. Athens: Ohio UP, 1971.

Millett, Kate. *Sexual Politics*. London: Hart-Davis, 1971.

Millgate, Michael. *Thomas Hardy: His Career as a Novelist*. London: Bodley Head, 1971.

Southerington, F. R. *Hardy's Vision of Man*. London: Chatto and Windus, 1971.

Stewart, J. I. M. *Thomas Hardy: A Critical Biography*. London: Oxford UP, 1971.

Burns, Wayne. "Flesh and Spirit in *Jude the Obscure*." *Recovering Literature* 1 (1972): 26–41.

Davie, Donald. "Hardy's Virgilian Purples." *Agenda* 10 (1972): 138–56. Reprinted in *The Poet in the Imaginary Museum*. Edited by Barry Alpert. Manchester: Carcanet, 1977. 221–235.

Giordano, Frank R., Jr. "*Jude the Obscure* and the *Bildungsroman*." *Studies in the Novel* 4 (1972): 580–91.

"Hardy the Novelist: A Reconsideration" (W. D. Thomas Memorial Lecture, University College, Swansea [1966]). Reprinted in *The Nineteenth Century Novel: Critical Essays and Documents*, Edited by Arnold Kettle. London: Heinemann Educ. Books, 1972. 262–273.

Hellstrom, Ward. "Hardy's Scholar-Gipsy." *The English Novel in the Nineteenth Century: Essays on the Literary Mediation of Human Values*. Edited by G. Goodin. Chicago: U of Illinois P, 1972. 196–213.

Miller, J. Hillis. "History as Repetition in Thomas Hardy's Poetry: The Example of 'Wessex Heights'." *Victorian Poetry*, Stratford-upon-Avon Studies 15 (1972): 223–53. Reprinted in *Post-Structuralist Readings of English Poetry*. Edited by Christopher Norris and Richard Machin. Cambridge: Cambridge UP, 1987.

Bloom, Harold. *The Anxiety of Influence: A Theory of Poetry*. New York: Oxford UP, 1973.

Burstein, Janet. "The Journey Beyond Myth in *Jude the Obscure*." *Texas Studies in Literature and Language* 15 (Fall, 1973): 499–515. Reprinted in *Thomas Hardy (Modern Critical Views)*. Edited by Harold Bloom. New York: Chelsea House, 1987. 19–36.

Davie, Donald. *Thomas Hardy and British Poetry*. London: Routledge and Kegan Paul, 1973.

Rachman, Shalom. "Character and Theme in Hardy's *Jude the Obscure*." *English* 22 (1973): 45–53.

Salter, K. W. "Lawrence, Hardy and 'The Great Tradition.'" *English* 22 (1973): 60–65.

Williams, Raymond. *The Country and the City*. London: Chatto and Windus, 1973.

Cassis, A. F. "A Note on the Structure of Hardy's Short Stories." *Colby Library Quarterly*, 10th ser. (1974): 287–96.

Creighton, T. R. M., ed. *Poems of Thomas Hardy: A New Selection*. London: Macmillan, 1974.

Eagleton, Terry. "Introduction" to *Jude the Obscure*. London: Macmillan, 1974. Reprinted in *Thomas Hardy: Modern Critical Views*. Edited by Harold Bloom (1987: 61–71), and re-entitled "The Limits of Art."

Furbank, P. N. "Introduction." *Tess of the D'Urbervilles*. London: Macmillan ["New Wessex Edition"], 1974).

Gregor, Ian. *The Great Web: The Form of Hardy's Major Fiction*. London: Faber and Faber, 1974.

Grigson, Geoffrey. *The Contrary View: Glimpses of Fudge and Gold*. London: Macmillan, 1974.

Hardy, Thomas. "Preface" to *The Return of the Native* (1878). As reprinted in the "New Wessex Edition." Edited by George Woodcock. London: Macmillan, 1974.

Morton, Peter R. *"Tess of the D'Urbervilles*. A Neo-Darwinian Reading." *Southern Review* [Adelaide] 7 (1974): 38–50.

Southerington, F. R. *"The Return of the Native*: Thomas Hardy and the Evolution of Consciousness." In *Thomas Hardy and the Modern World: Papers Presented at the 1973 Summer School*. Edited by F. B. Pinion. Dorchester, The Thomas Hardy Society Ltd., 1974. 37–47.

Vigar, Penelope. *The Novels of Thomas Hardy: Illusion and Reality*. London: Athlone Press, 1974.

Zietlow, Paul. *Moments of Vision: The Poetry of Thomas Hardy*. Cambridge, MA: Harvard UP, 1974.

Barthes, Roland. *S/Z*. Trans. Richard Miller. London: Cape, 1975.

Beatty, C. J. P.[Claudius]. "Introduction." *Desperate Remedies*. London: Macmillan ["New Wessex Edition"], 1975.

Bloom, Harold. *A Map of Misreading*. New York: Oxford UP, 1975.

Gittings, Robert. *Young Thomas Hardy*. London: Heinemann, 1975. Reprinted Harmondsworth: Penguin, 1978.

Havely, Cicely. *Thomas Hardy*. Milton Keynes: Open Univ., 1975.

Jacobus, Mary. "Sue the Obscure." *Essays in Criticism*, 25 (1975): 304–28.

Kramer, Dale. *Thomas Hardy: The Forms of Tragedy*. London: Macmillan, 1975.

Lerner, Laurence. *Thomas Hardy's 'The Mayor of Casterbridge': Tragedy or Social History?* London: Chatto and Windus, 1975.

Ricks, Christopher. "A Note on *Little Gidding*." *Essays in Criticism* 25 (1975): 145–7.

Rogers, Kathleen. "Women in Thomas Hardy." *Centennial Review* 19 (1975): 249–58.

Thurley, Geoffrey. *The Psychology of Hardy's Novels: The Nervous and the Statuesque.* Queensland: Queensland UP, 1975.

The Genius of Thomas Hardy. Edited by Margaret Drabble. London: Weidenfeld and Nicholson, 1976.

Budmouth Essays on Thomas Hardy. Edited by F. B. Pinion. Dorchester: The Thomas Hardy Society Ltd., 1976.

Baudrillard, Jean. *L'Echange Symbolique et la Mort.* Paris: Gallimard, 1976.

Eagleton, Terry. *Criticism and Ideology: A Study in Marxist Literary Theory.* London: Verso, 1976.

Goode, John. "Women and the Literary Text." In *The Rights and Wrongs of Women.* Edited by Juliet Mitchell and Anne Oakley. Harmondsworth: Penguin, 1976.

Hawkins, Desmond. *Hardy: Novelist and Poet.* Newton Abbot: David and Charles, 1976.

Ingham, Patricia. "The Evolution of *Jude the Obscure.*" *Review of English Studies* 27 (1976): 27–37, 159–69.

Leavis, F. R. *Thought, Words and Creativity.* London: Chatto and Windus, 1976.

Orel, Harold. *The Final Years of Thomas Hardy, 1912–28.* London: Macmillan, 1976.

Paulin, Tom. "Time and Sense Experience: Hardy and T. S. Eliot." In *Budmouth Essays on Thomas Hardy.* Ed. F. B. Pinion. Dorchester: The Thomas Hardy Society Ltd., 1976. 192–204.

Perkins, David. *A History of Modern Poetry: From the 1890s to the High Modernist Mode.* Cambridge, MA: Harvard UP, 1976.

Pinion, F. B. *A Commentary on the Collected Poems of Thomas Hardy.* London: Macmillan, 1976.

Stevens Cox, Gregory. "The Hardy Industry." In *The Genius of Thomas Hardy.* Edited by Margaret Drabble. London: Weidenfeld and Nicholson, 1976. 170–181.

Stewart, J. I. M. "The Major Novels." In *The Genius of Thomas Hardy.* Edited by Margaret Drabble. 1976. 56–66.

Sutherland, John. *Victorian Novelists and Publishers.* London: Athlone Press, 1976.

Alexander, Michael. "Hardy Among the Poets." In Lance St. John Butler, ed. *Thomas Hardy After Fifty Years.* London: Macmillan, 1977. 49–63.

Buck-Morss, Susan. *The Origin of Negative Dialectics.* Brighton: Harvester, 1977.

Butler, Lance St. John, "How It is for Thomas Hardy." *Thomas Hardy after Fifty Years.* London: Macmillan, 1977. 53–76.

Casagrande, Peter J. "Hardy's Wordsworth: A Record and a Commentary." *English Literature in Transition* 20 (1977): 210–37.

Cockshut, A. O. J. *Man and Woman: A Study of Love and the Novel 1740–1940.* London: Collins, 1977.

Fernando, Lloyd. *The "New Woman" in the Late Victorian Novel.* London: Pennsylvania State UP, 1977.

Grigson, Geoffrey. "The Poems." in *The Genius of Thomas Hardy.* Edited by Margaret Drabble. London: Weidenfeld and Nicholson, 1977. 80–93.

Holloway, John. *The Proud Knowledge: Poetry, Insight and the Self 1620–1920.* London: Routledge and Kegan Paul, 1977.

Johnson, H. A. T. "'Despite Time's Derision': Donne, Hardy and the 1913 Poems." *Thomas Hardy Yearbook* 6 (1977): 7–20.

Kinkead-Weekes, Mark. "Lawrence on Hardy." In *Thomas Hardy after Fifty Years.* Edited by Lance St. John Butler. London: Macmillan, 1977. 90–103.

Lucas, John. *The Literature of Change.* Brighton: Harvester, 1977.

Page, Norman. *Thomas Hardy.* London: Routledge, 1977.

Richardson, James. *Thomas Hardy: The Poetry of Necessity.* London: Macmillan, 1977.

Shelley, P. B. "Preface" to *Prometheus Unbound.* In *Selected Poems,* ed. Timothy Webb. London: Dent, 1977.

Wain, John. *Professing Poetry.* London: Macmillan, 1977.

Bayley, John. *An Essay on Hardy.* Cambridge: Cambridge UP, 1978.

Blake, Kathleen. "Sue Bridehead: 'The Woman of the Feminist Movement.'" *Studies in English Literature* 18 (1978): 703–26. Reprinted in *Thomas Hardy.* Edited by H. Bloom (1987). 81–102.

Butler, Lance St. J. *Thomas Hardy.* Cambridge: Cambridge UP, 1978.

Cunningham, Gail. *The "New Woman" and the Victorian Novel.* New York: Harper and Row, 1978.

Gittings, Robert. *The Older Hardy.* London: Heinemann, 1978.

Howe, Irving. *Thomas Hardy* (1966). Chapter on "*Jude*" reprinted in *Jude the Obscure.* Edited by Norman Page. New York: W. Norton, 1978. 395–406.

Mahar, Margaret. "Hardy's Poetry of Renunciation." *ELH* 45 (1978): 303–24. Reprinted in *Thomas Hardy* (Modern Critical Views). Edited by Harold Bloom. New York: Chelsea House, 1987. 155–173.

Murfin, Ross C. "New Words: Swinburne and the Poetry of Thomas Hardy." *Swinburne, Hardy, Lawrence and the Burden of Belief.* London: U of Chicago P, 1978. Reprinted in *Thomas Hardy.* Edited by Harold Bloom. 1987. 137–153.

Wright, David., ed. *Thomas Hardy: Selected Poetry.* London: Penguin, 1978.

Howe, Irving. "Hardy the Obscure." *New York Times Book Review* (7 May 1978): 11.

Ellmann, Mary. *Thinking about Women.* London: Virago, 1979.

Enstice, Andrew. *Thomas Hardy: Landscapes of the Mind.* London: Macmillan, 1979.

Gibson, James, and Trevor Johnson, eds. *Thomas Hardy. Poems.* Macmillan Casebook Series. London: Macmillan, 1979.

Gittings, Robert and Jo Manton. *The Second Mrs Hardy.* London: Heinemann, 1979.

Goode, John. "Sue Bridehead and the New Woman." In *Women Writing and Writing about Women.* Edited by Mary Jacobus. Beckenham: Croom Helm, 1979.

Johnson, Trevor. "'Pre-Critical Innocence' and the Anthologist's Hardy." *Victorian Poetry,* 17 (1979): 9–29.

Kramer D., ed. *Critical Approaches to Thomas Hardy.* London: Macmillan, 1979.

Levine, George. *The Realistic Imagination.* Chicago: Chicago UP, 1979.

Lodge, David. "*Jude the Obscure*: Pessimism and Fictional Form." In *Critical Approaches to the Fiction of Thomas Hardy.* Edited by Dale Kramer. London: Macmillan, 1979. 193–201.

Lerner, Lawrence. *Love and Marriage: Literature and its Social Context.* London: Chatto and Windus, 1979.

Mulhern, Francis. *The Moment of 'Scrutiny'.* London: NLB, 1979.

Richards, I. A. "Some Notes on Thomas Hardy's Verse Forms." *Victorian Poetry* 17 (1979): 1–8.

Stubbs, Patricia. *Women and Fiction: Feminism and the Novel, 1880–1920.* Brighton: Harvester, 1979.

The Poetry of Thomas Hardy. Edited by Clements, Patricia and Juliet Grindle. London: Vision Press, 1980.

Thomas Hardy: The Writer and His Background. Edited by Norman Page. London: Bell and Hyman, 1980.

Auerbach, Nina. "The Rise of the Fallen Woman." *Nineteenth Century Fiction* 35 (1980): 29–52.

Belsey, Catherine. *Critical Practice.* London: Methuen, 1980.

Bergonzi, Bernard, ed. *Poetry 1870 to 1914.* London: Longman, 1980.

Clements, P. "Unlawful Beauty: Order and Things in Hardy's Poetry." In *The Poetry of Thomas Hardy.* Edited by Clements and Grindle. 1980. 137–154.

Cook, Cornelia. "Thomas Hardy and George Meredith." In *The Poetry of Thomas Hardy*. Edited by Clements and Grindle. 1980. 83–100.

Gibson, James. "Hardy and His Readers." In *Thomas Hardy: The Writer and His Background*. Edited by Norman Page. 1980. 192–218.

Grundy, Isobel. "Hardy's Harshness." In *The Poetry of Thomas Hardy*. Edited by Clements and Grindle. 1980. 1–17.

McCarthy, R. "Hardy's Baffled Visionary: A Reading of 'A Sign-Seeker.'" *Victorian Poetry* 18 (1980): 85–90.

Newman, S. C. "Emotion Put into Measure: Meaning in Hardy's Poetry." In *The Poetry of Thomas Hardy*. Edited by Clements and Grindle. 1980. 33–51.

Wickens, Glen. "Hardy's Inconsistent Spirits and the Philosophical form of *The Dynasts*." In *The Poetry of Thomas Hardy*. Edited by Clements and Grindle. 1980. 101–118.

Browne, Merle E. *Double Lyric: Divisiveness and Communal Creativity in Recent English Poetry*. London: Routledge and Kegan Paul, 1980.

Björk, Lennart A. "Hardy's Reading." In *Thomas Hardy: The Writer and His Background*. Edited by Norman Page. London: Bell and Hyman, 1980. 102–127.

Collins, Philip. "Hardy and Education" In *Thomas Hardy: The Writer and His Background*. Edited by Norman Page. London: Bell and Hyman, 1980. 41–75.

Hynes, Samuel. "The Hardy Tradition in Modern English Poetry." In *Thomas Hardy: The Writer and His Background*. Edited by Norman Page. London: Bell and Hyman, 1980. 173–191.

Langland, Elizabeth. "A Perspective of One's Own: Thomas Hardy and the Elusive Sue Bridehead." *Studies in the Novel* 12 (Spring, 1980): 12–28.

McCarthy, Robert. "Hardy and 'The Lonely Burden of Consciousness': The Poet's Flirtation with the Void." *English Literature in Transition* 23 (1980): 89–98.

Morrison, Blake. *The Movement: English Poetry and Fiction of the 1950s*. Oxford: Oxford UP, 1980.

Weiss, Theodor. "The Many-Sidedness of Modernism." *Times Literary Supplement*, 1 February 1980: 124–5.

Winter, Michael. "A Note Towards An Historical and Class Analysis of Thomas Hardy's Novels." *Literature and History* 6 (1980): 174–81.

Williams, Raymond and Merryn Williams. "Hardy and Social Class." In *Thomas Hardy: the Writer and His Background*. Edited by Norman Page. London: Bell and Hyman, 1980. 29–40.

Björk, Lennart A. "Hardy's Reading." In *Thomas Hardy: The Writer and His Background*. Edited by Norman Page. London: Bell and Hyman, 1980. 102–127.

Page, Norman. "Hardy and the English Language." In *Thomas Hardy: The Writer and His Background*. London: Bell and Hyman, 1980. 150–172.

Robinson, Roger. "Hardy and Darwin." In *Thomas Hardy: The Writer and His Background*. Edited by Norman Page. London: Bell and Hyman, 1980. 128–149.

Taylor, Richard H. "Thomas Hardy: A Reader's Guide." In *Thomas Hardy: The Writer and His Background*. Edited by Norman Page. London: Bell and Hyman, 1980. 219–258.

Barthes, Roland. "Theory of the Text." *Untying the Text: A Post Structuralist Reader*. Edited by Robert Young. London: Routledge, 1981.

Childers, Mary. "Thomas Hardy, the Man Who 'Liked' Women." *Criticism* 23, no. 4 (1981): 317–34.

Eagleton, Terry. *Walter Benjamin: or Towards a Revolutionary Criticism*. London: Verso, 1981.

Edmond, Rod. "Death Sequences: Hardy, Patmore and the New Domestic Elegy." *Victorian Poetry* 19 (1981): 151–65.

Fischler, Alexander. "An Affinity for Birds: Kindness in Hardy's *Jude the Obscure*." *Studies in the Novel* 13 (1981): 250–65.

Peck, John. "Hardy and Joyce: A Basis for Comparison." *Ariel*, 12 (1981): 71–85.

Sonstroem, David. "Order and Disorder in *Jude the Obscure*." *English Literature in Transition (1880–1920)*, 24, no.1 (1981): 6–15.

White, Allon. *The Uses of Obscurity: The Fiction of Early Modernism*. London: Routledge and Kegan Paul, 1981.

Williams, Raymond. *Politics and Letters: Interviews with New Left Review*. London: Verso, 1981.

Belsey, Catherine. "Re-Reading the Great Tradition." *Re-Reading English*. London: Methuen, 1982. 121–35.

Brady, Kristin. *The Short Stories of Thomas Hardy*. London: Macmillan, 1982.

Casagrande, Peter J. "'Old Tom and New Tom': Hardy and His Biographers." *Thomas Hardy Annual* 1 (1982), 1–32.

Jacobus, Mary. "Hardy's Magian Retrospect." *Essays in Criticism* 32 (1982): 258–79.

Jefferson, Douglas and Graham Martin, eds. *The Uses of Fiction: Essays on the Modern Novel in Honour of Arnold Kettle*. Milton Keynes: Open UP, 1982.

Millgate, Michael. *Thomas Hardy: A Biography*. Oxford: Oxford UP, 1982.

Paulin, Tom. "Words, in all their Intimate Accents." *Thomas Hardy Annual* 1 (1982): 84–9.

Seymour Smith, Martin. *Robert Graves: His Life and Work*. London: Hutchinson, 1982.

Lucas, John. "Thomas Hardy, Donald Davie, England and the English." *Thomas Hardy Annual* 1 (1982): 134–151.

Poster, Mark. "Semiology and Critical Theory: from Marx to Baudrillard." *The Question of Textuality: Strategies of Reading in Contemporary American Criticism*. Bloomington: Indiana UP, 1982.

Robinson, Peter. "In Another's Words: Thomas Hardy's Poetry." *English* 31 (1982): 221–46.

Casagrande, Peter. *Unity in Hardy's Novels: 'Repetitive Symmetries.'* London: Macmillan, 1982.

Smith, Stan. *Inviolable Voice: History and Twentieth Century Poetry*. Dublin: Gill and Macmillan, 1982.

Taylor, Richard. *The Neglected Hardy: Thomas Hardy's Lesser Novels*. London: Macmillan, 1982.

Williams, Raymond. "Region and Class in the Novel." In *The Uses of Fiction: Essays on the Modern Novel in Honour of Arnold Kettle*. Edited by Douglas Jefferson and Graham Martin. Milton Keynes: Open UP, 1982. 59–68.

Baldick, Chris. *The Social Mission of English Criticism, 1848–1932*. Oxford: Clarendon Press, 1983.

Beer, Gillian. *Darwin's Plots: Evolutionary Narrative in Darwin, George Eliot, and Nineteenth-Century Fiction*. London: Routledge and Kegan Paul, 1983.

Chapman, Raymond. "'A True Representation': Speech in the Novels of Thomas Hardy." *Essays and Studies* (1983). Edited by Beatrice White. London: John Murray, 1983. 40–55.

Davis, Philip. *Memory and Writing from Wordsworth to Lawrence*. Liverpool: Liverpool UP, 1983.

Easthope, Anthony. *Poetry as Discourse*. London: Methuen, 1983.

Gifford, Henry. "Hardy in his Later Poems." In *From James to Eliot. New Pelican Guide to English Literature 8*. Edited by Boris Ford. London: Penguin, 1983. 166–79.

Goetz, W. R. "The Felicity and Infelicity of Marriage in *Jude the Obscure*." *Nineteenth Century Fiction* 38 (1983): 189–213.

Johnson, Bruce. *True Correspondence: A Phenomenology of Hardy's Novels*. Tallahassee: UP of Florida, 1983.

Larkin, Philip. *Required Writing: Miscellaneous Pieces 1955–1982*. London: Faber and Faber, 1983.

Leavis, Q. D. *The Englishness of the English Novel. Collected Essays. Vol 1*. Edited by G. Singh. Cambridge: Cambridge UP, 1983.

Neill, Edward. "Modernism and Englishness: Reflections on Auden and Larkin." *Essays and Studies* (1983). Edited by Beatrice White. London: John Murray, 1983. 79–93.

Saldivar, Ramon. "*Jude the Obscure*: Reading and the Spirit of the Law," *ELH* 50 (1983): 607–25; Reprinted in Harold Bloom, ed. *Thomas Hardy* (Modern Critical Views. New York: Chelsea House, 1987. 103–118.

Springer, Marilyn. *Hardy's Use of Allusion*. London: Macmillan, 1983.

Widdowson, Frances. *Going Up Into the Next Class: Women and Elementary Teacher Training, 1840–1894*. London: Hutchinson, 1983.

Ackroyd, Peter. *T. S. Eliot: A Biography*. London: Hamish Hamilton, 1984.

Boumelha, Penny. *Thomas Hardy and Women: Sexual Ideology and Narrative Form*. Brighton: Harvester Press, 1984.

Elliott, Ralph W. V. *Thomas Hardy's English*. Oxford: Basil Blackwell, 1984.

Miller, J. Hillis. "Thomas Hardy, Jacques Derrida and the 'Dislocation of Souls.'" In *Taking Chances: Derrida, Psychoanalysis and Literature*. Edited by J. H. Smith and W. Kerrigan, 135–145. Baltimore: Johns Hopkins, 1984.

Hardy, Thomas. *The Life and Work of Thomas Hardy*. Edited by Michael Millgate. London: Macmillan, 1984.

Hynes, Samuel, ed. *Thomas Hardy*. ("Oxford Authors" Series). Oxford: Oxford UP, 1984.

Weinstein, Philip M. "The Spirit Unappeased and Peregrine: *Jude the Obscure*." In *The Semantics of Desire: Changing Models of Identity from Dickens to Joyce*. Princeton: Princeton UP, 1984; reprinted in *Thomas Hardy*. Edited by Harold Bloom. New York: Chelsea House, 1987. 119–135.

Beer, Patricia. *Wessex: A National Trust Book*. London: Hamish Hamilton, 1985.

Eagleton, Terry. "Capitalism, Modernism and Postmodernism." *New Left Review*, 152 (1985), 60–73; rpr. in *Postmodernism: A Reader*, ed. Patricia Waugh. London: Edward Arnold, 1992.

Lawrence, D. H. *A Study of Thomas Hardy and Other Essays*. Cambridge: Cambridge UP, 1985.

Miller, J. Hillis. *The Linguistic Moment: From Wordsworth to Stevens*. Princeton: Princeton UP, 1985.

Miller, J. Hillis. "Topography and Tropography in Thomas Hardy's 'In Front of the Landscape.'" In *Identity of the Literary Text*. Edited by M. J. Valdes and O. Miller. Toronto: Toronto UP, 1985. 73–91; also in *Post-structuralist Readings of English Poetry*. Edited by Richard Machin and Christopher Norris. Cambridge: Cambridge UP, 1987.

Sacks, Peter. "Hardy: 'A Singer Asleep' and Poems of 1912–13." In *The English Elegy: Studies in the Genre from Spenser to Yeats*. Baltimore: Johns Hopkins UP, 1985. 227–259.

Snell, K. D. M. "Thomas Hardy, Rural Dorset, and the Family." *Annals of the La-bouring Poor: Social Change and Agrarian England 1660–1900*. Cambridge: Cambridge UP, 1985. 374–410.

Wotton, George. *Thomas Hardy: Towards a Materialist Criticism*. Dublin: Gill and Macmillan, 1985.

Bullen, J. B. *The Expressive Eye: Fiction and Perception in the Work of Thomas Hardy*. Oxford: Oxford UP, 1986.

De Man, Paul. *The Resistance to Theory*. Manchester: Manchester UP, 1986.

Eagleton, Terry. "The Idealism of American Criticism." *Against the Grain: Essays 1975–1985*. London: Verso, 1986.

Feltes, N. N. *Modes of Production of Victorian Novels*. Chicago: Chicago UP, 1986.

Hawkes, Terence. *That Shakespeherian Rag: Essays on a Critical Process*. London: Methuen, 1986.

The Ideology of Englishness: National Identity in the Arts, Politics and Society 1880–1920. Edited by Robert Colls and Philip Dodd. London: Croom Helm, 1986.

Lucas, John. "Thomas Hardy: Voices and Visions." *Modern English Poetry from Hardy to Hughes: A Critical Survey*. London: B. T. Batsford, 1986. 22–49.

Morgan, William. "The Novel as Risk and Compromise, Poetry as Safe Haven: Hardy and the Victorian Reading Public." *Victorian Newsletter* 69 (1986): 1–3.

Paulin, Tom. *Thomas Hardy: The Poetry of Perception*. 2nd ed. London: Macmillan, 1986.

Robson, W. W. *A Prologue to English Literature*. London: B. T. Batsford, 1986.

Spender, Stephen. *Journals 1939–1985*. London: Faber and Faber, 1986.

Taylor, Dennis. "Hardy and Wordsworth." *Victorian Poetry* 24 (1986): 441–54.

Deleuze, G. and C. Parnet. *Dialogues*. As Translated by H. Tomlinson and B. Hammerson. London: Athlone Press, 1987.

Widdowson, Peter. "Hardy, 'Wessex,' and the Making of a National Culture." *Thomas Hardy Annual*, 4 (1986). Edited by Norman Page. 45–69.

Thomas Hardy. ["Modern Critical Views"]. Edited by Harold Bloom. New York: Chelsea House, 1987.

Thomas Hardy's Jude the Obscure ["Modern Critical Views"]. Edited by Harold Bloom. New York: Chelsea House, 1987.

Casagrande, Peter J. *Hardy's Influence on the Modern Novel*. London: Macmillan, 1987.

Empson, William. Review of G. M. Young's edition of a *Selected Poems* of Hardy (*New Statesman*, 14 September 1940). Reprinted in *Argufying: Essays on Lit-erature and Culture*. Edited by John Haffenden. London: Chatto and Windus, 1987. 421–423.

Empson, William. Review of Wayne C. Booth's *A Rhetoric of Irony* in the *Journal of General Education* (Winter, 1975) and the *New York Review of Books* (July, 1975), reprinted in *Argufying*, Edited by John Haffenden. 1987. 178–183.

Kenner, Hugh. *The Mechanic Muse.* New York: Oxford UP, 1987.

Millgate, Michael. "The Tragedy of Unfulfilled Aims." [Re-titled] in Bloom (1987: 7–17) from *Thomas Hardy: His Career as a Novelist.* London: The Bodley Head, 1971. 317–335.

Ricks, Christopher. *New Oxford Book of Victorian Verse.* Oxford: Oxford UP, 1987.

Auden, W. H. "A Literary Transference." *Southern Review* 6 (1940–41): 78–86. Reprinted in *Hardy: A Collection of Critical Essays.* Edited by Albert J. Guerard, 135–142, and in Bloom, *Thomas Hardy* (1987), above.

Casagrande, Peter J. *Hardy's Influence on the Modern Novel.* Basingstoke: Macmillan, 1987.

Parrinder, Patrick. *The Failure of Theory: Essays on Criticism and Contemporary Fiction.* Brighton: Harvester Press, 1987.

Shaw, W. David. *The Lucid Veil: Poetic Truth in the Victorian Age.* London: Athlone Press, 1987.

Armstrong, Tim. "Supplementarity: Poetry as the Afterlife of Thomas Hardy." *Victorian Poetry* 26 (1988): 381–94.

Eagleton, Terry. "General Editor's Preface" to *Thomas Hardy: the Offensive Truth.* By John Goode. Oxford: Blackwell, 1988.

Easthope, Anthony. *British Post-Structuralism.* London: Routledge, 1988.

Durant, Alan. "Pound, Modernism and Literary Criticism." In *Futures for English.* Edited by Colin McCabe. Manchester: Manchester UP, 1988. 154–166.

Goode, John. *Thomas Hardy: The Offensive Truth.* Oxford: Basil Blackwell, 1988.

Hardy, Thomas. *The Collected Letters of Thomas Hardy.* Edited by R. L. Purdy and Michael Millgate. Oxford: Oxford UP, 1978–88.

Keith, W. J. *Regions of the Imagination: The Development of British Rural Fiction.* Toronto: U of Toronto P, 1988.

Morgan, Rosemarie. *Women and Sexuality in the Novels of Thomas Hardy.* London: Routledge, 1988.

Neill, Edward. "A Nice Idea." [Review of Harold Orel, *The Unknown Thomas Hardy*]. *Essays in Criticism* 38 (1988): 162–6.

Orel, Harold. *The Unknown Thomas Hardy: Little-Known Aspects of His Life and Work.* London: Macmillan, 1988.

Pickrel, Paul. "*Jude the Obscure* and the Fall of Phaethon." *Hudson Review* 39 (1988): 231–50.

Langenbach, James. *Stone Cottage: Pound, Yeats and Modernism.* New York: Oxford UP, 1988.

Barrell, John. "Geographies of Hardy's Wessex." *Journal of Historical Geography* 8 (1982): 347–61. Reprinted in *Tess of the D'Urbervilles.* Edited by Peter Widdowson. Macmillan "Casebook" Series. London: Macmillan, 1989. 157–171.

Alternative Hardy. Edited by Lance St. John Butler. London: Macmillan, 1989.

Brooke-Rose, Christine. "Ill Wit and Sick Tragedy: *Jude the Obscure.*" In *Alternative Hardy.* Edited by Lance St. John Butler. London: Macmillan, 1989. 26–48.

Ingham, Patricia. "Provisional Narratives: Hardy's Final Trilogy." In *Alternative Hardy.* Edited by Lance St. John Butler. London, Macmillan, 1989. 49–73.

Davie, Donald. *Under Briggflats: A History of Poetry in Great Britain 1960–1988.* Manchester: Carcanet, 1989.

Easthope, Anthony. *Poetry and Phantasy.* Cambridge: Cambridge UP, 1989.

Griffiths, Eric. *The Printed Voice of Victorian Poetry.* Oxford: Clarendon Press, 1989.

Hawkins, Desmond. *Hardy at Home. The People and Places of His Wessex.* London: Barrie and Jenkins, 1989.

Hands, Timothy. *Thomas Hardy: Distracted Preacher? Hardy's Religious Biography and its Influence on His Novels.* Basingstoke: Macmillan, 1989.

Ingham, Patricia. *Thomas Hardy: A Feminist Reading.* Brighton: Harvester, 1989.

Miller, J. Hillis. "Prosopopoeia in Hardy and Stevens." In *Alternative Hardy.* Edited by Lance St. John Butler. London: Macmillan, 1989. 110–127.

O'Neill, Patricia. "Thomas Hardy: Poetics of a Postromantic." *Victorian Poetry* 27 (1989): 129–156.

Reed, John R. *Victorian Will.* Athens: Ohio UP, 1989.

Schur, Owen. "A Dwelling's Character: from Pastoral to the Country House in Hardy." *Victorian Pastoral: Tennyson, Hardy and the Subversion of Forms.* Columbus: Ohio State UP, 1989. 200–218.

Steig, Michael. *Stories of Reading: Subjectivity and Literary Understanding.* London: Johns Hopkins UP, 1989. 183–201.

Stevenson, Anne. *Bitter Fame: A Life of Sylvia Plath.* London: Viking, 1989.

Taylor, Dennis. *Hardy's Poetry, 1860–1928.* 2nd. ed. London: Macmillan, 1989.

Turner, Paul. *Victorian Poetry, Drama and Miscellaneous Prose 1832–1890.* Oxford: Clarendon Press, 1989.

Widdowson, Peter. *Hardy in History: A Study in Literary Sociology.* London: Routledge, 1989.

Wright, Terence. *Hardy and the Erotic.* Basingstoke: Macmillan, 1989.

Ardis, Ann. *New Women, New Novels: Feminism and Early Modernism.* New Brunswick, NJ: Rutgers UP, 1990.

Beer, Gillian. "Finding a Scale for the Human: Plot and Writing in Hardy's Novels." In *Critical Essays on Thomas Hardy.* Edited by Dale Kramer. Boston: G. K. Hall, 1990.

Chapman, Raymond. *The Language of Thomas Hardy.* London: Macmillan, 1990.

Collins, Deborah L. *Thomas Hardy and His God: A Liturgy of Unbelief.* London: Macmillan, 1990.

Draper, R. P. "*Jude the Obscure.*" In Dale Kramer (ed.) *Critical Essays on Thomas Hardy: The Novels.* Boston: G. K. Hall, 1990.

Green, Brian. "Darkness Visible: Defiance, Derision and Despair in Hardy's 'In Tenebris' Poems." *The Thomas Hardy Journal,* 6 (1990): 126–146.

Kermode, Frank. *An Appetite for Poetry: Essays in Literary Interpretation.* London: Fontana, 1990.

Lodge, David. *After Bakhtin: Essays on Fiction and Criticism.* London: Routledge, 1990.

Maynard, Katherine Kearney. *Thomas Hardy's Tragic Poetry: The Lyrics and 'The Dynasts'.* Iowa City: Iowa UP, 1990.

Moore, Kevin Z. *The Descent of the Imagination: Postromantic Culture in the Later Novels of Thomas Hardy.* London: New York UP, 1990.

Morgan, William W. "Thomas Hardy." in *Victorian Poetry* 28 (1990): 201.

Riesen, Beat. *Thomas Hardy's Minor Novels.* New York: Peter Lang, 1990.

Witek, Terri. "Repetition in a Land of Unlikeness: What 'Life Will not be Balked of' in Thomas Hardy's Poetry." *Victorian Poetry* 28 (1990): 119–128.

Armstrong, Tim. "Hardy's Dantean Purples." *Thomas Hardy Journal* 7 (May, 1991): 47–54.

Dibattista, Maria. *First Love: The Affections of Modern Fiction.* Chicago: Chicago UP, 1991.

Garson, Marjorie. *Hardy's Fables of Integrity: Woman, Body, Text* Oxford: Clarendon Press, 1991.

Gewanter, David. "'Undervoicings of Loss' in Hardy's Elegies to his Wife." *Victorian Poetry* 29 (1991): 193–207.

Goode, John. "Hardy and Marxism." *Critical Essays on Thomas Hardy: the Novels.* Edited by Dale Kramer. Boston: G. K. Hall, 1990. 21–38.

Johnson, Trevor. *A Critical Introduction to the Poems of Thomas Hardy.* London: Macmillan, 1991.

Johnson, Trevor. "'Ancestral Voices': Hardy and the English Poetic Tradition." *Victorian Poetry* 29 (1991): 47–62.

Kamuf, Peggy. *A Derrida Reader: Between the Blinds.* London: Harvester Wheat-sheaf, 1991.

Kramer, Dale. *Tess of the D'Urbervilles.* Cambridge: Cambridge UP, 1991.

Miller, J. Hillis. *Tropes, Parables, Performatives: Essays on Twentieth Century Litera-ture.* Brighton: Harvester Press, 1991.

Ramazani, Jahan. "Hardy's Elegies for an Era: 'By the Century's Deathbed.'" *Vic-torian Poetry,* 29 (1991): 131–143.

Rose, Jacqueline. *The Haunting of Sylvia Plath.* London: Virago, 1991.

Sexton, Melanie. "Phantoms of His Own Figuring: The Movement towards Re-covery in Hardy's Poems." *Victorian Poetry,* 29 (1991): 209–226.

Ward, J. Powell. *The English Line: Poetry of the Unpoetic from Wordsworth to Larkin.* London: Macmillan, 1991.

Whitford, Margaret. *Luce Irigaray: Philosophy in the Feminine* London Routledge, 1991.

Armstrong, Tim. "Hardy, Thaxter and History as Coincidence in 'The Conver-gence of the Twain.'" *Victorian Poetry,* 30 (1992): 29–42.

Fisher, Joe. *The Hidden Hardy.* London: Macmillan, 1992.

Booth, James. *Philip Larkin: Writer.* London: Harvester Press, 1992.

Gibson, James. *Thomas Hardy: Selected Short Stories and Poems.* London: Dent [Everyman], 1992.

Jameson, Fredric. "Periodising the Sixties." In *The Ideologies of Theory: Essays 1971–86.* Reprinted in *Postmodernism: A Reader,* ed. Patricia Waugh. London: Ed-ward Arnold, 1992.125–152.

Lock, Charles. *Thomas Hardy.* Bristol: Bristol Classical Press, 1992.

Miller, J. Hillis. *Ariadne's Thread: Story Lines.* London: Yale UP, 1992.

Millgate, Michael. *Testamentary Acts: Browning, Tennyson, James, Hardy.* Oxford: Clarendon Press, 1992.

Morgan, Rosemarie. *Cancelled Words: Re-Discovering Thomas Hardy.* London: Routledge, 1992.

Pinion, F. B. *Thomas Hardy: His Life and Friends.* London: Macmillan, 1992.

Janmohammed, Abdul R. "Worldliness-Without-World, Homelessness-as-Home: Toward a Definition of the Specular Border Intellectual." In Sprinker, Michael, ed. *The Edward Said Reader.* Oxford: Blackwell, 1992. 196–221.

Armstrong, Isobel. *Victorian Poetry: Poetry, Poetics and Politics.* London: Rout-ledge, 1993.

Armstrong, Tim, ed. *Thomas Hardy: Selected Poems.* London: Longman, 1993.

Cunningham, Valentine. *In the Reading Jail: Postmodernity, Texts and History.* Blackwell: Oxford, 1993.

Ebbatson, Roger. *Hardy: The Margin of the Unexpressed*. Sheffield: Sheffield UP, 1993.

Gervais, David. *Literary Englands: Versions of "Englishness" in Modern Writing*. Cambridge: Cambridge UP, 1993.

Higonnet, Margaret R., ed. "Introduction" to *The Sense of Sex: Feminist Perspectives on Hardy*. Chicago: U of Illinois P, 1993.

Langland, Elizabeth. "Becoming a Man in *Jude the Obscure*." In *The Sense of Sex: Feminist Perspectives on Hardy*. Edited by Margaret Higonnet. Chicago: U of Illinois P, 1993. 32–48.

Maynard, John. "Conclusion: Hardy's *Jude*: Disassembling Sexuality and Religion." In *Victorian Discourses on Sexuality and Religion*. Cambridge: Cambridge UP, 1993.

Mitchell, Judith. "Hardy's Female Reader." In *The Sense of Sex: Feminist Perspectives on Hardy*. Edited by Margaret Higonnet. 172–187.

Reilly, Jim. *Shadowtime: History and Representation in Hardy, Conrad and George Eliot*. London: Routledge, 1993.

Said, Edward. *Culture and Imperialism*. London: Chatto and Windus, 1993.

Taylor, Dennis. *Hardy's Literary Language and Victorian Philology*. Oxford: Clarendon Press, 1993.

Thomas, Harry, ed. *Thomas Hardy: Selected Poems*. London: Penguin, 1993.

Ward, J. P. *Thomas Hardy's Poetry*. Milton: Keynes: Open Univ, 1993.

New Perspectives on Thomas Hardy. Edited by Charles P. C. Pettit. London: Macmillan, 1994.

Butler, Lance St. J. "'Bosh' or: Believing Neither More Nor Less." In *New Perspectives on Thomas Hardy*. Edited by Charles P. C. Pettit. 101–116.

Casagrande, Peter. "'Something more to be Said': Hardy's Creative Process and the Case of *Tess and Jude*." In *New Perspectives on Thomas Hardy*." Edited by Charles P. C. Pettit. 16–40.

Gibson, James. "'The Characteristic of All great Poetry — The General Perfectly Reduced in the Particular': Thomas Hardy." In *New Perspectives on Thomas Hardy*. Edited by Charles P. C. Pettit. 1–15.

Hardy, Florence E. *The Life of Thomas Hardy*, reprinted London: Studio Books, 1994 [2vols.].)

Jackson, Tony E. *The Subject of Modernism: Narrative Alterations in the Fiction of Eliot, Conrad, Woolf and Joyce*. Ann Arbor: U of Michigan P, 1994.

Johnson, Trevor. "'Thoroughfares of Stones': Hardy's 'Other' Love Poetry." In *New Perspectives on Thomas Hardy*. Edited by Charles P. C. Pettit. London: Macmillan, 1994. 58–79.

Pinion, F. B. "Questions Arising from Hardy's Visits to Cornwall." In *New Perspectives on Thomas Hardy*. Edited by Charles P. C. Pettit. London: Macmillan, 1994. 191–208.

Raine, Craig. "Conscious Artistry in *The Mayor of Casterbridge*." In *New Perspectives on Thomas Hardy*. Edited by Charles P. C. Pettit. London: Macmillan, 1994. 156–71.

Schweik, Robert. "The 'Modernity' of Hardy's *Jude the Obscure*." In *A Spacious Vision: Essays on Hardy*. Edited by Phillip V. Mallet and

Ronald P. Draper. Newmill: The Patten Press, 1994. 49–63.

Seymour-Smith, Martin. *Hardy*. London: Bloomsbury, 1994.

Emig, Rainer. *Modernism in Poetry: Motivations, Structures and Limits*. London: Longman, 1995.

Heaney, Seamus. *The Redress of Poetry: Oxford Lectures*. London: Faber and Faber, 1995.

Kranidis, Rita S. *Subversive Discourse: The Cultural Production of Late Victorian Feminist Novels*. London: Macmillan, 1995.

Langbaum, Robert. *Thomas Hardy in Our Time*. London: Macmillan, 1995.

Moses, Michael Valdes. *The Novel and the Globalization of Culture*. Oxford: Oxford UP, 1995.

Royle, Nicholas. *After Derrida*. Manchester: Manchester UP, 1995.

Cohen, Tom. "The Ideology of Dialogue: the Bakhtin/de Man (Dis)Connection." *Cultural Critique* 33 (Spring, 1996): 41–86.

Langbaum, Robert. *Thomas Hardy in Our Time*. Basingstoke: Macmillan, 1995.

Thomas, Brian. *The Return of the Native: Saint George Defeated*. New York: Twayne Publishers, 1995.

Wilson, Keith. *Thomas Hardy and the Stage*. London: Macmillan, 1995.

Celebrating Thomas Hardy: Insights and Appreciations. Edited by Charles P. C. Pettit. London: Macmillan, 1996.

Gibson, James. *Thomas Hardy: A Literary Life*. London: Macmillan, 1996.

Green, Brian. *Hardy's Lyrics: Pearls of Pity*. London: Macmillan, 1996.

Hynes, Samuel, ed. *Thomas Hardy: Selected Poetry*. Oxford: Oxford UP, 1996.

Jedrzejewski, Jan. *Thomas Hardy and the Church*. Basingstoke: Macmillan, 1996.

Millgate, Michael. *Letters of Emma and Florence Hardy*. Oxford: Clarendon Press, 1996.

Osborne, Peter and Anne Beezer, eds. *A Critical Sense: Interviews with Intellectuals*. London: Routledge, 1996.

Beer, Gillian. "Hardy and Decadence." In *Celebrating Thomas Hardy*. Edited by Charles P. C. Pettit. London: Macmillan, 1996. 90–102.

Blishen, Edward. "Hardy, *The Hand of Ethelberta*, and Some Persisting English Discomforts." In *Celebrating Thomas Hardy*. Edited by Charles P. C. Pettit. London: Macmillan, 1996. 177–195.

Butler, Lance St. J. "Stability and Subversion: Thomas Hardy's Voices." In *Celebrating Thomas Hardy*. Edited by Charles P. C. Pettit. London: Macmillan, 1996. 39–53.

Blythe, Ronald. "Thomas Hardy and John Clare: A Soil Observed, A Soil Ploughed." In *Celebrating Thomas Hardy*. Edited by Charles P. C. Pettit. London: Macmillan, 1996. 54–67.

Curtis, Simon. "Hardy, George Moore and the 'Doll' of English Fiction." in *Celebrating Thomas Hardy*. Edited by Charles P. C. Pettit. London: Macmillan, 1996. 103–114.

Gibson, James. "Thomas Hardy's Poetry: Poetic Apprehension and Poetic Method." In *Celebrating Thomas Hardy*. Edited by Charles P. C. Pettit. London: Macmillan, 1996. 1–21.

Eagleton, Terry. *The Illusions of Postmodernism*. Oxford: Blackwell, 1996.

Lerner, Lawrence. "Moments of Vision — and After." In *Celebrating Thomas Hardy*. Edited by Charles P. C. Pettit. London: Macmillan, 1996. 22–38.

Levi, Peter. "Hardy's Friend William Barnes." In *Celebrating Thomas Hardy*. Edited by Charles P. C. Pettit. London: Macmillan, 1996. 68–89.

Millgate, M. "Wives All: Emma and Florence Hardy." in *Celebrating Thomas Hardy*. Edited by Charles P. C. Pettit. London: Macmillan, 1996. 115–135.

Morgan, Rosemarie. "Bodily Transactions: Toni Morrison and Thomas Hardy in Literary Discourse." In *Celebrating Thomas Hardy*. Edited by Charles P. C. Pettit. London: Macmillan, 1996. 136–158.

Ricks, Christopher. "A Note on Hardy's 'A Spellbound Palace.'" In *Essays in Appreciation*. Oxford: Clarendon Press, 1996. 235–44.

Rothermel, Peter. "The Far and the Near: On Reading Thomas Hardy Today." In *Celebrating Thomas Hardy*. Edited Charles P. C. Pettit. London: Macmillan, 1996. 159–176.

Xie, Shaobo. "History and Utopian Desire: Fredric Jameson's Dialectical Tribute to Northrop Frye." *Cultural Critique* 34 (Fall, 1996): 115–142.

Hughes, John. *Lines of Flight: Reading Deleuze with Hardy, Gissing, Conrad, Woolf*. Sheffield: Sheffield Academic Press, 1997.

Turner, Paul. *The Life of Thomas Hardy*. Oxford: Blackwell, 1998.

Widdowson, Peter. *On Thomas Hardy. Late Essays and Earlier*. London: Macmillan, 1998.

Index

Abercrombie, Lascelles, 8, 97–98
Ackroyd, Peter, 15
Adorno, Theodor, ix, 76
After Strange Gods (Eliot), 70
Agenda, 7
"Aldcliffe, Miss" (*Desperate Remedies*), 43
Alexander, Michael, 67
Alice in Wonderland (Carroll), 35; Cheshire Cat in, 67
alienation, 9
Allen, Walter, 118
Althusser, Louis, 11, 99, 105
Amis, Kingsley, 53
"anamnesis," 32
Anderson, Perry, 38, 42
antiquarianism, 34
aporia, 56, 101
appropriation, 38
Archer, William, 28, 64
Ardis, Anne, 94
Armstrong, Isobel, 33
Armstrong, Tim, 39, 56, 60, 74
Arnold, Matthew, 25, 32, 77, 92, 93, 102, 105
Auden, W. H., 4, 76, 80, 96
Auerbach, Nina, 98
Augustans, 72
Aurelius, Marcus, 41
Austen, Jane, 94

Bailey, J. O., 6, 60, 76
Bakhtin, M. M., 42, 103
Baldick, Chris, 34
Balzac, Honoré de, 99
Barber, D. F., 18
Barnes, William, 43, 64, 71, 77
Barrell, John, 39
Barrie, J. M., 13

Barthes, Roland, ix, 6, 21, 28, 31
Bartlett, Phyllis, 93
"Bathsheba," (*Far from the Madding Crowd*), 16
Baudrillard, Jean, 31
Bayley, John, 29, 66, 93, 100
Beach, Joseph Warren, 8
Beatty, C. J. P., 43
Beckett, Samuel, 72
Beer, Gillian, 43
Beer, Patricia, 3
Beethoven, Ludwig van, 90
Belsey, Catherine, 34, 42
Benjamin, Walter, viii, ix, 29, 40
Benvenuto, Richard, 120
Bergonzi, Bernard, 57
"Bertram, Sir Thomas" (Jane Austen), 101
Bildungsroman, 90
Bjork, Lennart A., 38
Blackmur, R. P., 28, 73
Blake, Kathleen, 27, 90, 92, 96
Blake, William, 41, 93, 97
Blishen, Edward, 22, 23, 24
Bloom, Harold, 23, 25, 29, 71, 74, 75, 93, 103
Blunden, Edmund, 28, 64
Blythe, Ronald, 26
body, the, 96
"Boldwood" (*Far from the Madding Crowd*), 16
Booth, James, 53
Booth, Wayne C., 82
Boumelha, Penny, 89, 105
Bove, Paul, vii–viii, 5
Bowra, C. M., 71
Brady, Kristin, 113n.
Bredin, Hugh, 79
Brennecke, Ernest, viii, 14

bricolage, 100
bricoleur, 37, 64
Bridges, Robert, 63
Bronte, Charlotte, 102
Brooke-Rose, Christine, 89–105
Brooks, Jean R., 96
Brown, Douglas, 37, 63
Browne, Merle E., 53
Browning, Robert, 15, 71, 72, 75, 77, 95
Brunel, Isambard Kingdom, 37, 53
"Brunnhilde" (Wagner), 96
Buck-Morss, Susan, 123
Bullen, J. B., 130
Burke, Edmund, 77, 99
Burns, Wayne, 94
Burstein, Janet, 105
Butler, Lance St. John, 40, 41, 42, 72, 95

canons, 7
Carlyle, Thomas, 78
Casagrande, Peter J., 27, 33, 74, 100-01
Cassis, A. F., 113
Cecil, David, Lord, 8
Chapman, Raymond, 111
Chase, Mary Ellen, 119
Chesterton, G. K., 10, 19n. 37
Childers, Mary, 97
Clare, John, 26
class, 28, 99
Clements, P., 87n.
clerisy, 102, 105
Clifford, Emma, 108
clinamen, 75, 93
Clodd, Edward, 100
Cockshut, A. O. J., 96
Cohen, Tom, 43
Coleman, Terry, 6
Coleridge, Samuel Taylor, 53
collage, 37
Collins, Deborah L., 46, 90

Collins, Philip, 10, 50n.
Colls, Robert, 50n.
commodity, 8
Comte, Auguste, 38, 95
conservatism, 31, 40, 53
Cook, Cornelia, 74
"Coriolanus," 101
counter-text, 99
Cox, Gregory Stevens, 44
Creighton, T. R. M., 54, 56
critiography, 31, 98
culture, 7, 104
Cunningham, Gail, 98
Cunningham, Valentine, 34, 63
Curtis, Simon, 44
"Cytherea," 43

Dante, 58
Darwin, Charles, ix, 14, 38, 57, 60, 69
Davidson, Donald, 106n.
Davie, Donald, 6, 21, 25, 36, 41, 53, 55, 57, 58, 59, 66, 67, 68, 72, 73, 99
Davis, Philip, 60
De Man, Paul, 22, 104
De Sola Pinto, Vivian, 117
Deacon, Lois, 6
deconstruction, 5, 7, 29
Deleuze, Gilles, xi, 89
Derrida, Jacques, ix, 30, 56, 69, 99
Desperate Remedies, 11, 15, 43, 97
Deutsche, Babette, 117
dialect, 99
Dibattista, Maria, 95
Dickinson, Emily, 79
Diderot, Denis, 101
discourse, 21, 25, 40
Dodd, Philip, 50n.
Dodsworth, Martin, 73
Donne, John, 70, 75
"Dorsetshire Labourer, The," 32
Drabble, Margaret, 18n.

"Dracula" (Stoker), 99
Draper, R. P., 90
Dryden, John, 65
Durant, Alan, 38
"Dynasts, The," 34

Eagleton, Terry, 31, 40, 93, 95, 104
Easthope, Anthony, 34, 38
Ebbatson, Roger, 22, 29, 34, 51n.
Edmond, Rod, 74
Eliot, T. S., 2, 13, 15, 30, 36, 39, 53, 55, 59, 61, 69, 70, 72, 73, 75, 76, 103
"Eliot, George," 36, 60, 102
Ellis, Havelock, 91
Ellmann, Mary, 98
Emerson, Ralph Waldo, 70
Emig, Rainer, 35
Empson, William, 54, 55, 80, 82n.
"Engineer(ing)," 663, 64, 68
Enlightenment, The, 32
Enstice, Andrew, 96

Far from the Madding Crowd, 41, 97, 104
"Farfrae, Donald" (in *The Mayor of Casterbridge*), 43
Feltes, N. N., 22
feminism, 94
feminist, 95, 96
Fernando, Lloyd, 96
Firor, Ruth, 50n.
Fischler, Alexander, 107n.
Fischer, Joe, 22, 41, 43, 90, 98, 104
Fitzgerald, F. Scott, 41
Ford, Ford Madox, 76
Ford, John (dramatist), 58
formation, 10, 16
Foucault, Michel, ix, 95, 96
Four Quartets (Eliot), 63
Fraser, G. S., 72
Freud, Sigmund, 93

Frye, Northrop, 10, 29, 75
Furbank, P. N., 89

Garson, Marjorie, 9, 23, 29, 30, 92, 95, 99, 100
Garwood, Helen, 19
Gervais, David, 37
Gewanter, David, 68
Gibson, James, 3, 22, 24, 25, 26, 32, 56
Gielgud, Sir John, 78
Gifford, Henry, 62
Gilder, Jeanette, x
"Gillingham" (in *Jude*), 99
Giordano Jr., Frank R., 106n.
Gittings, Robert, 1, 3, 4, 5, 11, 12, 13, 23, 95
Goetz, W., 101
Goode, John, xi, 10, 22, 27, 33, 39, 41, 61, 90, 96, 98, 100, 104
Goodheart, Eugene, 108n.
Gosse, Edmund, 48n., 101
Graves, Robert, xi, 12, 57
Gray, Thomas, 15, 55, 73
Green, Brian, 80
Gregor, Ian, 93
Griffiths, Eric, 25, 72, 77–78
Grigson, Geoffrey, 57–58
Grindle, Juliet, 87n.
Grundy, Isobel, 126
Guerard, Albert J., 89
"haecceitas," 14
Hand of Ethelberta, The, 8, 22, 24
Hands, Timothy, 46n.
Hannigan, D. F., 91
Hardy, Emma (wife), 12, 14, 42, 59, 60, 68
Hardy, Florence E. (wife), 12, 14
Hardy, Evelyn, 8
Hassett, Michael E., 92, 101
Havely, Cicely, 64
Hawkes, Terence, 34
Hawkins, Desmond, 64

Hawthorne, Nathaniel, 13
Heaney, Seamus, 54
hegemony, 65, 97
Heidegger, Martin, 72
Heilman, R. B., 93
Hellstrom, Ward, 92
"Henchard, Michael," (*The Mayor of Casterbridge*), 41
Herbert, George, 75
Herbert, Lucille, 12
Higonnet, Margaret R., 23, 104
Hill, Geoffrey, 78
Holland, Norman, 95
Holloway, John, 72, 112n.
Hopkins, Gerard Manley, 14, 65, 67, 75
Hornback, Bert G., 102
Hough, Graham, 50n., 63
Housman, A. E., 61
Howe, Irving, 61, 100, 102
Howells, W. D., 91
Hughes, John, xi, 89, 91
Hume, David, 14, 38, 54, 57
Huxley, T. H., 59, 60
Hyatt, Alfred, 3
Hyde, W. J., 93
Hynes, Samuel, 12, 56, 64, 65, 73
hysteria, 98

Ibsen, H., 100
ideology, x, 25, 26, 32, 60, 78–79
image, viii, 16, 24, 37, 38, 53, 56, 72
imagination, 102
"Imaginative Woman, An" (story), 16
Indiscretion in the Life of an Heiress, An, 8
Ingham, Patricia, 22, 10
intention, 9, 30, 90, 92, 95, 97
interpellation, 10, 105
interrogative texts, 8, 101
intertextuality, 15, 17, 25, 33, 71, 93

Irigaray, Luce, 17

Jackson, Tony E., 103
Jacobus, Mary, 27, 93, 94
James, Henry, ix, 62, 67, 68, 72, 103
Jameson, Fredric, 1, 2, 31
Janmohammed, Abdul R., 51n.
Jedrzejewski, Jan, 24, 29, 30
Jehovah's witness, anti-, 67
Jefferies, Richard, 27
Jefferson, Douglas, 52
"Jocelyn" (*The Well-Beloved*), 37
Johnson, Bruce, 105
Johnson, H. A. T., 59
Johnson, Lionel, 8
Johnson, Trevor, 54, 74
Joyce, James, 6, 91, 103
"Jude," 8, 35, 41, 89–106 *passim*
Jude the Obscure, 27, 39, 40, 41, 69, 89–106 *passim*

Kafka, Franz 103
Kamuf, Peggy (ed. *Derrida Reader*), 82n.
Kant, Immanuel, 60
Kegan Paul, Charles, 14
Keith, W. J., 51n.
Kenner, Hugh, 39
kenosis, 75
Kermode, Frank, ix, 30, 37
Kettle, Arnold, 7
Kingsley, Charles, 94
Kinkead-Weekes, Mark, 124
"Kraken, The" (Tennyson), 99
Kramer, Dale, 27, 39, 98
Kranidis, Rita S., 94

Lacan, Jacques, 9, 100
Langbaum, Robert, 36, 61
Langenbach, James, 70
Langland, Elizabeth, 104
Laodicean, A, 43
Larkin, Philip, 53, 54, 56, 57, 63

Lawrence, D. H., 8, 27, 35, 36,
    37, 69, 94, 98
Le Galliene, Richard, 91
Leavis, F. R., 28, 35, 36, 54, 62,
    64, 67, 68, 69, 73, 74
Leavis, Q. D., 34, 107n.
Lerner, Lawrence, 26, 95, 112n.
Levi, Peter, 43
Levine, George, 125
Lewis, C. Day, 73
Lewis, C. S., 58
"liberticide," 32
Life of Thomas Hardy, The, 42
Litz, A. Walton, 61
Lock, Charles, 7, 23, 30
Locke, John, 97
Lodge, David, 35, 89, 104
Lowell, Robert, ix, 100
Lubbock, Percy, ix
Lucas, John, 56, 66

Macbeth, George, 68
McCarthy, Robert, 72

Macdowell, Arthur, 68–69
Macherey, P., 99
Mahar, Margaret, 72–73
Mahler, Gustav (composer), 90
Mallarmé, Stephane, 62
Malthus, Thomas, 95
Marsden, Kenneth, 62, 69, 74
Marx, Karl, 15
marxist, 29, 75
masochism, 96
Maupassant, Guy de, 44
Maxwell, J. C., 37
May, Charles E., 120
Mayor of Casterbridge, The, 37, 43,
    103
Maynard, Katherine Kearney, 133
Maynard, John, 35, 94
Meredith, George, 71, 74
metaphor, 37, 79
metonymy, 79

Mill, J. S., 14, 60, 66
Mill on the Floss, The ("George
    Eliot"), 67
Miller, J. Hillis, 16, 23, 25, 31,
    32, 40, 54, 59, 76
Millett, Kate, 110n.
Millgate, Michael, 1, 4, 5, 7, 11,
    13, 22, 29, 91, 93, 100, 102
Milton, John, 8, 10, 39, 92
mimesis, 103
misogyny, 98
Mitchell, Judith, 45n.
Mizener, Arthur, 103
modernism, 34, 70, 76, 103, 104
modernist, 16, 35, 38, 56
modernity, 29, 72, 103
Moore, George, 44
Moore, Kevin Z., 2, 23, 32, 40,
    92, 99, 105
Morgan, Rosemarie, 3, 24, 42, 94,
    95, 99
Morgan, William, 80, 93
Morris, William, 41
Morrison, Blake, 81n.
Morrison, Toni, 42
Morton, Peter R., 50n.
Moses, Michael Valdes, 29
Moule, Horace, 15, 50n.
"Movement, The," 53, 76
"Much Wittering," 22
Mulhern, Francis, 34
Munch, Edvard, 89
Murfin, Ross C., 74
"mythic subtext," 9

narrative, 103
narrator, 94
Neill, Edward, 33, 53
Neiman, Gilbert, 118
Newey, Vincent, 96
Newton, Sir Isaac, 97
Nietzsche, Friedrich, 16, 29, 67,
    73, 87, 93
nostalgia, vii, 29, 31, 38, 99

oedipality, 23
Oliphant, Mrs. M., x, 91
O'Neill, Patricia, 79
Orel, Harold, 7
organicism, 105
Osborne, Peter, 51n.
overdetermination, 98

Page, Norman, 10, 33, 63, 64
Pair of Blue Eyes, A, 11
Palgrave, Francis T., 56, 75
Paris, Bernard J., 103
Parnell, Charles, 100
Parnet, C., 106n.
parochialism, 33
Parrinder, Patrick, 107n.
Patmore, Coventry, 71, 74, 77, 94
patrimony, 63
Paulin, Tom, 54, 58, 59, 65, 70,
    75
Peck, John, 102, 103
Perkins, David, 71
Pettit, Charles P. C., 6, 22, 24, 25,
    26, 27, 28, 30, 36, 39
pharmakon, 101
phenomenology, 16, 105
"Phillotson" (in *Jude*), 92, 96, 99
phoneme, 56
Pickrel, Paul, 89, 90
Pinion, F. B., 6, 76
Piper, John, 32
Pope, Alexander, 40
Porter, Katherine Anne, 62, 63
Portrait of the Artist (Joyce), 35
Poster, Mark, 48
postmodernism, 44, 63
postmodernist, 38
poststructuralism, 54
Pound, Ezra, ix, 53, 69, 72, 75,
    76
precursor, 35, 71
Proust, Marcel, 96
Purdy, R. L., 5

Quiller-Couch, Sir Arthur, 75

Rachman, Shalom, 108n.
radicalism, 31, 92
radicality, 31
Rainbow, The (Lawrence), 94
Raine, Craig, 2, 37–38
Ramazani, Jahan, 55
Reed, John R., 102
regionalism, 41
Reilly, Jim, 33
repetition, 9, 73, 89
representation, xi, 9, 16, 21, 31,
    32, 33, 34, 77, 91, 92, 93, 94,
    98, 104, 88, 90, 91, 94, 95,
    100, 104
Return of the Native, The, 9
ressentiment, 23, 40, 44, 95
revolutionary, 98
Richards, I. A., 74
Richardson, James, 72, 73, 74
Ricks, Christopher, 4, 70, 77
Riesen, Beat, 49n.
Robinson, Peter, 68
Robinson, Roger, 50n.
Robson, W. W., 35
Rogers, Kathleen, 97
romanticism, 23, 29, 92, 101, 105
Romola ("George Eliot"), 34
Rose, Jacqueline, 4
Rothermel, Peter, 28
Royle, Nicholas, 84
Rover, Constance, 95
Rutland, W. R., 75

Sacks, Peter, 25, 55
sadism, 96
Said, Edward, 40, 41
Saldivar, Ramon, 92, 101
Salter, K. W., 109n.
Schoenberg, Arnold, vii
Schopenhauer, Arthur, 2, 14, 38,
    60, 100

Schur, Owen, 77
Schwartz, Barry N., 107n.
Schwartz, Delmore, 70
Schweik, Robert, 136
semiotics, 92, 105
Serres, Michel, 72
Sexton, Melanie, 59
sexuality, 36, 43, 94, 96
Seymour-Smith, Martin, 3, 10, 11
   12, 13, 23, 24, 57, 101
Shakespeare, William, viii, 39, 53,
   56, 63, 72, 73, 92
Shaw, W. David, 79
Shelley, Percy Bysshe, 10, 15, 16,
   23, 27, 31, 40, 57, 69, 71, 73,
   79, 89, 93, 94, 103
Sidney, Sir Philip, 27
signifieds, 106
signs, 92, 104
simulacrum, 92
Smiles, Samuel, 53
Smith, Stan, 128
Snell, K. D. M., 29, 32
Sonstroem, David, 127
sous rature, 33
Southerington, F. R., 7, 50n.
Southworth, J. G., 113
Spann, Marcella, 76
Spender, Stephen, 72
Springer, Marilyn, 129
Steig, Michael, 93, 95
Stephen, Leslie, 23, 99
Sterne, Lawrence, 74
Stevens, Wallace, 30, 54, 67, 70,
   75, 81, 95
Stevens Cox, Gregory, 44n.
Stevenson, Anne, 4
Stevenson, R. L., 67
Stewart, J. I. M., 7
Strachey, Lytton, 62, 63
Strauss, Richard (composer), 90
structuralism, ix
Stubbs, Patricia, 125
subtext, 10

"Sue (Bridehead)," 86–102 *passim*
Sully, James, 60
Suspense (Conrad), 34
Sutherland, John, 11
Swinburne, Algernon, 71, 73, 74

Tasso, Torquato, 27
Taylor, Dennis, 48n., 54, 62, 64–
   65, 74, 77
Taylor, Richard H., 19n., 49n., 62
teleologies, 33
temporality, 65
Tennyson, Alfred Lord, 15, 44,
   57, 75, 77, 99
Tess of the D'Urbervilles, 27, 33,
   41, 103
text, 89, 90, 97, 98, 101
textuality, 23, 28, 68, 92, 104
Thackeray, William Makepeace,
   102
Thatcher, David, 55
Thomas, Dylan, 53, 54, 56, 57,
   76, 80
Thomas, Edward, 37
Thomas, Harry, 56
Thurley, Geoffrey, 89
Tolkien, J. R. R., 58
tragedy, 102
Tredell, Nicholas, viii
tropes, 32
Trumpet-Major, The, 33–34
"Tulliver, Maggie" ("George
   Eliot"), 67
Turner, Paul, 14, 15, 43, 77
Tyrell, R. Y., 97

Under the Greenwood Tree, 9, 11,
   14, 100

Van Doren, Mark, 54, 56
Vigar, Penelope, 109
Virgil, 15, 58, 59

Wagner, Richard, 79

Wain, John, 67
Wakefield, Bishop of, 91
Waller, E., 32
Ward, J. Powell, 37, 63
Watkins, Vernon, 57
Watson, George, 25
Weber, Carl, viii, 14, 75
Weber, Max, 1
Weinstein, Philip M., 27, 105
Weiss, Theodor, 58, 61
Well-Beloved, The, 6, 14, 37
Wells, H. G., 91
Whitford, Margaret, 17
Whitman, Walt, 75
Wickens, Glen, 34
Widdowson, Frances, 46n.
Widdowson, Peter, 8, 12, 22, 23, 24, 34, 38, 39, 41, 54, 75, 99, 104
"Wildeve, Damon" (in *The Return of the Native*), 9
Williams, Merryn, 10
Williams, Randall, 111n.
Williams, Raymond, xi, 3, 10, 13, 22, 28–29, 39, 104
Wilson, Harold, 66
Wilson, Keith, 136
Winter, Michael, 126
Witek, Terri, 73
"Wittering, Much," 22
Women in Love (Lawrence), 94
Woodlanders, The, 43
Woolf, Virginia, 67
Wordsworth, William, 33, 67, 71, 74
Wotton, George, 8, 10, 22, 69, 99, 104
Wright, David, 56
Wright, Terence, 5
Wyatt, Sir Thomas, 75

Xie, Shaobo, 48n.

Yeats, W. B., ix, 13, 53, 54, 57, 59, 61, 63, 67, 69, 73
Young, G. M., 56, 63

Zabel, Morton Dauwen, 35
Zietlow, Paul, 60, 64
Zizek, Slavoj, 40
Zola, Emile, 44